2d Edition

Keyboarding Speed And Control Builders

Lee R. Beaumont
Professor of Business, Emeritus
Indiana University of Pennsylvania

Ronald D. Johnson
Professor of Business Administration
Department of General Business and Finance
Sam Houston State University

Franklin H. Dye, Supervisor
Vocational Education for the Handicapped
State of Louisiana Department of Education

Published by

T08   **SOUTH-WESTERN PUBLISHING CO.**

CINCINNATI   WEST CHICAGO, ILL.   DALLAS   PELHAM MANOR, N.Y.   PALO ALTO, CALIF.

Copyright © 1985
by South-Western Publishing Co.
Cincinnati, Ohio

ISBN: 0-538-20080-4

Library of Congress Catalog Card Number: 84-50337

2 3 4 5 6 7 H 10 9 8 7 6 5

Printed in the United States of America

PREFACE

Keyboarding Speed/Control Builders is a supplemental book of special skill-building drills and timed writings designed to improve keyboarding facility with straight, script, statistical, and rough-draft copy. It provides a flexible package of drill materials which can be used (1) as a supplement to any basic textbook for individuals who need additional emphasis on basic skills; (2) as a source of basic skillbuilding practice to accompany individualized problem/production materials that place their total emphasis on the development of problem/production competence; (3) as a refresher program for individuals with prior instruction but without keystroking power to support the intensive development of problem/production skills.

Organization and Content

Since efficient techniques are the foundation of all good keyboarding performance, drill materials designed to modify and refine movement patterns to make them more efficient must be a part of any program to build speed and control. Experience and research indicate, however, that the best approach to building speed and accuracy (control) is through the use of drills in which only *one* of the two elements is emphasized, thus providing opportunities for practice toward a single goal.

This book, divided into two major parts, contains 60 carefully structured lessons suitable for 20-30 minutes of intensive skill-building practice. Part 1 includes drills specifically designed to increase SPEED; Part 2, to improve CONTROL. Within each of these two parts, the difficulty of timed-writing copy increases after each 10 lessons. This simple-to-complex progression of copy permits the use of the book at different skill levels, depending upon the intent of instruction and level of skill development.

Lesson structure of Part 1. Each of the 30 lessons of Part 1 consist of a keyboard review, a technique builder, a basic skill builder, a special speed builder, and a set of paragraphs for speed development. The major thrust, therefore, is on techniques with appropriate speed.

Lesson structure of Part 2. Each of the 30 lessons of Part 2 consist of a keyboard review, a technique builder, a basic control builder, a special control builder, and a set of paragraphs for control development. These lessons are designed to integrate technique refinement and keyboarding with accuracy.

Basis for Copy Difficulty Controls

The paragraph materials that are designed for speed/control building and measurement have been controlled for difficulty using three difficulty indices: syllable intensity, average word length, and percentage of high-frequency words. Experimentation has shown that these 3 factors when controlled simul-

taneously affect significantly the speed of performance in keyboarding: the easier the copy, the higher the speed; the more difficult the copy, the lower the speed.

Computer analyses of the language of business, as well as the general vocabulary, have identified the frequency with which specific letters, figures, letter combinations, figure combinations, and words occur in the normal use of language. The special drills in *Keyboarding Speed/Control Builders* are composed of the combinations identified by these analyses to ensure realistic practice on those combinations that *will* occur in everyday business communications — not merely those that *may* occur. The relative stroking difficulties of the various types of combinations have also been determined by experimentation.

Emphasis on Techniques of Performance

Because poor techniques of keyboard performance underlie the development of both speed and control, the lessons give special attention to basic techniques in a recurring cycle of emphasis on first one, then another, technique. In addition, marginal technique reminders are provided even for those drills whose basic purposes are not primarily technique refinement.

Pacing Tactics Employed

It is common knowledge that keyboarding skill increases very slowly unless pressure is applied to force the stroking combinations close together in time. It is equally well known that individuals whose stroking rates are forced to high levels will inevitably make errors and must be led by forced drop back in speed to bring their stroking patterns under control. The materials in *Keyboarding Speed/Control Builders,* therefore, are structured to provide the pressure to "spurt" for speed followed by a drop back to refine the motion patterns. The tactics employed for this purpose include: guided writings, skill-comparison writings, progressive-length writings (1-, 3-, and 5-minute writings), and skill transfer writings.

Acknowledgements

The design of this book is based on the findings of a number of research studies, including: the vocabulary studies of Dr. J.E. Silverthorn and Dr. Devern J. Perry; the word- and letter-combination analyses and the copy difficulty studies of Dr. Jerry W. Robinson; the figure-symbol frequency study of Dr. George S. Grill; and the "chaining" study of Dr. Thomas E. Langford. The authors gratefully acknowledge the contributions of each of these studies to the development and sequencing of the materials contained in *Keyboarding Speed/Control Builders.*

Each Speed Builder in Part 1 contains the following sections: (1) a keyboard review, (2) a technique builder, (3) a basic skill builder, (4) a special speed builder, and (5) a set of paragraphs for speed development. Some effective ways of using the materials are suggested below.

Keyboard review. Each *Keyboard review* consists of an alphabetic sentence, a figure sentence, and a figure/symbol sentence. These sentences may be used as preparatory material to limber up the fingers and to establish the correct "mind set" for the remainder of the speed-building session. The alphabetic sentence provides a complete review of the letters on the keyboard and can be used through an informal error analysis to determine which letters have not been mastered. Since all the numbers are used in the figure sentences and commonly used symbols are combined with figures in the figure/symbol sentences, these drill lines will build proficiency in these two difficult skill areas affecting keyboarding fluency.

Technique builder. The *Technique builders* are designed to improve basic keyboarding techniques that are so essential for developing speed—keystroking and efficient use of the manipulative parts of the keyboard. The keystroking drills should be used to refine the techniques of stroking the keys. Emphasis should be on quick, sharp, direct strokes with the fingers curved, the wrists low, and the hands quiet, almost motionless.

In the stroking drills, those sentences which include double-letter sequences and third-row reaches will result in higher stroking rates. These sentences should be used as *goal-setting* sentences for 1-minute writings on the more difficult sentences containing direct-reach, adjacent-key, and first- or bottom-row sequences. The goal should be to equal the rate attained on the easier copy.

In the drills on the manipulative parts, concentrate on the elimination of time-consuming pauses when using the space bar, the return key, the shift keys and lock, and the backspace key. Practice these special drills until the manipulation of these keyboard parts becomes a smooth, fluent response within overall keyboarding performance.

Basic speed builder. The *Basic speed builders* provide concentrated practice on balanced-hand 2-letter combinations and commonly used words, easy 3-letter stroking patterns, and common phrases. In addition, the drills provide an opportunity to practice keyboarding from script. The opening lines of each drill consist of a preview of the basic elements which make up the sentences that follow. Maintain a smooth stroking rate when keyboarding these drills with the goal of improving stroking rhythm.

Special speed builder. The *Special speed builders* include speed spurt sentences, skill comparison sentences and paragraphs, guided writings, and skill transfer paragraphs.

Spurt writings can be used to force more rapid stroking. Increase the "spurts" from 15" to 20" to 30" to 1' to maintain higher stroking rates for increased periods of time. In any self-directed pacing for spurt writing and goal typing, become familiar with the copy through unpaced practice; try two or three pacings, adjusting the goal if necessary; drop back for isolated practice of those words or stroking combinations that cause difficulty; then pace the keyboarding again to reach a new goal.

The skill comparison drills in Special Speed Builders 5, 12, 15, 20, 27 and 30 provide opportunities for keyboarding copy of contrasting difficulty. Follow the marginal cues in attempting to reach individual goals for keyboarding the more difficult copy.

Guided writing paragraphs in Special Speed Builders 6, 13, 21, and 28 consist of triple-controlled copy progressing from easy to low-average to average difficulty designed for self-paced or teacher-paced practice. Detailed procedures are outlined in the margin alongside each timed writing.

Special Speed Builders 7, 14, 22, and 29 provide opportunities for skill transfer rate comparisons in key-boarding straight-copy timed writings and writings from script, rough-draft, and statistical copy. Marginal cues call for establishing a base rate on straight-copy paragraphs and practicing figures in isolation before comparing rates achieved on the more difficult copy.

Speed paragraphs. The *Speed paragraphs* in Part 1 consist of triple-controlled timed writings on straight, statistical, and rough-draft copy, progressing from easy to low-average to average difficulty. Following efforts to achieve a higher speed with repeated 1-minute attempts on each paragraph, the student is challenged to attain the same rate or better through a 3-minute writing on both paragraphs combined.

The following chart compares copy difficulty indices for speed and control paragraphs in Parts 1 and 2:

Difficulty level	Syllable intensity	Average word length (strokes)	Percent of high frequency words
E—Easy	1.2	5.1	90
LA—Low average	1.4	5.4	85
A—Average	1.5	5.7	80
HA—High average	1.7	6.0	75
D—Difficult	1.8	6.3	70

30c • Basic control builder: common phrases

Keyboard the phrases *as units* while you strive for control and continuity.

1 the city | to this | order to | be able to | I can | we hope | at your | in any
2 we would like | just to | your request | have had | the most | fulfill your
3 In order to be able to fulfill your request, we hope you call us.
4 We would like to have had the opportunity just to visit the city.

30d • Special control builder: guided paragraph writing

1 Take a 1' writing on the ¶; determine *gwam*.

2 Add 4-6 *gwam* to this base rate to set a new goal rate.

3 Take two 1' guided writings on the ¶; determine *gwam* on the better writing.

all letters used | D | 1.8 si | 6.3 awl | 70% hfw

One characteristic usually sought in a promotable person is the ability to speak and write effectively using proper English. Personnel managers, however, often emphasize the fact that too many employees are unable to prepare written communications that are clear, concise, and free of grammar errors. Just how expert are you in this trait? For most of us, acquiring this skill involves studying sound principles of written communications which have proven effective in the past and then applying these rules every day in an educated manner.

30e • Control paragraphs

(straight copy)

1 Two 1' writings on each ¶; strive to increase accuracy on the second writing.

2 One 5' writing on both ¶s combined; determine *gwam*.

all letters used | D | 1.8 si | 6.3 awl | 70% hfw

	gwam 1'	5'

Ever since the automobile was invented, Americans have found that | 13 | 3 | 35
owning one can become both a necessity and also a luxury. Unless good | 27 | 5 | 38
public transportation is available in the larger cities, practically | 41 | 8 | 41
everyone who commutes to work each day definitely needs a vehicle; or | 55 | 11 | 43
that individual must depend upon others for a ride. Millions of people | 70 | 14 | 46
spend hours every workday behind the steering wheel of an automobile. | 83 | 17 | 49

Changing gas prices and availability have prompted many larger | 13 | 19 | 52
vehicle owners to adjust their lifestyles. Some have realized that | 26 | 22 | 54
a small car with better gas economy satisfies their needs adequately. | 40 | 24 | 57
Others have opted to form carpools to lower commuting costs. Every | 54 | 27 | 60
year when the new automobiles come off the assembly lines, numerous | 67 | 30 | 63
Americans face the question of what size vehicle to buy. | 79 | 32 | 65

gwam 1' | 1 | 2 | 3 | 4 | 5 | 6 | 7 | 8 | 9 | 10 | 11 | 12 | 13 | 14 |
5' | 1 | 2 | 3 |

SPEED BUILDER 1

1a • Keyboard review

Practice once slowly; a second time for speed; a third time for control.

alphabet 1 Brox said the lucky girls have hit the jackpot with amazing frequency.

figures 2 Major FM stations broadcast here on 98.6, 102.3, 104.7, and 105.2 MHZ.

fig/sym 3 As fractions, 62.5% is 5/8, 37.5% is 3/8, 75% is 3/4, and 90% is 9/10.

| 1 | 2 | 3 | 4 | 5 | 6 | 7 | 8 | 9 | 10 | 11 | 12 | 13 | 14 |

1b • Technique builder: stroking (reach strokes)

Reach up to the 3d row and down to the bottom row without moving the hands.

j-h; d-e 1 jhj jog jug hub high other month ded do due deal desk deed ledge added

l-o; f-t 2 lol of old loss loan look solo ftf at fit far often after lofty rafter

k-i; f-r 3 kik is if his skid kill skill like frf fro fry farm from refund friend

4 This month his friend helped them adjust lofty rafters in my old farm.

5 I told the fellow that I had a deed to this house in an old jelly jar.

6 After she fails to get the loan, she may ask for a refund on the deal.

| 1 | 2 | 3 | 4 | 5 | 6 | 7 | 8 | 9 | 10 | 11 | 12 | 13 | 14 |

1c • Basic skill builder: balanced-hand two-letter combinations (digraphs)

Practice each two-letter combination 3 or 4 times before keyboarding the words which follow each combination.

1 th these brother both he healthy check ache an annual change plan

2 or order support editor en entire trend dozen nd and mandate land

3 to today stocks into ti times sitting until ur urges further tour

4 My brother urged the editor to have an annual health check today.

5 The manager will support the change to order our stocks annually.

6 Until further notice, the time for the land tour will not change.

1d • Special speed builder: speed spurts (balanced hand)

Practice each sentence as fast as possible to build stroking speed.

1 The social sorority may suspend the girls and make them pay a penalty.

2 The tutor may form a theory to handle the big problem for the auditor.

3 When did the rich girl pay the firm for the ruby and the formal gowns?

4 She may risk the title to the land to make the goals for a big profit.

5 The firm may pay for the workbox if and when they do their work right.

6 Did he go with the eight girls of the sorority to the ritual downtown?

7 If they work with proficiency and vigor, they may make their big goal.

8 The rigid amendment to the proviso may signal a problem for the firms.

| 1 | 2 | 3 | 4 | 5 | 6 | 7 | 8 | 9 | 10 | 11 | 12 | 13 | 14 |

29e • Control paragraphs

(statistical copy)

1 Two 1' writings on each ¶; strive for improved control rate on the second writing.

2 One 5' writing on both ¶s combined; determine *gwam*.

| all letters used | D | 1.8 si | 6.3 awl | 70% hfw |

gwam 1' 5'

Recently, the Agriculture Department revealed plans to offer the — 13 | 3 | 38
complete or partial sale of 6,000,000 acres of National Forest Service — 25 | 5 | 41
property. This possible sale does include 3.2% of the 190.8 million — 37 | 7 | 43
acres within the system. Forest Service property is situated within — 51 | 10 | 46
39 states. Land chosen for possible sale includes 36% of U.S. forests — 63 | 13 | 48
in Ohio, 27% of that in Illinois, and 24% of that in Mississippi; but — 76 | 15 | 51
the amount of acreage involved in most states is considerably smaller. — 90 | 18 | 54

Alaska unquestionably leads all the other states in the number of — 13 | 21 | 56
national forest acreage with 23,119,525. With 20,427,455 acres, Idaho — 23 | 23 | 58
ranks second. It is not too amazing that California placed third with — 38 | 25 | 61
20,413,044. Despite its size, Texas actually does not fall within the — 49 | 28 | 63
top 10. Considering the percentage of forest property qualifying for — 63 | 30 | 66
possible sale, however, Texas and an adjacent state, Oklahoma, could — 76 | 33 | 69
stand to lose 20% and 21% respectively should the sale be approved. — 88 | 36 | 71

gwam 1' | 1 | 2 | 3 | 4 | 5 | 6 | 7 | 8 | 9 | 10 | 11 | 12 | 13 | 14 |
gwam 5' | 1 | 2 | 3 |

CONTROL BUILDER 30

30a • Keyboard reivew

Practice once slowly; a second time for speed; a third time for control.

alphabet 1 I wonder if Kay ever realized the jumping exercise can be quite tough?

figures 2 Mail in Boxes 312, 784, 965, and 1005 was destroyed in the May 2 fire.

fig/sym 3 Specs for #0-87 are: paper, 16.5" (419.1 mm); line, 13.2" (335.2 mm).

| 1 | 2 | 3 | 4 | 5 | 6 | 7 | 8 | 9 | 10 | 11 | 12 | 13 | 14 |

30b • Technique builder: stroking

Keep fingers vertical, not slanting, over home keys as you practice this drill.

direct reaches

1 After the symphony, my uncle served a special brunch to the directors.
2 My unusual brochures brought many new tourists to my recreation parks.
3 A huge iceberg broke into many pieces as it went under the icebreaker.

adjacent keys

4 Water skiing in the choppy waters at Port Avalon was Luisa's decision.
5 In her opinion, our secretarial pool should receive a superior rating.
6 Lu's mother violently opposed her decision to travel with a pop group.

| 1 | 2 | 3 | 4 | 5 | 6 | 7 | 8 | 9 | 10 | 11 | 12 | 13 | 14 |

1e • Speed paragraphs

(straight copy)

1 Two 1' writings on each ¶; strive to increase speed on the second writing.
2 One 3' writing on both ¶s combined; determine *gwam*.

all letters used | E | 1.2 si | 5.1 awl | 90% hfw

gwam 1' | 3'

	1'	3'	
Through the years, people all over the world have shown quite an	13	4	68
interest in the moon and the stars. We want to know about space. Not	27	9	73
until the invention of the telescope a little more than two hundred	41	14	78
years ago did we get a close look at objects in space. With improved	55	18	82
telescopes, we have been able to learn more about what is out there.	69	23	87
People have long wanted to go out into space so that we can explore it.	83	28	92
It has taken many years of work to begin to make that dream come true.	97	32	97
An early means of travel was to have a horse pull a wagon. The	13	37	101
train, the ship, and also the car increased the distance and the speed	27	41	106
at which we could travel. Then, in the early years of our century,	41	46	110
the first machine that could fly was made. Since this development,	54	51	115
progress has been amazing. We now have jets that take us all over the	69	55	119
world, and we have rockets that can carry us into space. We have been	83	60	124
able to make the dream of many come true, to travel in space.	95	64	128

gwam 1' | 1 | 2 | 3 | 4 | 5 | 6 | 7 | 8 | 9 | 10 | 11 | 12 | 13 | 14 |
gwam 3' | 1 | 2 | 3 | 4 | 5 |

SPEED BUILDER 2

2a • Keyboard review

Practice once slowly; a second time for speed; a third time for control.

alphabet 1 The six groups objected to the frenzied activity at my weekly inquest.

figures 2 We must paint rooms 107, 135, 248, 260, and 354 no later than July 29.

fig/sym 3 We paid charges of $34.50, $6.79, $28.10, and $9.30 on Account #86975.

| 1 | 2 | 3 | 4 | 5 | 6 | 7 | 8 | 9 | 10 | 11 | 12 | 13 | 14 |

2b • Technique builder:
stroking (adjacent keys)

Keep fingers curved and upright as you practice this drill.

1 re review increase shore io prior radio operations er erected were her

2 po port policy importance as ask base last op open hope proper develop

3 we were between power ui quite requirement suit rt part artery support

4 Her weekly news service hopes to offer reports for his radio stations.

5 We were told to develop a basic policy to stop her operations quickly.

6 Policies which require the erection of power lines are broad in scope.

| 1 | 2 | 3 | 4 | 5 | 6 | 7 | 8 | 9 | 10 | 11 | 12 | 13 | 14 |

29a • Keyboard review

Practice once slowly; a second time for speed; a third time for control.

alphabet 1 Vicente disqualified two zealous bikers for excitedly jumping the gun.

figures 2 Be sure to add Extensions 276, 398, 413, and 506 to your new listings.

fig/sym 3 Model Z-203-948 measures 15″ x 30″ x 46″ and sells for $78 discounted.

| 1 | 2 | 3 | 4 | 5 | 6 | 7 | 8 | 9 | 10 | 11 | 12 | 13 | 14 |

29b • Technique builder: manipulative control

Center each line horizontally. Use your right index finger on the backspace key for better control.

1 Back to the Basics in Business Education
2 A Recurring Phenomenon: The Computer Craze
3 The National Collegiate Association for Secretaries (NCAS)
4 Word Processing and Its Impact on Small Businesses
5 Keyboarding Speed/Control Builders

29c • Basic control builder: one-hand three-letter combinations (trigraphs)

Practice each three-letter combination 3 or 4 times before keyboarding the words which follow each combination. Concentrate on the trigraphs in the words.

1 ese these deserve research reservations age rage averaged engaged
2 omp pomp compare company companion era erase herald erratic opera
3 rom from aroma chrome romantic red redo erred redeemed reductions
4 Much pomp will herald the performance of the engaged opera stars.
5 Figures from my company show large reductions on chrome fixtures.
6 Your very erratic companions may cancel these opera reservations.

29d • Special control builder: opposite fingers

Concentrate on each pair of opposite-finger letters as you practice this drill.

1 ty nightly exactly quarterly tightly yt yachts youth enjoyment layouts
2 ru rough routine rumors running ur urges urgent during purpose current
3 sl sales sleek slightly slyly ls lasts lists also lusty listen lessons
4 Nightly, the youth seeks enjoyment by running the yacht in the inlets.
5 Rumor has it that your quarterly report lists sales at a current high.
6 The sleek sled was slightly damaged during the rough turn in the road.
7 The lass turned away slyly when the joyful youth let out a lusty yell.
8 Be sure to listen to the lesson so you can draw the last layout right.

| 1 | 2 | 3 | 4 | 5 | 6 | 7 | 8 | 9 | 10 | 11 | 12 | 13 | 14 |

2c • Basic skill builder: balanced-hand two-letter combinations (digraphs)

Practice each two-letter combination 3 or 4 times before keyboarding the words which follow each combination. *Think* the two-letter combinations.

1 of office softer roof nt into continue want is issue poison basis
2 le letter flew file me mention comment same fo found perform info
3 ic icy bicycle chic it item position profit ng angle danger doing
4 Did the letter mention her position or performance in the office?
5 At issue is a letter in my office file which mentions the danger.
6 I want the info in the file on the profits from the chic bicycle.

2d • Special speed builder: speed spurts (double letters)

Practice each sentence as fast as possible to build stroking speed. Work for continuous movement of the carriage (carrier).

1 She will be happy to offer to meet with the planning committee weekly.
2 My staff will soon suggest that I assist the community in its efforts.
3 I will call the bookkeeping errors to the attention of the commission.
4 To assist the community, the committee will offer millions of dollars.
5 Anna will address a letter to the attention of the college bookkeeper.
6 Following the weekly meeting, the staff will pay all accounts in full.

| 1 | 2 | 3 | 4 | 5 | 6 | 7 | 8 | 9 | 10 | 11 | 12 | 13 | 14 |

2e • Speed paragraphs (straight copy)

1 Two 1' writings on each ¶; strive to increase speed on the second writing.
2 One 3' writing on both ¶s combined; determine *gwam*.

all letters used | E | 1.2 si | 5.1 awl | 90% hfw

	gwam 1'	3'
There were some problems that had to be solved before travel into	13	4 69
space was feasible. In the early days, it was thought that the air on	27	9 73
earth extended to the moon and beyond, so that the sole problem would be	42	14 79
to make a machine which could travel far into space. When we realized	56	19 84
that the air around us extends only several hundred miles, we knew that	71	24 88
not even a jet could travel into space. Our plans to go out in space	85	28 93
had to wait while we built the right sort of ship for space travel.	98	33 97
The means which was to be used to let us travel from here to outer	13	37 102
space has been known to us for many years. This was a rocket which does	28	42 107
not require air in order to move. It was not until just before the	43	47 111
second world war, though, that a rocket which could go a few thousand	56	51 116
feet into the air was built. Two problems to confront were getting	70	56 121
enough force to send the rocket away from earth and making a ship of	84	60 125
materials which would not be destroyed by heat as it returned home.	98	65 130

```
gwam 1' | 1 | 2 | 3 | 4 | 5 | 6 | 7 | 8 | 9 | 10 | 11 | 12 | 13 | 14 |
     3' |   1   |     2     |     3     |     4     |     5     |
```

28c • Basic control builder: common phrases

Maintain proper technique and control as you keyboard these phrases. Read and keyboard the phrases *as units*.

1 some of | we know | have to | for your letter | copy of the | that you will
2 more than | part of | enjoy your | this will | under the | your interest in
3 Thank you for your letter expressing your interest in the camera.
4 We know that you will enjoy your copy of the book more than ever.

28d • Special control builders

(homonym hurdles)

Keyboard each sentence at a controlled rate. Concentrate on these homonyms as you improve control.

1 to too two tare tear weekly weakly capital capitol feat feet bear bare
2 pare pair pear knot not principal principle roles rolls bazaar bizarre
3 do dew due rains reigns reins taut taught rite right write wait weight
4 She taught my girls to keep the reins taut whenever it rains severely.
5 The two were too busy to notice your bizarre items sold at the bazaar.
6 Wait before you add more weight; it may already be right for the rite.

| 1 | 2 | 3 | 4 | 5 | 6 | 7 | 8 | 9 | 10 | 11 | 12 | 13 | 14 |

28e • Control paragraphs

(rough-draft copy)

1 Two 1' writings on each ¶; strive to increase your control rate on the second writing.
2 One 5' writing on both ¶s combined; determine *gwam*.

| all letters used | 1.8 si | 6.3 awl | 70% hfw |

	gwam 1'	5'
Through the years, various *dramatic* changes have often occurred because	12	2	36
of machines. the impact of automation on society canbe truly	24	5	38
seen in shorter work weeks or considerable less time spent in	36	7	41
the home performing house hold duties. Consequently, women	47	9	43
continue to have an ever increasing amount of extra liesure	60	12	45
time. Learning how to handle additoinal freetime can become	71	14	48
sincerely a challenge to the person who prefers to stay busy.	84	17	50
Today, more then ever before all of us certainly ponder	11	19	53
the importants of haveing some interesting hobbys. To travel	24	22	55
can satisfy some people who are phiscally able and who could	36	24	57
handle all the expenses. For others, quiet pursuit of hidden,	48	26	60
creative talent, laying dormant because lack of time now may	60	29	62
initiate a quality of life unexpected totally. Having taken	73	31	65
inventory, determines the hobbies you possess.	84	34	67

SPEED BUILDER 3

3a • Keyboard review

Practice once slowly; a second time for speed; a third time for control.

alphabet 1 Frank will adjust a lever to equalize pressure in this oxygen chamber.

figures 2 Warehouse A34962 has 1,250 square feet and 18,750 cubic feet of space.

fig/sym 3 Oki sold items that cost $9.50, $13.24, and $76.08--a total of $98.82.

| 1 | 2 | 3 | 4 | 5 | 6 | 7 | 8 | 9 | 10 | 11 | 12 | 13 | 14 |

3b • Technique builder: stroking (direct reaches)

Make the long reaches without returning to the home row as you practice this drill.

1 To serve notice for my brass sale, we announced many price reductions.

2 A large shiny truck swerved left of center under a bridge into my car.

3 I used many effective programs to bring my company under a debt limit.

4 I used my special checking accounts to pay many of my charge accounts.

5 We doubt my young group received any extra music instruction recently.

6 Young men must obtain a special permit to serve in many reserve units.

| 1 | 2 | 3 | 4 | 5 | 6 | 7 | 8 | 9 | 10 | 11 | 12 | 13 | 14 |

3c • Basic skill builder: balanced-hand two-letter combinations (digraphs)

Practice each two-letter combination 3 or 4 times before keyboarding the words which follow each combination. Keep the hands and arms quiet; use *finger* action.

1 co come record acorn al allow dealer local ro room product patrol

2 me near knew alone wi with otherwise wit pr price express prepare

3 si sixty assist basis ri rich bring trip ch chief exchange church

4 Local dealers knew that the product would allow for rich profits.

5 He may wish to prepare a basis for the exchange of color schemes.

6 He alone knew the true basis for the sixty price changes we made.

3d • Special speed builder: speed spurts (common words)

Practice each line as fast as possible to build stroking speed. Keep hands quiet; keep fingers curved and upright.

1 the of to and in you a for we your is that be will this are on have it

2 as our with I or at by yours if not very from which all us truly would

3 has an can any dear order time was one been these may do please office

4 they so new but now year there business more no letter their other who

5 If it is your job to do so, would you please send their letters to me.

6 All of us would like to have more business this year if we can get it.

7 In reply to your business letter, we will ship your new order on time.

8 They can make your will, and I can send it to your office at any time.

| 1 | 2 | 3 | 4 | 5 | 6 | 7 | 8 | 9 | 10 | 11 | 12 | 13 | 14 |

27e • Control paragraphs

(straight copy)

1 Two 1′ writings on each ¶; strive to improve accuracy on the second writing.
2 One 5′ writing on both ¶s combined; determine *gwam*.

all letters used | D | 1.8 si | 6.3 awl | 70% hfw

gwam 1′ | 5′

The issuing of a unique public law has created unusual provisions   13 | 3 | 42
for students with various disabilities to return to the typical class-   27 | 5 | 44
room. The mandated procedure has been referred to as mainstreaming.   41 | 8 | 47
Through a series of sessions with school officials, parents, and each   55 | 11 | 50
student, plans are initiated to enable the learner to take part in all   69 | 13 | 53
regular classes along with other pupils. Diligent attempts are made   83 | 17 | 56
to secure what has been defined as the least restrictive environment.   97 | 19 | 58

For years, typing teachers have been slightly aware, but yet not   13 | 22 | 61
totally informed, of ways in which handicapped students can definitely   27 | 25 | 64
benefit from instruction at the keyboard. Various reach patterns can   41 | 28 | 67
be taught the learner with a finger or a hand missing. Several devices   56 | 30 | 70
have also been proven useful to enable students with other disabilities   70 | 33 | 72
to adjust as quickly as possible to positioning themselves at any kind   84 | 36 | 75
of keyboard console. A little extra effort realizes maximum results.   98 | 39 | 78

gwam 1′ | 1 | 2 | 3 | 4 | 5 | 6 | 7 | 8 | 9 | 10 | 11 | 12 | 13 | 14 |
gwam 5′ | 1 | 2 | 3 |

CONTROL BUILDER 28

28a • Keyboard review

Practice once slowly; a second time for speed; a third time for control.

alphabet 1 Hazel quit exercising daily last week just before seeing improvements.

figures 2 Locks on Rooms 138, 294, and 607 were broken during a June 5 break in.

fig/sym 3 He should star (*) Orders #4-36, #5-87, and #36-90 for 12/10 delivery.

| 1 | 2 | 3 | 4 | 5 | 6 | 7 | 8 | 9 | 10 | 11 | 12 | 13 | 14 |

28b • Technique builder:

stroking (rows)

Make each reach without moving the other fingers out of position as you practice this drill.

3d row 1 We wrote you, too, your two youth groups were to tour the Purdy Tower.

2 Were we tipped quietly to typewrite our story of the territory treaty?

home row 3 Gladys was aghast as Silas joshed Hilda while they walked to the hall.

4 Sally, a shy lass, was glad Sheff's aged dad had a full staff at work.

bottom row 5 Mannix excavated the caved-in zone where the mammoth bones were found.

6 Zebras can become extinct without expert care, my zoo keeper verified.

| 1 | 2 | 3 | 4 | 5 | 6 | 7 | 8 | 9 | 10 | 11 | 12 | 13 | 14 |

3e • Speed paragraphs

(statistical copy)

1 Two 1′ writings on each ¶; strive to increase speed on the second writing.
2 One 3′ writing on both ¶s combined; determine *gwam*.

| all letters used | E | 1.2 si | 5.1 awl | 90% hfw |

| | gwam 1′ | 3′ |

The first object to circle the world was put into space by the — 13 | 4 | 62
Russians in 1957. Its weight was 184 pounds, and it stayed in space — 27 | 8 | 66
for 57 days. This was followed very quickly by a second one of 1,121 — 37 | 12 | 70
pounds with a dog in it. Early in 1958, this country put its first sat- — 51 | 17 | 75
ellite into space. Its weight was only 31 pounds, and it was in space — 64 | 21 | 79
for 112 days. The first man went into space in 1961. From 1961 to — 75 | 25 | 83
1965, 24 men were sent into space, two of them for more than 330 hours. — 87 | 29 | 87

Efforts in 1957 and 1958 to get to the moon were not successful. — 11 | 33 | 91
In 1959, a Russian ship reached it after a 36-hour trip. In the years — 24 | 37 | 95
1961, 1962, 1963, and 1964, many ships went by or reached the moon. A — 35 | 41 | 99
ship flew around the moon in 1966 and came as close as 120 miles to its — 48 | 45 | 103
surface. In 1968, this country sent two men in a ship that went around — 62 | 50 | 108
the moon 10 times and returned. Next, we amazed the world in 1969 by — 74 | 54 | 112
sending two men who spent 21 hours and 36 minutes working on the moon. — 87 | 58 | 116

```
gwam  1' | 1 | 2 | 3 | 4 | 5 | 6 | 7 | 8 | 9 | 10 | 11 | 12 | 13 | 14 |
      3' |    1    |     2    |      3     |      4    |      5    |
```

SPEED BUILDER 4

4a • Keyboard review

Practice once slowly; a second time for speed; a third time for control.

alphabet	1	Why did Vi expect to find quartz rocks in the bottom of the glass jar?
figures	2	Please revise pages 8, 10, 24, 37, 51, 96, and 104 as soon as you can.
fig/sym	3	He made scores of 81.3%, 92.6%, 84.7%, and 85.0%--an average of 85.9%.

```
| 1 | 2 | 3 | 4 | 5 | 6 | 7 | 8 | 9 | 10 | 11 | 12 | 13 | 14 |
```

4b • Technique builder: stroking

Concentrate on the words as you practice this drill.

adjacent keys	1	Prior to their proposed sale, he has agreed to drop radio advertising.
	2	The shop union was anxious to report the progress on the new policies.
double letters	3	It is essential that all letters in a business office be written well.
	4	Sally shipped the tools, wood, and glass we need by express last week.
direct reaches	5	My secretary must check the charges made excessively on many accounts.
	6	Accountants managed my special checking account at your branch office.

```
| 1 | 2 | 3 | 4 | 5 | 6 | 7 | 8 | 9 | 10 | 11 | 12 | 13 | 14 |
```

CONTROL BUILDER 27

27a • Keyboard review

Practice once slowly; a second time for speed; a third time for control.

alphabet 1 The Board was quick to explain every major hazardous flying condition.

figures 2 Send your request to 7208 Oak Drive or 9365 Yale Street by October 14.

fig/sym 3 Your Policy #280-95734 (amended) calls for quarterly premiums of $146.

| 1 | 2 | 3 | 4 | 5 | 6 | 7 | 8 | 9 | 10 | 11 | 12 | 13 | 14 |

27b • Technique builder: manipulative control

(aligning on lines)

1 Keyboard 5 horizontal lines 35 spaces wide using the underline key.
2 Pull paper release lever forward and remove paper.

3 Reinsert paper. Using the variable line finder, align the paper and keyboard each sentence of the paragraph over a horizontal line.
4 Check alignment by comparing the above example.

Check your work using this example.

To relay the best impression, learn

how to insert all data on a printed

form using the proper machine parts

correctly. Practice and a good eye

will help you to master this skill.

27c • Basic control builder: one-hand three-letter combinations (trigraphs)

Practice each three-letter combination 3 or 4 times before keyboarding the words. Read and key the trigraphs *as units.*

1 ted elated interested selected slated rec direct received correct
2 der under order derive thunderous ess less stress address lessons
3 sta stay statement stadium stage oul should would fouled shoulder
4 I'm elated he has been selected to address those most interested.
5 Thunderous sounds in the stadium cheered the southpaw to victory.
6 Your correct statement should show less money received than this.

27d • Special control builder: common word endings

Practice each combination ending before keyboarding the sentences.

1 ability reality facility responsibility initial spatial circumstantial
2 bound sound round sight right fright might event prevent count recount
3 inject reject project inform perform either neither inferior superiors
4 monogram telegram select reflect radical logical quire inquire acquire
5 The rules may require me to acquire the lead story from the head cook.
6 In reality, they have the ability to prevent an event in our facility.
7 They have the right to inform you of official circumstantial evidence.
8 A logical decision would be to reject an inferior project immediately.

| 1 | 2 | 3 | 4 | 5 | 6 | 7 | 8 | 9 | 10 | 11 | 12 | 13 | 14 |

Control Builder 27

4c • Basic skill builder: balanced-hand two-letter combinations (digraphs)

Practice each two-letter combination 3 or 4 times before keyboarding the words which follow each combination. Make quick, snappy strokes.

1 us use trust status nc once income dance ns answer transfer turns
2 di did additions radio la land delay gala pa payment repairs span
3 ot other hotels shot fi find affirm outfit em emblem theme system
4 I answered that other hotels used radio music for the gala dance.
5 He must find a system to make payment for the repair of the span.
6 In addition, there may be a delay in the use of the music system.

4d • Special speed builder: speed spurt sentences

Practice each sentence as fast as possible to build stroking speed. Work for smooth, quick stroking.

balanced-hand
1 The duty of the panel is to dismantle the ancient chapel or halt work.
2 The emblem is an authentic memento of the visit to the rich coalfield.

double letters
3 I still feel we can add three employees to the staff of the committee.
4 Will all these book offers be in effect for an additional three weeks?

common words
5 Do you have the time to do the letters and orders they want this week?
6 We all hope you will be able to be with them when they go to the city.

| 1 | 2 | 3 | 4 | 5 | 6 | 7 | 8 | 9 | 10 | 11 | 12 | 13 | 14 |

4e • Speed paragraphs

(rough-draft copy)

1 Two 1' writings on each ¶; strive to increase speed on the second writing.
2 One 3' writing on both ¶s combined, determine *gwam*.

all letters used | E | 1.2 si | 5.1 awl | 90% hfw

| | gwam 1' | 3' |

There is no doubt that we now know *so much* more about our world 13 | 4 | 59
and this solar system because of our *trips into space* ~~space trip~~. In the field 27 | 9 | 64
of science, *a great deal of data* ~~much information~~ has been obtained and is being 39 | 13 | 68
studied ~~studies~~. Studies of the moon's *sur* face alone have given us a lot 53 | 18 | 72
of data not just about the moon but about the earth. *and its history* Samples 68 | 23 | 78
bought back from the moon will be under study for years to come. 81 | 27 | 82

Few of us may realize that *quite* a lot of *the* items on the market 13 | 31 | 86
now were *first made* for use in the space program. *For* Example, satellites now 29 | 37 | 92
are used to send TV *signals and to speed up* ~~and telephone~~ calls. Surveys made from 44 | 42 | 97
space of the earth and the air have made weather fore casts 56 | 46 | 101
better and have *helped us in* ~~aided~~ our production of food, power, and other 70 | 50 | 105
things. Tools *once* used in the space program are now in daily use. 83 | 55 | 110

26c • Basic control builder: common phrases

Practice each phrase 3 or 4 times before keyboarding the sentences.

1 *this time | to do | we will | of course | wish to | you that | if you | as well*

2 *I know | which is | with our | have the | will not | enclosed is | as soon as*

3 *is in | is to | and to | to go | to assure | one of the | we will be | the next*

4 *As soon as I know one of the boats is in, we will be ready to go.*

5 *Of course, we wish to assure you that we will not stop this time.*

6 *The long report which is to appear in the next issue is enclosed.*

26d • Special control builder: word building

Practice each line at a controlled rate. As you keyboard each line, concentrate on the word endings with each new word.

1 hope hoped hoping hopeful receive received receiving receivership firm

2 firmly firmed firmness high higher highly highest budge budget budgets

3 budgeted budgetary all allot allotted allotment know knowing knowledge

4 The growing firm is hopeful of receiving a higher budgetary allotment.

5 Knowing that receivership was imminent, the judge allotted extra time.

6 Please certify that needless items have been cut from the high budget.

| 1 | 2 | 3 | 4 | 5 | 6 | 7 | 8 | 9 | 10 | 11 | 12 | 13 | 14 |

26e • Control paragraphs

(straight copy)

1 Two 1' writings on each ¶; strive to increase your accuracy on the second writing.
2 One 5' writing on both ¶s combined; determine *gwam*.

all letters used | D | 1.8 si | 6.3 awl | 70% hfw

gwam 1'   5'

Students who eventually plan to seek entry-level positions in a   13   3 | 41
field of business usually ask how they should be preparing themselves   27   5 | 44
for such positions. With the job competition today, career-oriented   41   8 | 46
students would do well to acquire various abilities that continue to   54   11 | 49
be in high demand. Thorough preparation in mathematics is a definite   68   14 | 52
advantage. Likewise, anyone who possesses a thorough background in   82   16 | 55
computers should easily land a high-paying spot with a business firm.   96   19 | 57

An essential skill so often disregarded, however, is the viable   13   22 | 60
skill of being able to typewrite. The person who can keyboard with   26   24 | 63
accuracy and proof copy equally well will always be in demand in this   40   27 | 66
electronic era. As businesses continue to utilize additional data and   55   30 | 68
word processing equipment, talented operators of this equipment will   68   33 | 71
always be sought. Since much of the data processed deal with numbers,   83   36 | 74
the quest will continue for those extremely accurate with figures.   96   38 | 77

gwam 1' | 1 | 2 | 3 | 4 | 5 | 6 | 7 | 8 | 9 | 10 | 11 | 12 | 13 | 14 |
5' | 1 | 2 | 3 |

5a • Keyboard review

Practice once slowly; a second time for speed; a third time for control.

alphabet 1 Victoria may win the special grand prize of an exquisite sable jacket.

figures 2 The square root of 23 is 4.7958315 whereas the cube root is 2.8438670.

fig/sym 3 Bob noted that Room 125 is 9'3" x 11'6" and Room 170 is 10'6" x 18'4".

| 1 | 2 | 3 | 4 | 5 | 6 | 7 | 8 | 9 | 10 | 11 | 12 | 13 | 14 |

5b • Technique builder: manipulative control (space bar)

Space with a down-and-in motion of the right thumb as you practice this drill.

1 Al the and to for may is but fix it pay due or own men by did box with

2 if big air us end six an she cut do fit go so bid map me oak them both

3 he sir rug make than am of bus tie when also go lay man form wish then

4 Al and the six men may make a box of oak for us if they wish to do so.

5 He may also make the men go with me to the bus to cut and fit the rug.

6 Both of them may wish to pay us for a map if they go by air or by bus.

| 1 | 2 | 3 | 4 | 5 | 6 | 7 | 8 | 9 | 10 | 11 | 12 | 13 | 14 |

5c • Basic skill builder: balanced-hand two-letter combinations (digraphs)

Practice each two-letter combinations 3 or 4 times before keyboarding the words which follow each combination. Speed up the stroking of the two-letter combinations.

1 ut utmost route out so social resort also ow owner downtown below

2 su supply assures pursue os costs prose autos ai air chairs plaid

3 th these either with he hear their apostrophe an any brands ocean.

4 The owner of a social resort on the ocean bought my plaid chairs.

5 Sue assured me that either route led to a show of autos downtown.

6 I hear they will supply either one of these brands at below cost.

5d • Special speed builder: skill comparison sentences

Practice each sentence for 30" or 1'. Strive to achieve the same rate on all the sentences.

balanced-hand 1 The firm may pay for an audit to end the big problem of the coalfield.

2 He paid for the autos the girls kept to go downtown to their sorority.

one-hand 3 Kinuyo was aware bad debts created greater stress on minimum reserves.

4 A decrease in minimum tax rates attracted scarce reserves in my union.

short words 5 It is true that most of us may lose our jobs soon if the farm is sold.

6 As of this date, all of the bonds have been sold for cash by the bank.

long words 7 Increased radio advertising attracts considerable additional business.

8 Trade associations publish articles concerning outstanding activities.

| 1 | 2 | 3 | 4 | 5 | 6 | 7 | 8 | 9 | 10 | 11 | 12 | 13 | 14 |

25e • Control paragraphs

(straight copy)

1 Two 1' writings on each ¶; strive to improve accuracy on the second writing.

2 One 5' writing on both ¶s combined; determine *gwam*.

all letters used | D | 1.8 si | 6.3 awl | 70% hfw

	gwam 1'		5'
Backpacking is an outdoor activity that young and old alike seem	13	3	41
to enjoy. Hiking into the wilderness for several days can be extremely	27	5	43
relaxing. How strenuous such an activity becomes depends upon every	41	8	46
individual. The younger, more physically able person may prefer to	55	11	49
backpack personally every item necessary for the trip. Others, and	68	14	51
especially older, retired persons, would just as soon have a packer	82	16	54
and pack train handle all the provisions except for the day pack.	95	19	57
When a packer is hired, backpack parties can become quite large.	13	22	60
Considering the expense, a larger group is usually necessary to cut	27	24	62
actual costs for any one individual. Despite the size of the group,	41	27	65
it is always possible to travel together in smaller combinations and	54	30	68
experience the thrill of enjoying rugged scenery and an unsurpassed	68	33	70
solitude with family and close friends. Azure skies, snowy distant	82	35	73
peaks, and brilliant wildflowers entice new hikers every summer.	94	38	76

gwam 1' | 1 | 2 | 3 | 4 | 5 | 6 | 7 | 8 | 9 | 10 | 11 | 12 | 13 | 14 |

5' | 1 | 2 | 3 |

CONTROL BUILDER 26

26a • Keyboard review

Practice once slowly; a second time for speed; a third time for control.

alphabet **1** The lively crowd was quick to praise five zany, ambidextrous jugglers.

figures **2** Check No. 125, dated 7/6/87, completed the payment on Account #340-291.

fig/sym **3** Effective 3/1/86, $295.60 will be drawn monthly from Account #202-074.

| 1 | 2 | 3 | 4 | 5 | 6 | 7 | 8 | 9 | 10 | 11 | 12 | 13 | 14 |

26b • Technique builder:

stroking (third and fourth fingers, both hands)

Make these finger reaches without moving the hands or arms as you practice the sentences.

1 The quartet will appeal to headquarters for its small quota of quartz.

2 Our opponent is optimistic the owners will allow for popular opinions.

3 Townspeople oppose postponement of a parade in their quaint old plaza.

4 Azaleas are popular by a pool, but Polly wanted poppies planted there.

5 She quietly questioned the quota of zippers and extra, new allowances.

6 I awoke early, aware we must await repair of the wagon spoke and axle.

| 1 | 2 | 3 | 4 | 5 | 6 | 7 | 8 | 9 | 10 | 11 | 12 | 13 | 14 |

5e • Speed paragraphs

(straight copy)

1 Two 1' writings on each ¶; strive to increase speed on the second writing.
2 One 3' writing on both ¶s combined; determine *gwam*.

all letters used | E | 1.2 si | 5.1 awl | 90% hfw

	gwam 1'	3'	

No country can survive without law and order. When people began · 13 | 4 | 69

to organize and to live and work as a group, they found that a set of · 27 | 9 | 73

laws to control the group was needed. If we had not had these laws, we · 41 | 14 | 78

would have made little or no progress. It is quite certain that if each · 56 | 19 | 83

of us did just as he or she pleased with no thought for the rights of · 70 | 23 | 88

others, chaos would result. Laws are set up to protect the group and, at · 85 | 28 | 93

the same time, provide as much freedom for the individual as possible. · 99 | 33 | 97

It has been said that the only thing certain is that we can expect · 13 | 37 | 101

to have change. Our laws follow the progress of the group and, in the · 28 | 42 | 106

course of time, as the group changes so do the laws. Although the · 41 | 47 | 111

changes in society may be slow, the laws change as we try to make our · 55 | 51 | 116

social conditions better and to insure equal justice for all of our · 69 | 56 | 120

citizens. As the years go by, we can expect even more change as we · 82 | 60 | 125

change our views about how people should act in our society. · 94 | 64 | 129

gwam 1' | 1 | 2 | 3 | 4 | 5 | 6 | 7 | 8 | 9 | 10 | 11 | 12 | 13 | 14 |
gwam 3' | | 1 | | 2 | | 3 | | 4 | | 5 | |

SPEED BUILDER 6

6a • Keyboard review

Practice once slowly; a second time for speed; a third time for control.

alphabet 1 Ziegman quit his job waxing cars to avoid being fired for sloppy work.

figures 2 Call 876-9425 to arrange for the meetings on August 6, 13, 20, and 27.

fig/sym 3 Add these items to our new catalog: #47 ($1.35 each) and #69 ($2.80).

| 1 | 2 | 3 | 4 | 5 | 6 | 7 | 8 | 9 | 10 | 11 | 12 | 13 | 14 |

6b • Technique builder:

stroking (double letters)
Strike the double letters quickly as you practice these sentences.

1 Eddy took three kickoffs for the offense and bobbled all of them.

2 Annie borrowed a glass bowl filled with coffee, eggs, and apples.

3 The caddie will find the ball in a muddy pool just off the green.

4 Apparently, the school roof cannot support the additional weight.

5 All committees will meet weekly to discuss bookkeeping loopholes.

6 The new football puzzles in the book took skill and added effort.

25a • Keyboard review

Practice once slowly; a second time for speed; a third time for control.

alphabet	1	Zane expects to pass five new bylaws quickly during the joint meeting.
figures	2	The dismissal bells may ring at 8:35, 9:17, and 10:26 a.m. on the 4th.
fig/sym	3	Part #428-6 (*old #159-3) is now selling for $6.70 effective 10/25/83.

| 1 | 2 | 3 | 4 | 5 | 6 | 7 | 8 | 9 | 10 | 11 | 12 | 13 | 14 |

25b • Technique builder:
stroking (second finger, both hands)

Make the second-finger reaches without moving the other fingers out of position as you practice this drill.

1 Clara succeeded in keeping the edict, but her editor declined to help.
2 Mel liked the idea to erect a dike but decided to accede to the edict.
3 A low cloud ceiling blocked a decent view of the recent lunar eclipse.
4 I am keenly aware of the recent kidding Cecelia received at Rebecca's.

| 1 | 2 | 3 | 4 | 5 | 6 | 7 | 8 | 9 | 10 | 11 | 12 | 13 | 14 |

25c • Basic control builder:
one-hand three-letter combinations (trigraphs)

Practice each three-letter combination 3 or 4 times before keyboarding the words which follow each combination.

1 pre prefer prepare pretend suppress tte attend plotted committees
2 rea really unreal realize reappraise eve every believe everything
3 ear early nearly appeared rearrange rat rate underrated rationale
4 She may prefer to prepare for her act early to attend to details.
5 Without a rationale, he may pretend to believe everything passed.
6 She realized she had really suppressed them when they retaliated.

25d • Control paragraph

(rough-draft copy)

all letters used | D | 1.8 si | 6.3 awl | 70% hfw

1 Two 1' writings on the ¶; strive to increase accuracy on the second writing.

2 One 5' writing on the ¶; determine gwam.

	gwam 1'	5'
Regardless of economics, conditions, the job outlook for ~~the new~~ business	13	3	29
graduates can be a promising ~~one~~ for those who have readied them-	27	5	32
selves well for a variety of initial work experiences, ~~who have~~ the ability to	41	8	35
be flexible, to be ~~ready~~ qualified for that single position that is available	56	11	38
within the company, ~~or~~ makes the value of an applicant immediately apparent	70	14	41
to the employer. Success is realized by workers who ~~may~~ strive	85	17	44
to ~~accel~~ excel immediately in their first jobs and endeavoring to ~~toil~~ work to maxi-	99	20	47
mize ~~there~~ their both the potential. Possessing ambition to be a success and	113	23	49
a willing to acquire the right pre requisites, will surely doors open	127	25	52
those that otherwise might ~~not usually open~~ remain closed.	134	27	54

6c • Basic skill builder: balanced-hand two-letter combinations (digraphs)

Practice each two-letter combination 3 or 4 times before keyboarding the words which follow each combination. *Think* the two-letter combinations.

1 *bl black payable cable am amounts name logjam wo workers flowers power*

2 *ry rye hungry machinery tu turn returnable attitude ia via liar liable*

3 *id ideas bridge valid if differs verify tariff ep epic department keep*

4 *Pay a valid tariff on the machinery via cable if we are liable for it.*

5 *To avoid a logjam, workers on the cable bridge returned the machinery.*

6 *The department workers realize valid attitudes and ideas might differ.*

6d • Special speed builder: guided paragraph writing

1 Take a 1′ writing on the ¶; determine *gwam*. This is your base rate.

2 Add 4-6 words to your base rate to determine your goal rate. Find ¼′ goals for new writings at your goal rate (example: 48 = 12, 24, 36, 48).

3 Take 1′ writings as ¼′ guides are called until you reach your goal rate.

all letters used | E | 1.2 si | 5.1 awl | 90% hfw

There are very few people in our country today who do not find it essential to work in order to make a living. It is quite true that work is the foundation of all human existence and that it is a measure of life. If you reflect for a moment, you will realize that there would be no progress without work. Without work, we would not have the comforts or the goods which we enjoy in our daily lives.

6e • Speed paragraphs

(straight copy)

1 Two 1′ writings on each ¶; strive to increase speed on the second writing.

2 One 3′ writing on both ¶s combined; determine *gwam*.

all letters used | E | 1.2 si | 5.1 awl | 90% hfw

gwam 1′ | 3′

	1′	3′
The ability to express the right words when you speak or write is	13	4 / 59
one of the basic qualities you need for success in business. There have	28	9 / 63
been many studies made which show that skill in the use of words has an	42	14 / 68
effect on the success one achieves and the pay he or she earns. If you	57	19 / 73
are able to use the words which say clearly the ideas you have in mind,	71	24 / 78
you will be welcome in the world of business.	80	27 / 81
How well can you express your ideas when you speak or write? Do	13	31 / 85
you speak and write clearly so that you are easily understood? Or do	27	36 / 90
you give others a fuzzy or mistaken impression of the thought you would	41	40 / 95
like to communicate? When you state any idea, you must be sure it	55	45 / 99
is clear. If you improve your word power so that you can use the best	69	50 / 104
words to express your thoughts, you are on your way to job success.	83	54 / 108

gwam 1′ | 1 | 2 | 3 | 4 | 5 | 6 | 7 | 8 | 9 | 10 | 11 | 12 | 13 | 14 |
3′ | 1 | 2 | 3 | 4 | 5 |

24c • Basic control builder:
common phrases

Maintain proper technique and control as you keyboard these phrases. Read and keyboard the phrases *as units.*

1 to try | as the | I hope | interested in | have the | that I opportunity to
2 this matter | as to | number of | when we | the new | your interests | not be
3 we are | look forward | they may | copies of | happy to | the time | are able
4 I hope that I have the opportunity now to check into this matter.
5 They may not be interested in a number of copies of this catalog.
6 I look forward to the time when we are able to try the new motor.

24d • Special control builder:
transition traps

Work for smooth stroking transition between each pair of words as you practice this drill. Strive for continuity as you keyboard the sentences.

1 club bought leagues seek extra athletes travel ledgers everyone except
2 state exciting two oldest to organize team members my youth only young
3 five excellent civic campground for ready airmail letters fancy yachts
4 My youth club bought five excellent trucks for ready use at two camps.
5 Several leagues seek to organize extra athletes as night team members.
6 These old travel ledgers state exciting facts about two tourist traps.

| 1 | 2 | 3 | 4 | 5 | 6 | 7 | 8 | 9 | 10 | 11 | 12 | 13 | 14 |

24e • Control paragraphs

(statistical copy)

1 Two 1′ writings on each ¶; strive for improved control rate on the second writing.
2 One 5′ writing on both ¶s combined; determine *gwam.*

| all letters used | D | 1.8 si | 6.3 awl | 70% hfw |

gwam 1′ | 5′

According to Census Bureau calculations, a bachelor's degree is — 13 | 3 | 37
worth approximately $300,000 in extra lifetime salaries for today's — 25 | 5 | 40
young men. A recently tabulated survey reveals that today's 18-year- — 38 | 8 | 42
old man who completes a college degree will accumulate $329,000 more — 50 | 10 | 44
during his lifetime than men that same age receiving only their high — 64 | 13 | 47
school diplomas. Based upon reported salaries from inquiries in 1979, — 77 | 15 | 50
1980, and 1981, women in the same category can expect to earn $242,000. — 87 | 17 | 52

The Bureau's extrapolations indicate that today's 18-year-old man — 13 | 20 | 54
with a college diploma can anticipate earning $1,190,000 over his life- — 25 | 23 | 57
time compared with $861,000 for a male counterpart who just completed — 37 | 25 | 59
high school. Likewise, women in a similar category also can realize — 51 | 27 | 62
earnings from $381,000 with any secondary diploma to $523,000 with a — 61 | 30 | 64
college degree. Bureau tabulations indicate that the average male — 74 | 32 | 66
works for 38 years, compared to 28 years for the average female. — 86 | 34 | 69

gwam 1′ | 1 | 2 | 3 | 4 | 5 | 6 | 7 | 8 | 9 | 10 | 11 | 12 | 13 | 14 |
5′ | 1 | 2 | 3 |

SPEED BUILDER 7

7a • Keyboard review

Practice once slowly; a second time for speed; a third time for control.

alphabet	1	Overworked people fight tension by relaxing quietly in a warm Jacuzzi.
figures	2	On May 2, we shipped 4,390 tons; but on May 15, we shipped 6,875 tons.
fig/sym	3	On March 31, J & M Co. (478-9200) merged with Marks & Sons (596-8100).

| 1 | 2 | 3 | 4 | 5 | 6 | 7 | 8 | 9 | 10 | 11 | 12 | 13 | 14 |

7b • Technique builder: manipulative control

(element return)

Set the left margin at 30 (pica) or 36 (elite); set a tab stop at center *plus 10.* Keyboard the lines as directed.

tab ⟶ To return
the element,_____ tab _____⟶ make
a quick_____ tab _____⟶ little-finger
reach_____ tab _____⟶ to the
return_____ tab _____⟶ without
moving_____ tab _____⟶ other fingers.

7c • Basic skill builder: balanced-hand two-letter combinations (digraphs)

Practice each two-letter combination 3 or 4 times before keyboarding the words which follow each combination. Read and key the digraphs *as units.*

1 *vi views evils provide wh when which whether ie ties pried parties*
2 *ir ivory live drive ol old folder fool ci city civil special acid*
3 *na names nation snap banana ir irk tire require ay may stay today*
4 *The city may require both parties to provide the special folders.*
5 *Where are the names of those who live or drive in the city today?*
6 *They tried to provide our views on the evils of the nation today.*

7d • Special speed builder: skill transfer paragraphs

1 One 1' writing on ¶1; determine *gwam.*
2 Take 1' writings on ¶2 until you equal or exceed your *gwam* on ¶1.

all letters used | E | 1.2 si | 5.1 awl | 90% hfw   gwam 1'

You might expect that money would head the list of the rewards that 14
workers want most from their jobs. Yet, in many cases, money is far 27
from the top of the list. In one study of ten key factors, workers said 42
they felt the most important factor was a show of appreciation for the 56
work they had done. 60

Most firms realize now that the need to feel important is 12
a strong one for most of us. In reply to questions asked about 23
what they seek from a job, most people ranked money fifth. The 36
type kind of job a person has, his annual or her income and social status, 49
as well as other personal factors, have some effect on the replies answers. 61

23e • Control paragraphs

(rough-draft copy)

1 Two 1' writings on each ¶; strive to increase your control rate on the second writing.

2 One 5' writing on both ¶s combined; determine *gwam*.

all letters used	D	1.8 si	6.3 awl	70% hfw

	gwam 1'	5'	
Care(i)ng for the ~~old age~~ *elderly* has become, and rightfully should	11	2	35
be, a national con(s)(c)ern. As ~~modern~~ *miracle* medicines are ~~invented, so~~ *discovered*	24	5	38
many Citizens are able to live longer ~~and much~~ *more* more productive	36	7	40
life(s). ~~The problem for~~ *a challenge to* the nation is tobe continually al(l)ert	48	10	43
too ways to p(r)ovide not only adequ(ate) medic(al) care but al(l)so	60	12	45
adequate hous(e)ing and unique li(e)suretime activit(ies) that ~~does~~ *will*	72	14	48
promo(te a) he(a)lthy, happy, and secure(d) enviro(n)ments for all.	83	17	50
Much publi(s)(c)ity is usually given to ~~the need for~~ *the necessity of* funding the	11	19	52
soca(i)l programs de(a)ling with the ~~old age~~ *elderly*. Re(s)(c)ently, much ~~of~~	24	21	54
~~the~~ sup(p)ort for the(se) programs has ~~dropped~~ *shifted* to the local ~~level~~ *agencies*	36	24	57
where mone(ys) (y)(ies) often are inadequ(ate). Consequently, Volunt(t)eers	48	26	59
are ne(e)ded who will give gener(o)usly of ~~there~~ *their* time and ~~any~~ talent(s)	60	29	62
in serving the ~~old age~~ *elderly*. it may a ma(i)ze you how excit(e)ing and	72	31	64
que(i)tly rewa(r)ding just such volunteer work ~~is~~ *can be.*	82	33	66

CONTROL BUILDER 24

24a • Keyboard review

Practice once slowly; a second time for speed; a third time for control.

alphabet	1	Just next week Hoby's quaint cafes may serve pizza and wine regularly.
figures	2	Their enrollment figure jumped from 19,764 to over 23,580 in 10 years.
fig/sym	3	A 10-pitch model is 22.4" x 19.2" x 7.6" (568 mm x 487 mm x 193.5 mm).

| 1 | 2 | 3 | 4 | 5 | 6 | 7 | 8 | 9 | 10 | 11 | 12 | 13 | 14 |

24b • Technique builder:
stroking (first finger, both hands)

Make the first-finger reaches without moving the hands as you practice this drill.

1 The attorneys for both parties agreed to settle the case out of court.
2 Thirteen men were not immune to the irritating virus, but others were.
3 The committee referred to the comments attached to the hurried offers.
4 The unmarried youths regret not vying for that tennis trophy tomorrow.
5 A firm made an attractive offer and received many fitting suggestions.
6 You guaranteed the jobber was holding my shipment another four months.

| 1 | 2 | 3 | 4 | 5 | 6 | 7 | 8 | 9 | 10 | 11 | 12 | 13 | 14 |

7e • Speed paragraphs

(straight copy)

1 Two 1' writings on each ¶; strive to increase speed on the second writing.
2 One 3' writing on both ¶s combined; determine *gwam*.

all letters used | E | 1.2 si | 5.1 awl | 90% hfw

gwam 1' | 3'

What is an office? In the early days of this century, an office — 13 | 4 | 67

was simply a room with stools and high desks where the workers were — 27 | 9 | 71

usually all men. It was the job of these men to write letters, reports, — 41 | 14 | 76

and forms and to keep records of all types by hand. The only equipment — 56 | 19 | 81

used was pen, ink, and paper. Simple filing and calculations were also — 70 | 23 | 86

done by hand. All in all, it was quite a simple job in which the major — 84 | 28 | 90

task was to produce papers of some kind. — 92 | 31 | 93

The office of today is far more complex. The desks and chairs are — 13 | 35 | 98

still used, but some of the workers are women. Although they still pre- — 27 | 40 | 102

pare letters, forms, and reports and keep records of all kinds, many — 42 | 45 | 107

do so on electronic machines, such as the one you may be using, as well — 56 | 50 | 112

as some kind of computer, big or small, to analyze and process data. — 70 | 54 | 116

The office is now the source of data which is so vital to the day-to-day — 85 | 59 | 121

work of the business and the success it achieves. — 94 | 62 | 125

gwam 1' | 1 | 2 | 3 | 4 | 5 | 6 | 7 | 8 | 9 | 10 | 11 | 12 | 13 | 14 |
gwam 3' | 1 | 2 | 3 | 4 | 5 |

SPEED BUILDER 8

8a • Keyboard review

Practice once slowly; a second time for speed; a third time for control.

alphabet 1 Joy said the big shop was quiet after six bronze clocks chimed twelve.

figures 2 On August 10, 5,928 voted for the proposal and 4,367 voted against it.

fig/sym 3 Mark Invoice #86 for Tri-State Co. "Paid 12/19 ($40.35) by Check #75."

| 1 | 2 | 3 | 4 | 5 | 6 | 7 | 8 | 9 | 10 | 11 | 12 | 13 | 14 |

8b • Technique builder: stroking

(reach strokes)

Make each reach without moving the other fingers out of position as you practice this drill.

s-w; j-n 1 sws sweeps swim switch wish wise jnj June jangle junior enjoin janitor

f-g; j-u 2 fgf fog flag fight figure gift golf juj judge jump jury justice adjust

d-c; ;-p 3 dcd dock decide addict cod clad cadet ;p; pop; pup; trip; wrap; sweep;

s-x; j-m 4 sxs six sax sex axis exist express jmj jam Jim jamb jump major majesty

5 Jan plans to join the cadets on their trip; Jim decided to go golfing.

6 Did the janitor decide to adjust or switch the six flags on the docks?

7 That judge enjoined a jury to decide on the justice of the major case.

8 A majority of the six cadets plan to switch to a trip on that express.

| 1 | 2 | 3 | 4 | 5 | 6 | 7 | 8 | 9 | 10 | 11 | 12 | 13 | 14 |

23a • Keyboard review

Practice once slowly; a second time for speed; a third time for control.

alphabet 1 Jeff quizzed two boys about a vehicle normally parked right next door.

figures 2 The large lot at 8976 Elm is 140 feet wide and at least 235 feet deep.

fig/sym 3 After 12/30, Regulation 567(c) supercedes 498(b), affecting 392 cases.

| 1 | 2 | 3 | 4 | 5 | 6 | 7 | 8 | 9 | 10 | 11 | 12 | 13 | 14 |

23b • Technique builder:
stroking (rows)

Practice the sentences with smooth rhythm; keep hand and arms quiet.

3d row 1 Were you aware your first priority was to write two etiquette reports?

2 I opted to try to sell our upper property prior to our trip to Europe.

home row 3 Galah was glad she had shell glasses as Dallas also had shell glasses.

4 Dallah's dad had a sad day as a jagged shard of glass slashed his leg.

bottom row 5 A brave man zeroed in on a cave exit where I saw a brown grizzly bear.

6 My zoo has mazes of shrubbery carved in the images of zebras and oxen.

| 1 | 2 | 3 | 4 | 5 | 6 | 7 | 8 | 9 | 10 | 11 | 12 | 13 | 14 |

23c • Basic control builder:
one-hand three-letter
combinations (trigraphs)

Practice each three-letter combination 3 or 4 times before keyboarding the words which follow each combination. Read and key the trigraphs *as units*.

1 res rest arrest interest reserve ver very verify reverse inverted

2 ere here where erected elsewhere ave have behave avenues averaged

3 ers hers matters personal customers own ounces amounts discounted

4 The rest can verify my interest in where the sign may be erected.

5 Personal amounts discounted to customers averaged more this year.

6 The police may arrest those who do not behave here and elsewhere.

23d • Special control builder

(long words)

Work for continuity of stroking while still maintaining control as you keyboard these long words.

10-12 letters 1 agreements employment recommended utilization outstanding considerable

2 managerial merchandise cooperation requirements publication interested

12-14 letters 3 extraordinary conscientious responsibility professional administrators

4 accomplishment dependability satisfactorily approximately endorsements

sentences 5 He recommended a managerial position with considerable responsibility.

6 Her extraordinary accomplishment clearly reveals she is conscientious.

sentences 7 Were all the administrators interested in my professional publication?

8 Employment agreements called for outstanding professional cooperation.

| 1 | 2 | 3 | 4 | 5 | 6 | 7 | 8 | 9 | 10 | 11 | 12 | 13 | 14 |

8c • Basic skill builder: balanced-hand two-letter combinations (digraphs)

Practice each two-letter combination 3 or 4 times before keyboarding the words which follow each combination. Keep fingers curved and wrists low; use quick snap strokes

1 ap approve disappear mishap ke keep workers awake ty types style sixty
2 qu quickly acquaint banquet bo bonds hobo labor bu buy ambulance debut
3 ov overlook improves above ig ignores figure big uc luck buckle reduce
4 We quickly approved the improved style of the buckle the workers made.
5 Did they labor over the figures and buy ambulances at a reduced price?
6 I approve of the big banquet for the sixty workers who had no mishaps.

| 1 | 2 | 3 | 4 | 5 | 6 | 7 | 8 | 9 | 10 | 11 | 12 | 13 | 14 |

8d • Special speed builder: speeds spurts (balanced hand)

Practice each sentence as fast as possible to build stroking speed.

1 Their fury and dismay may fuel the proxy fight when they pay the firm.
2 When did the auditor sign the formal amendment to the endowment proxy?
3 If I am too busy, Len may hand the amendment to Akeo to sign by proxy.
4 Duty with the signal corps may entitle the ensign to the lapel emblem.
5 Their neighbor kept a big box of hay and eight bushels of corn for me.
6 The sorority paid the firm to make the six oak signs and eight panels.

| 1 | 2 | 3 | 4 | 5 | 6 | 7 | 8 | 9 | 10 | 11 | 12 | 13 | 14 |

8e • Speed paragraphs

(rough-draft copy)

1 Two 1' writings on each ¶; strive to increase speed on the second writing.
2 One 3' writing on both ¶s combined; determine *gwam.*

all letters used | E | 1.2 si | 5.1 awl | 90% hfw

	gwam 1'	3'
In the business office today, people must know how to type.	12	4	59
A great many positions *jobs now* require the use of the key board for	24	8	63
all *kinds of* work. Most of the work done for *a* business is in some way	38	13	68
linked to a computer *of some kind* some way. Skill at a keyboard is *the* needed *s thus*	53	18	72
in order to *record and* process data. All workers who deal with data and	67	22	77
words, and all those at all levels of management must know how to typewrite.	82	27	82
We realize that there are many jobs for typists in busi-	11	31	86
ness and that the *good* typist *can* finds a job *quite* fast and *can* moves to a new	27	36	91
job with *relative* much ease. A *For* very good example *is* the position *is* the	38	40	95
same for *the* letters and *the* numbers on *a word* processors *it is* as on a typewriter;	55	46	101
only the symbols are moved. The *good* typist but needs *a* little prac-	69	50	105
tice *to learn how* to work one of these machines and make a job change.	83	55	110

22c • Basic control builder: common phrases

Keyboard the phrases and sentences while maintaining proper control and technique.

1 *the same | it was | would appreciate | you have | is not | so that | it would*
2 *that it | hope that | interest in | your help | all of | at this | during the*
3 *want to | this letter | on this | to a | which we | amount of | the following*
4 *All of us hope that you have an interest in the following offers.*
5 *She would appreciate your help during the switch to a new system.*
6 *This letter which we received reveals the same amount of pledges.*

22d • Special control builder

(direct reaches)

Practice each line at a controlled rate. Make direct reaches with minimum hand movement.

words
1 echo annuity unless numbing incorrect number bravely receive municipal
2 nullified nucleus ceremony under unusual ceiling effective understands
3 celebrate lunar economical nutritionist eclipse my intervals specifics

sentences
4 Jun has nullified my right to receive annuities at specific intervals.
5 A large ceremony was under way to celebrate the unusual lunar eclipse.
6 Unless Tammy was incorrect, rice is an effective, nutritive substance.

| 1 | 2 | 3 | 4 | 5 | 6 | 7 | 8 | 9 | 10 | 11 | 12 | 13 | 14 |

22e • Control paragraphs

(straight copy)

1 Two 1' writings on each ¶; strive to improve accuracy on the second writing.
2 One 5' writing on both ¶s combined; determine *gwam*.

all letters used | D | 1.8 si | 6.3 awl | 70% hfw

gwam 1' | 5'

For several years, Americans have been aware of the need to alter   13 | 3 | 40
radically their usual lifestyles with regards to daily nutrition and   27 | 5 | 43
exercise. Only recently, however, has any physical fitness movement   41 | 8 | 46
really taken hold across the nation. Exercise centers have sprung up   55 | 11 | 49
all over the country with unique equipment and special classes. These 69 | 14 | 51
centers offer patrons many options in guided exercise that range from 83 | 17 | 54
rigid workouts on machines to varied dance routines set to music.   96 | 19 | 57

Large business organizations now realize the importance of their   13 | 22 | 59
employees in sedentary jobs getting more exercise regularly. Numerous 27 | 25 | 62
incentives have been provided to encourage as many workers as possible 41 | 27 | 65
at all levels to get more exercise. It is not too unusual today for   55 | 30 | 68
some firms to have a workout facility right on the premises. Often   67 | 33 | 71
tied in with these corporate fitness programs are special lectures for 83 | 36 | 73
key executives dealing with stress management.   92 | 38 | 75

gwam 1' | 1 | 2 | 3 | 4 | 5 | 6 | 7 | 8 | 9 | 10 | 11 | 12 | 13 | 14 |
5' | 1 | 2 | 3 |

9a • Keyboard review

Practice once slowly; a second time for speed; a third time for control.

alphabet	1	Jacqueline broke dozens of very expensive wrought iron carriage lamps.
figures	2	The index increased from 156.9 on September 10 to 187.4 on October 23.
fig/sym	3	The vote was 407 (65%) "yes"; 198 (31%) "no"; and 26 (4%) "undecided."

| 1 | 2 | 3 | 4 | 5 | 6 | 7 | 8 | 9 | 10 | 11 | 12 | 13 | 14 |

9b • Technique builder: stroking (adjacent keys)

Strive for smooth, continuous stroking as you practice this drill.

1 oi oils invoice join nm inmate enmity solemn kl inkling weekly pickles
2 iu genius medium stadium lk milked talks walks uy buy buyers soliloquy
3 mn alumni hymns column sd Thursday wisdom df handful steadfast mindful
4 The buyer sent his weekly invoices for oil to the stadium on Thursday.
5 Mindful of alumni, the choir sang a solemn hymn prior to my soliloquy.
6 The inmate, a forger and a genius, joined the weekly talks on Tuesday.

| 1 | 2 | 3 | 4 | 5 | 6 | 7 | 8 | 9 | 10 | 11 | 12 | 13 | 14 |

9c • Basic skill builder: balanced-hand two-letter combinations (digraphs)

Practice each two-letter combination 3 or 4 times before keyboarding the words which follow each combination. Vary stroking speed to fit difficulty of copy.

1 th there mother eighth he head sheets niche an anyone brand spans
2 or original sport color en enters depends been nd end handle fund
3 to took factory photo ti titles still satin ur urban turns assure
4 The original of the color photo she took of the factory is there.
5 Assure them that anyone can turn onto the span to the urban area.
6 The color of the title sheet depends on the photos and the funds.

9d • Special speed builder: speed spurts (balanced hand)

Practice each line as fast as possible to build stroking speed. Keep hands and arms quiet; use *finger* action.

1 Did she make the proficient robot and sign the authentic title for it?
2 The firms may also amend or suspend the formal amendment to the proxy.
3 If he signals, row the visitor to the island for eight bushels of rye.
4 Did the busy neighbor lend them a hand to fix the auto and mend a rug?
5 They may make an oak shelf for ancient bowls their neighbor lent them.
6 An auditor held the proxy for the auto firm and the title to the land.
7 When did the formal panel name the girl prodigy heir to the endowment?
8 The city may pay the firm a small profit for all the land by the dock.

| 1 | 2 | 3 | 4 | 5 | 6 | 7 | 8 | 9 | 10 | 11 | 12 | 13 | 14 |

21e • Control paragraphs

(straight copy)

1 Two 1' writings on each ¶; strive to improve accuracy on the second writing.
2 One 5' writing on both ¶s combined; determine *gwam*.

all letters used	D	1.8 si	6.3 awl	70% hfw

	gwam 1'	5'
The typewriter has undergone innumerable changes ever since the	13	3 | 40
first "writing machine" was invented over a century and a half ago.	27	5 | 43
Typists were amazed when the manual typewriter gave way to the electric	41	8 | 46
model. And yet, perhaps an even more radical change was the invention	55	11 | 49
of the element, eliminating many extra parts necessary with the type-	69	14 | 51
bar machines. And now the print wheel is commonplace on the numerous	83	17 | 54
electronic typewriters readily available from vendors today.	95	19 | 57
Lately, manufacturers of office equipment have been forecasting	13	22 | 59
eventual removal of the common typewriter on top of each worker's	26	24 | 62
desk. Instead, office personnel--including the top echelon--may well	40	27 | 65
have an electronic word processor of some sort within easy reach for	54	30 | 67
handling various kinds of data input and output. In order to adjust	68	33 | 70
to unique changes taking place within tomorrow's offices, individuals	82	35 | 73
must be alert constantly to ways in which to stay abreast.	93	38 | 75

gwam 1' | 1 | 2 | 3 | 4 | 5 | 6 | 7 | 8 | 9 | 10 | 11 | 12 | 13 | 14 |
5' | 1 | | 2 | | 3 |

CONTROL BUILDER 22

22a • Keyboard review

Practice once slowly; a second time for speed; a third time for control.

alphabet 1 Five extra shallots were pickled quickly for my big jaunt to Zanzibar.

figures 2 Flight 287 left the gate at 10:43 p.m.; Flight 569 is to be cancelled.

fig/sym 3 Box #5 measured 24" x 36" x 18" and contained 970 trays ($13.95 each).

| 1 | 2 | 3 | 4 | 5 | 6 | 7 | 8 | 9 | 10 | 11 | 12 | 13 | 14 |

22b • Technique builder: manipulative control

(tabulation)

Keyboard the table 70 spaces wide and leave 4 spaces between the columns. Keep eyes on copy as you strive for smooth transition between tab and keys.

of	end	ink	fare	pink	autos	areas	myself	nature
be	lay	pin	cast	milk	socks	bears	change	family
so	pup	red	also	gets	plump	aware	freeze	handle
my	big	oil	sign	fact	works	nylon	played	better
at	sir	him	card	city	pupil	taxes	worthy	answer

9e • Speed paragraphs

(statistical copy)

1 Two 1' writings on each ¶; strive to increase speed on the second writing.
2 One 3' writing on both ¶s combined; determine *gwam*.

all letters and figures used | E | 1.2 si | 5.1 awl | 90% hfw

	gwam 1'		3'
In the early 1900s, the office began to grow in scope and size. In	13	4	59
1900, there were 870,000 people who held jobs as clerks of all types.	24	8	63
Of that group, 91% were men and only 9% were women. By 1920, the number	36	12	67
of clerks in the work force had grown to 3.38 million. In 1940, there	49	16	71
were almost 5 million clerks--a growth of more than 2,000% over the	61	20	74
figure in 1900. Only 19% of the clerks were men while 81% were women--	72	24	78
quite a big change from the picture in 1900.	80	27	81
What is the outlook for work in the office in the years ahead?	13	31	85
Experts say the job market in this field will rise through the 1990s	25	35	90
into the year 2000. They predict that the force of 18.8 million clerks	38	39	94
in 1980 will rise to about 23.9 million in 1990--a change of 26.8%. Of	48	42	97
this group, big demand will be for those who can type. From 3.8 million	62	47	102
in 1980, jobs for typists will increase by at least 28% and maybe 37% in	73	51	106
1990 to a total of at least 4.9 million or perhaps 5.2 million.	84	55	109

gwam 1' | 1 | 2 | 3 | 4 | 5 | 6 | 7 | 8 | 9 | 10 | 11 | 12 | 13 | 14 |
     3' | 1 | 2 | 3 | 4 | 5 |

SPEED BUILDER 10

10a • Keyboard review

Practice once slowly; a second time for speed; a third time for control.

alphabet 1 Key tax cuts revitalized performance as we bought new major equipment.

figures 2 Orders 4987, 5016, 5024, and 5137 were shipped by express on April 29.

fig/sym 3 "Crimson," a new shade (Stock #495307), will sell for $128.16 a gross.

| 1 | 2 | 3 | 4 | 5 | 6 | 7 | 8 | 9 | 10 | 11 | 12 | 13 | 14 |

10b • Technique builder: stroking

(reach strokes)

Reach with the finger, not the hand. Keep wrists low and relaxed as you practice this drill.

j-y; s-x 1 yjy joy jay Jerry justly majority xsx sax sox sixty six expose expects

a-z; f-b 2 zaz hazy azure zeal daze zag pizza bfb fib fabrics before bifocal buff

a-q; f-v 3 qaq Joaquin aqua quart quake equal vfv five favor fever flavors vivify

4 Jerry, a Red Sox buff, expects to enjoy five or six games during June.

5 Joy did Joaquin a favor and saved a bolt of azure blue fabric for him.

6 A majority of us enjoyed jam and jelly, but she raved about the pizza.

| 1 | 2 | 3 | 4 | 5 | 6 | 7 | 8 | 9 | 10 | 11 | 12 | 13 | 14 |

CONTROL BUILDER 21

21a • Keyboard review

Practice once slowly; a second time for speed; a third time for control.

alphabet 1 That very exquisite zodiac jewelry may go on display before next week.

figures 2 From a student body of 6,485, only 3,791 voted in the May 20 election.

fig/sym 3 Item #2-71 (at $36.95 each) may be reduced 40% for the January 8 sale.

| 1 | 2 | 3 | 4 | 5 | 6 | 7 | 8 | 9 | 10 | 11 | 12 | 13 | 14 |

21b • Technique builder: stroking (rows)

Make each reach without moving the other fingers out of position as you practice this drill.

3d row 1 Were you pretty sure you were to detour to your right to go to Topeka?

2 Thirty-three tourists were to go to Europe to tour your quiet retreat.

home row 3 Ask Hal's dad if a sad lad stashed aside a full glass flask last fall.

4 Dale Haskall added a dash of salt to a splash of soda for Dallas Falk.

bottom row 5 Max began to cram for the next quiz, convinced he could exceed Marvin.

6 Many are amazed the excise tax became a vested issue for heavy debate.

| 1 | 2 | 3 | 4 | 5 | 6 | 7 | 8 | 9 | 10 | 11 | 12 | 13 | 14 |

21c • Basic control builder: one-hand three-letter combinations (trigraphs)

Practice each three-letter combination 3 or 4 times before keyboarding the words which follow each combination.

1 you your young youthful ion ration nation relations international

2 ate late stated initiated ter sister after deter intern territory

3 ill still illness illogical illiteracy are area share arena aware

4 I was not aware of your illness until after your sister was here.

5 He stated that illiteracy in your nation was still a big problem.

6 Acts in a young territory may well deter international relations.

21d • Special control builder: word building

Practice each line at a controlled rate. As you keyboard each line, concentrate on the word endings with each new word.

1 create created creating creative creatively motive motivate motivation

2 motivational strike striker striking strikingly point pointed pointing

3 pointless debate debated debating learn learned learning learners even

4 event events eventful eventual eventually order orders orderly ordered

5 With such motivation, their learners were orderly but highly creative.

6 Eventually, the leaders debated if it was pointless to order a strike.

7 Their debate team strikingly pointed to current events in their favor.

8 Her motive was to create a learning event to motivate her large class.

| 1 | 2 | 3 | 4 | 5 | 6 | 7 | 8 | 9 | 10 | 11 | 12 | 13 | 14 |

10c • Basic skill builder: balanced-hand two-letter combinations (digraphs)

Practice each two-letter combination 3 or 4 times before keyboarding the words which follow each combination. Concentrate on the digraphs in the words.

1 cl claimed encloses uncle du dull during dues rm arm harmful dorm
2 do done doubt adopt sp special misspent clasps od body today food
3 ue dues fuel unique gh right though enough by byway bytes standby
4 Today, though, the farmer might adopt the unique fuel by-product.
5 Sue's uncle doubts the claim that the food in the dorm is unique.
6 Claudia wants to adopt a special plan that might double dues.

10d • Special speed builder: speed spurts
(common words)

Practice each line as fast as possible to build stroking speed. Strive for smooth, continuous stroking.

1 should service some them sincerely make out than about up each enclose
2 know were information me only when made sales also manager many he too
3 depend send good just am work get what my had price like copy such use
4 first how most his program amount under find help every want much give
5 I want the manager to send information about the price of his service.
6 We know we can depend upon you to give all workers the help they need.
7 The sales manager had a copy made of the study about sales and prices.
8 Find a copy of the program, send it to me, and enclose the amount due.

| 1 | 2 | 3 | 4 | 5 | 6 | 7 | 8 | 9 | 10 | 11 | 12 | 13 | 14 |

10e • Speed paragraphs
(straight copy)

1 Two 1' writings on each ¶; strive to increase speed on the second writing.
2 One 3' writing on both ¶s combined; determine gwam.

all letters used | E | 1.2 si | 5.1 awl | 90% hfw

gwam 1' | 3'

Are you making plans for your work in the future? Few individuals 13 | 4 | 67
give much thought to what they can expect to be doing in five, ten, or 28 | 9 | 72
twenty years. They are quite content to sit back and just let things 42 | 14 | 77
happen to them. If they are successful, it is only by luck. To assure 56 | 19 | 81
success, you must be able to study and rate the potential of a job. You 71 | 24 | 86
may find that a job meets your needs at first but offers little in the 85 | 28 | 91
way of progress in the years to come. 92 | 31 | 94

There are quite a few factors you must take into account when you 13 | 35 | 98
analyze a job. Pay is important, of course; but of equal concern is 27 | 40 | 103
the value of fringe benefits such as sick leave, the insurance paid by 41 | 45 | 107
the firm, and vacations with pay. Of even more concern to you are the 55 | 49 | 112
chances you will have to advance. While it is true that pay and bene- 69 | 54 | 117
fits are big factors, you may find it much better to take a job with 83 | 59 | 121
less pay at the start in favor of greater rewards in the future. 96 | 63 | 126

| gwam | 1' | 1 | 2 | 3 | 4 | 5 | 6 | 7 | 8 | 9 | 10 | 11 | 12 | 13 | 14 |
| | 3' | | 1 | | 2 | | 3 | | 4 | | 5 | | |

20c • Basic control builder: one-hand commonly used words

Practice the lines of one-hand words 3 or 4 times before keyboarding the following sentences.

1 get pin red bag bed was star fact stage rated only were nylon act
2 aware ill awarded average carefree regretted after my in you best
3 upon area oil join face milk fear pump reader hominy severe union
4 I was in a daze as I was awarded a red pin after my act on stage.
5 I regretted my carefree acts only after I was aware you were ill.
6 In fact, you are a star in a stage act; I was rated only average.

20d • Special control builder: guided paragraph writing

1 Take a 1' writing on the ¶; determine *gwam.*
2 Add 4-6 *gwam* to this base rate to set a new goal rate.
3 Take two 1' guided writings on the ¶; determine *gwam* on the better writing.

all letters used | HA | 1.7 si | 6.0 awl | 75% hfw

Every typing drill has meaning. Listen or read carefully to comprehend what you should accomplish from particular procedures. Then, adjust to the correct form and mental attitude as you zero in quickly on the entire process; and push yourself to excel. Only then will you be completely satisfied with the end results.

20e • Control paragraphs

(straight copy)

1 Two 1' writings on each ¶; strive to improve accuracy on the second writing.
2 One 5' writing on both ¶s combined; determine *gwam.*

all letters used | HA | 1.7 si | 6.0 awl | 75% hfw

	gwam 1'		5'
One of the most essential traits any individual possesses is self-	13	3	40
discipline--the ability to control your behavior, especially in unusual	28	6	43
situations. How would you rate yourself in this regard? When you are	42	8	46
asked to finish something within a definite time period--whether at	55	11	49
home or at school--are you able to conclude the assigned task without	69	14	52
putting it off until the last minute? In most situations, are you able	84	17	54
to proceed on your own without being prodded by others?	95	19	57
Oftentimes, self-discipline involves a more serious act or action	13	22	59
than simply completing a specific project on time. Certain actions we	27	24	62
must take in life usually require a great amount of self-discipline.	41	27	65
Have you ever tried to keep to special diets or follow difficult exer-	55	30	68
cise routines on a regular basis? It is important to realize that some	70	33	71
of the finer things in life eventually can occur if we really do possess	84	36	73
and sincerely try to utilize self-discipline.	93	38	75

gwam 1' | 1 | 2 | 3 | 4 | 5 | 6 | 7 | 8 | 9 | 10 | 11 | 12 | 13 | 14 |
5' | | 1 | | 2 | | 3 |

11a • Keyboard review

Practice once slowly; a second time for speed; a third time for control.

alphabet 1 Eve Jenks may pay for a quaint gazebo with your extra allocated funds.

figures 2 Typewriters 8, 19, 27, 36, 45, and 50 have been broken all this month.

fig/sym 3 Our ad on page 507 reads "4 x 8-ft. 1/2-in. drywall at $3.69 a panel."

| 1 | 2 | 3 | 4 | 5 | 6 | 7 | 8 | 9 | 10 | 11 | 12 | 13 | 14 |

11b • Technique builder: stroking

Keep fingers vertical, not slanting, over home keys as you practice this drill.

1 asa ask sales aspire asleep safely ioi ion riot prior elation national

2 ece echo each eclipse economy century unu unarm unable unaware unclear

3 dcd ducat docks cadet cadre caddie jnj junk join jitney jungles jinxed

4 Prior sales did eclipse the century mark to jolt the national economy.

5 Ava said no to your caddie in jeans who did ask if he could join them.

6 Prior to the riot, the cadet was unable to join the vast cadre safely.

| 1 | 2 | 3 | 4 | 5 | 6 | 7 | 8 | 9 | 10 | 11 | 12 | 13 | 14 |

11c • Basic speed builder: balanced-hand commonly used words

Strive for smooth, continuous keystroking action as you practice these sentences.

1 If they visit the big city, both men may go to the lake and fish.

2 Eight of the right men got their corps' six bushels off the land.

3 The handy pair throw with good form and work to make their goals.

4 The big dog and the ancient duck, an odd pair, slept by the dock.

5 The quantity of work to fix the rug and chair kept them all busy.

6 If they handle the risks, they may then spend all of the profits.

11d • Special speed builder: speed spurts

Practice each sentence as fast as possible to build stroking speed. Try to maintain the same fast stroking rate on each sentence.

balanced-hand 1 Visible signs of a profit may make them fight for their key amendment.

balanced-hand 2 The rich firms paid for the maps of downtown and the land by the lake.

double letters 3 Will the committee call their attention to the issue about free books?

double letters 4 The business office attached my letter to all staff employees' checks.

common words 5 In the future, all checks for payment should be mailed to that person.

common words 6 Please check the cost of these stock items and change the price today.

common words 7 Plan to help me make all those changes during the special spring show.

common words 8 If she will come to the sale today, help her find the items she needs.

| 1 | 2 | 3 | 4 | 5 | 6 | 7 | 8 | 9 | 10 | 11 | 12 | 13 | 14 |

(statistical copy)

1 Two 1' writings on each ¶; strive for improved control rate on the second writing.
2 One 5' writing on both ¶s combined; determine *gwam*.

all letters used | HA | 1.7 si | 6.0 awl | 75% hfw

gwam 1' | 5'

On October 9, 1982, another world "Ironman" contest was held in | 11 | 2 | 35
Hawaii. Athletes participating in this meet competed in three areas. | 25 | 5 | 38
They swam for 2.4 miles, biked for 112, and ran a grueling marathon | 38 | 8 | 40
(26.2 miles). Of the 775 who finally completed the meet, those partici- | 50 | 10 | 43
pants in the 26 to 29 age group actually did best. Top honors went to | 63 | 13 | 45
a man, 202, whose amazing official record shows he completed all three | 77 | 15 | 48
events in 9 hours, 8 minutes, and 23 seconds (9:08:23). | 85 | 17 | 50

The winning competitor easily swam 2.4 miles in 0:50:53, bicycled | 11 | 19 | 52
112 miles in 5:10:16, and ran 26.2 miles in 3:07:15. Quite close behind | 21 | 21 | 54
was 001, with a final time of exactly 9:28:28. He actually ended his | 33 | 24 | 56
swim just 0:10:06 after 202, completed the bicycle ride in 5:18:09, and | 44 | 26 | 58
ended the run in 3:08:21. The victorious woman competitor, number 50, | 56 | 28 | 61
finished ahead of 549 other competitors. Her final time was 10:54:08; | 68 | 31 | 63
her official time for the three events was 1:04:57, 5:50:36, and 3:58:35. | 78 | 33 | 65

gwam 1' | 1 | 2 | 3 | 4 | 5 | 6 | 7 | 8 | 9 | 10 | 11 | 12 | 13 | 14 |
gwam 5' | 1 | 2 | 3 |

CONTROL BUILDER 20

20a • Keyboard review

Practice once slowly; a second time for speed; a third time for control

alphabet 1 Jose quizzically kept trying, but excerpts from the sequel drew raves.
figures 2 Since 756-2890 is still busy, dial 754-3130 and ask for Extension 320.
fig/sym 3 Statements #459 ($32.78) and #160 ($8.95) were both marked "past due."

| 1 | 2 | 3 | 4 | 5 | 6 | 7 | 8 | 9 | 10 | 11 | 12 | 13 | 14 |

20b • Technique builder: manipulative control

(special symbols)

Strive for efficiency as you construct these special symbols.

1 For division signs, strike a colon; backspace, then type a hyphen (÷).
2 For any plus sign, type a diagonal; backspace, then type a hyphen (≠).
3 Make a paragraph sign using a small "l" struck over a capital "P" (℗).
4 Show multiplication by spacing before/after a lower case "x": 9 x 12.
5 Use an apostrophe for feet and quotation marks for inches: 25' x 18".
6 Typed diagonals with connected underlines become brackets: /surname/.

| 1 | 2 | 3 | 4 | 5 | 6 | 7 | 8 | 9 | 10 | 11 | 12 | 13 | 14 |

11e • Speed paragraphs

(straight copy)

1 Two 1' writings on each ¶; strive to increase speed on the second writing.
2 One 3' writing on both ¶s combined; determine *gwam*.

all letters used	LA	1.4 si	5.4 awl	85% hfw		gwam 1'	3'

	1'	3'	
You may know of people who have gotten perfect positions with very	13	4	63
little effort by just being in the right place at the right time. Most	28	9	68
of us, however, may find it prudent at strategic times in life to send	42	14	73
letters to possible employers. Since these letters become our foot in	56	19	77
the door, it is vital that precise care be taken in composing them.	70	23	82
Often the best job inquiries can be drafted after a thorough data sheet	84	28	87
has been prepared.	88	29	88
The first step in preparing a data sheet is to zero in on those	13	34	92
qualities that sell you best for the exact position you desire. Then,	27	38	97
list those traits in their order of emphasis using proper form that is	41	43	102
unique and neat. Be sure to make good use of white space and type a	55	48	106
letter-perfect copy. While some interviewers may desire the typed copy,	70	53	111
they most certainly will accept a duplicate copy if the copying process	84	57	116
is of fine quality.	88	59	117

gwam 1' | 1 | 2 | 3 | 4 | 5 | 6 | 7 | 8 | 9 | 10 | 11 | 12 | 13 | 14 |
3' | 1 | 2 | 3 | 4 | 5 |

SPEED BUILDER 12

12a • Keyboard review

Practice once slowly; a second time for speed; a third time for control.

alphabet 1 My friend willingly may have kept Jacque's crazy box kite from flying.

figures 2 Patterns 3049, 2158, and 6072 should be removed from that sewing book.

fig/sym 3 Document #39-04 (in folder A-56872) was recorded as missing on June 1.

| 1 | 2 | 3 | 4 | 5 | 6 | 7 | 8 | 9 | 10 | 11 | 12 | 13 | 14 |

12b • Technique builder: manipulative control

Improve control of these important service mechanisms as you practice the sentences.

1 Chi and Mary met Roy and Eleanor at the Blue Maze Theater in Loveland.

shift keys 2 Julio plugged Toys for Kids on TV; Lana plugged them at Rayfield Park.

3 Soon Jason, Mavis, Mary, and Wong will run in the Bluebonnet Marathon.

4 The red light flashed ON THE AIR, and Studio B of KUHN was OFF LIMITS.

shift lock 5 The address IOWA PARK TX takes ZIP CODE 76367; OLYMPIA WA takes 98506.

6 The BRYAN EAGLE and the CITY COURIER completed their merger last week.

| 1 | 2 | 3 | 4 | 5 | 6 | 7 | 8 | 9 | 10 | 11 | 12 | 13 | 14 |

19a • Keyboard review

Practice once slowly; a second time for speed; a third time for control.

alphabet	1	After Mac's lab quiz we six can jog to the lake and play in the waves.
figures	2	Lockers 2, 4, 6, 8 and 10 are rented; 3, 5, 7, and 9 are now reserved.
fig/sym	3	The book Eclipse (2d ed.) was reserved on 4/2, 5/7, 6/30, and 8/19/83.

| 1 | 2 | 3 | 4 | 5 | 6 | 7 | 8 | 9 | 10 | 11 | 12 | 13 | 14 |

19b • Technique builder: stroking (third and fourth fingers)

Make the third- and fourth-finger reaches without moving the hands as you practice this drill.

1 People are zealously opposed to planting azaleas next to the old pool.

2 Owls, squirrels, and zebras have overpopulated the poorly planned zoo.

3 Quail near the quaint quadrangle quietly zip across the popular plaza.

4 One quirk unquestionably is her possession of extremely queer apparel.

5 Exasperated, he postponed the quizzes following the apparent squabble.

6 Appalled by the powerful opposition, he quietly appealed for opinions.

| 1 | 2 | 3 | 4 | 5 | 6 | 7 | 8 | 9 | 10 | 11 | 12 | 13 | 14 |

19c • Basic control builder: one-hand commonly used words

Practice each line of one-hand commonly used words 3 or 4 times. Concentrate as you strive for smooth control.

1 in my as on saw you oil beat were case fact fate tax aces awarded

2 we after free state serve regards opinion better union was rebate

3 deserved minimum cards greatest upon abstract ploy plump wear pop

4 I was defeated, in my opinion, as you served Johnny better cards.

5 We were awarded a deserved tax rebate after I beat my dated case.

6 Afterwards, I stated my opinions as regarded minimum water rates.

19d • Special control builder: one-hand sentences

Practice each sentence at a controlled rate; strive for accuracy and continuity as you type.

1 In Linn's opinion, only a great monopoly ploy affects my gas reserves.

2 We were aware Johnny deserved a better ump as we saw him safe on base.

3 I reversed my opinion after my union agreed on a minimum wage in July.

4 Gregg was aware my cat was aggravated after a vet treated him at noon.

5 After I saw Baxter create a great stage act, I agreed few were better.

6 We saw Darce create a red Easter egg tree at a garret on State Street.

7 After I traded my car, I regretted my act as a better car was at Al's.

8 We gazed in awe as my pupils were treated to free desserts at Webbers.

| 1 | 2 | 3 | 4 | 5 | 6 | 7 | 8 | 9 | 10 | 11 | 12 | 13 | 14 |

12c • Basic speed builder: speed spurts (balanced hand)

Practice each sentence as fast as possible to build stroking speed. Maintain a smooth, snappy rhythm. Keep the action in the fingers, with quiet hands and arms.

1 The rich visitor did wish to pay for the fuel for their big auto.
2 Rush the ancient tusk to the downtown firm when he pays the duty.
3 The work of eighty island men did entitle them to a small profit.
4 May they sign a form to mend the chair and pay for half the work?
5 The element of risk is big, but she may wish to bid for the land.
6 The auditor may form a panel of eight and handle the proxy fight.

12d • Special speed builder: skill comparison sentences

Practice each sentence for 30″ or 1′. Strive to keyboard the other sentences as smoothly as you did the balanced-hand sentence.

balanced-hand 1 If the visitor paid for the chair by the aisle, she may lend it to me.
one-hand 2 As you are aware, exact deferred taxes on my estate are as you stated.
combination 3 The eager crew may start the work to fix the street when we join them.
3d row 4 Were there two or three tour routes your youth group preferred to try?
adjacent reaches 5 They were to join the weekly talk show to assess regions of the Yukon.
direct reach 6 Irv's brother declared that any city has numerous excellent musicians.

| 1 | 2 | 3 | 4 | 5 | 6 | 7 | 8 | 9 | 10 | 11 | 12 | 13 | 14 |

12e • Speed paragraphs

(straight copy)

1 Two 1′ writings on each ¶; strive to increase speed on the second writing.
2 One 3′ writing on both ¶s combined; determine *gwam*.

all letters used | LA | 1.4 si | 5.4 awl | 85% hfw

	gwam 1′		3′

One thing about data sheets often pointed out by people to whom 13 | 4 | 68
they are submitted is that many times the resumes look and sound too 27 | 9 | 73
much like those found in every textbook. While you may find it easy 40 | 13 | 77
to style yours after the example in your book, the best data sheet is 54 | 18 | 82
that which capitalizes on the unique features of more than one resume 68 | 23 | 87
while it also reveals format ideas of your own. The data sheet should 83 | 28 | 92
reflect well on the job seeker and be proper for the chosen job field. 97 | 32 | 96

When you prepare to use your completed data sheet, it is ideal 13 | 36 | 100
if you can type an original to include with each letter you send out to 27 | 41 | 105
seek an interview. If you must send copies instead, it is best to have 41 | 46 | 110
prints of your resume made through a photocopy process. Consider the 55 | 51 | 115
process called offset, which is a form of fairly low-cost printing. 69 | 55 | 119
You prepare perfect, camera-ready copy and have it printed; and the 82 | 60 | 124
end product should be as well received as your original would be. 95 | 64 | 128

gwam 1′ | 1 | 2 | 3 | 4 | 5 | 6 | 7 | 8 | 9 | 10 | 11 | 12 | 13 | 14 |
gwam 3′ | 1 | 2 | 3 | 4 | 5 |

18c • Basic control builder: one-hand commonly used words

Strive for smooth continuous stroking as you practice this drill.

1 *you was only case acted stated drafted started trade severe debts*
2 *I stated I acted only after I was aware you drafted a trade case.*
3 *A few tax cases tested after Easter created only a few red faces.*
4 *No, only you are aware I face severe bad debts on my vast estate.*

18d • Special control builders: letter drills (s–z)

Keyboard each sentence at a controlled rate. Concentrate on the emphasized letters and improved control as you repeat this drill.

s 1 Some sales surges satisfied statisticians the situation was softening.
t 2 Two tiny tots tiptoed through your tulips together talking constantly.
u 3 Understandably, understudy uncertainty ultimately led to your undoing.
v 4 Vandals verbalized various versions of violations that were valueless.
w 5 Weary but well-meaning workers welcomed the weekenders to Walla Walla.
x 6 Xavier College permits xeroxing extra text materials for examinations.
y 7 Yesterday youthful yachtsmen yearningly yelled at the yeoman to yield.
z 8 Zebras lost in hazy, zero-zero weather zanily zipped about at the zoo.

| | 1 | 2 | 3 | 4 | 5 | 6 | 7 | 8 | 9 | 10 | 11 | 12 | 13 | 14 | |

18e • Control paragraphs

(rough-draft copy)

1 Two 1′ writings on each ¶; strive to increase your control rate on the second writing.

2 One 5′ writing on both ¶s combined; determine *gwam*.

all letters used | HA | 1.7 si | 6.0 awl | 75% hfw

	gwam 1′	5′
It is amazing how many students who reach thier senior	11	2	29
years in school are undecided in regard as to the type of job	23	5	31
they wish to pursue upon gradation. Unfortunately, they're	35	7	34
often times expereincing delays in acquireing a good career	47	9	36
or in desieing upon an area of study should they finally opt	59	12	39
to attend college.	63	13	39
Hopefuly, you were fully told to begin earley analyzing	11	15	42
posible career fields based up on your intelligence, interests,	23	17	44
potentials. Beaware of tests availabel that will help dis-	36	20	46
cover various areas in which are you must likely to suceed.	48	22	49
Be come allert to grow in any new career feilds sothat your	60	24	51
able to make your possible decisions with available facts.	72	27	54

SPEED BUILDER 13

13a • Technique review

Practice once slowly; a second time for speed; a third time for control.

alphabet 1 Win's zymology lab often keeps several jars of exotic liquids on hand.

figures 2 Telephone Extensions 198, 234, 507, and 632 do not appear in the book.

fig/sym 3 The data sheet entry read: "12/69-3/70; 5/80-4/82, *Part-time Clerk."

| 1 | 2 | 3 | 4 | 5 | 6 | 7 | 8 | 9 | 10 | 11 | 12 | 13 | 14 |

13b • Technique builder: stroking (double letters)

Try to maintain the same even rhythm as you practice these sentences.

1 An additional supply of books shall arrive soon with an attached bill.

2 The business office shall issue a letter immediately to all employees.

3 In two weeks the committee will meet to discuss this personnel matter.

4 Effective now, all employees may apply for an additional open account.

| 1 | 2 | 3 | 4 | 5 | 6 | 7 | 8 | 9 | 10 | 11 | 12 | 13 | 14 |

13c • Basic speed builder: speed spurts (balanced hand)

Practice each sentence as fast as possible to build stroking speed. Use the left-right pattern of easy stroking to push for speed.

1 A panel may work with a world theme to title the sorority social.

2 If they do end their work by dusk, they may visit the big island.

3 When they mend the rug, make them rush it by air to the rug firm.

4 Their audit kept the auditor busy, but she did work for half pay.

13d • Special speed builder: guided paragraph writing

1 Take a 1' writing on ¶1; determine *gwam*.

2 Add 5 *gwam* to this base rate to set a new goal rate.

3 Take two 1' guided writings on ¶1; try to reach your goal rate.

4 Take two 1' guided writings on ¶2 in the same way.

5 Take two 3' writings on ¶s 1 and 2 combined; determine *gwam* on the better writing.

all letters used | LA | 1.4 si | 5.4 awl | 85% hfw

gwam 3'

In recent years, young and old alike have shown greater interest 4 | 46

in some kind of physical activity during their leisure time in an effort 9 | 51

to improve their quality of life. The forms of exercise may range from 14 | 56

walking at a fast pace to taking part in a jazzercise class. A new diet 19 | 61

often is part of any change in health habits. 22 | 64

Any changes in an individual's physical condition may be healthy 26 | 68

just as long as those changes are made slowly. It is easy to try too 31 | 73

hard to change one's physical status and cause more harm than good. 35 | 77

Anyone who may desire to make a drastic change in lifestyle needs to 40 | 82

consult with a doctor first. 42 | 84

gwam 3' | 1 | 2 | 3 | 4 | 5

17e • Control paragraphs

(straight copy)

1 Two 1′ writings on each ¶; strive to improve accuracy on the second writing.

2 One 5′ writing on both ¶s combined; determine *gwam*.

all letters used | HA | 1.7 si | 6.0 awl | 75% hfw

gwam 1′ | 5′

What is the best speed you ever recorded for three- or five-minute | 13 | 3 | 42
timed writings? How long is it since you achieved that top speed? Are | 28 | 6 | 44
you aware that many typing students usually reach a plateau in what ap- | 42 | 8 | 47
pears to be their rate of progress in their ability to keyboard straight- | 57 | 11 | 50
copy material? Whenever this situation occurs, it is usually beneficial | 71 | 14 | 53
to analyze specific factors affecting the pace at which any skill is | 85 | 17 | 56
obtained. Two main factors could be attitude and procedure. | 97 | 19 | 58

When we continue doing something that appears to be fairly routine, | 14 | 22 | 61
we frequently let our minds wander and just seem to neglect many proce- | 28 | 25 | 64
dures necessary for learning and showing growth in any skill. If your | 42 | 28 | 67
progress in typing appears to have hit that point, perhaps you should | 56 | 31 | 70
examine your attitude and refocus your attention on the essentials in | 70 | 33 | 72
making rapid progress. Then, zero in on specific exercises for speed | 84 | 36 | 75
and accuracy to help you acquire the daily growth you really desire. | 98 | 39 | 78

gwam 1′ | 1 | 2 | 3 | 4 | 5 | 6 | 7 | 8 | 9 | 10 | 11 | 12 | 13 | 14 |
5′ | 1 | | 2 | | 3 | |

CONTROL BUILDER 18

18a • Keyboard review

Practice once slowly; a second time for speed; a third time for control.

alphabet 1 Win analyzed and approved my tax benefits that do justify quick gains.

figures 2 Of 3,579 forms sent out, 1,862 were returned, with 40 very incomplete.

fig/sym 3 Gate receipts totaled $5,698 on July 4--a 30% ($271) profit this year.

| 1 | 2 | 3 | 4 | 5 | 6 | 7 | 8 | 9 | 10 | 11 | 12 | 13 | 14 |

18b • Technique builder:
stroking (second finger, both hands)

Make the second-finger reaches without moving the hands out of position as you practice this drill.

1 The cadets did succeed in sticking to the cadence, pleasing the cadre.

2 My initials indicate our decision to accept your idealistic editorial.

3 In keeping with your nice idea, we decided to order identical decking.

4 As I anticipated, declining indices initially influenced his decision.

5 Their illegal procedure during the kickoff ideally did kill the clock.

6 The identical cadets succeeded easily in deceiving my eccentric cadre.

| 1 | 2 | 3 | 4 | 5 | 6 | 7 | 8 | 9 | 10 | 11 | 12 | 13 | 14 |

13e • Speed paragraphs

(rough-draft copy)

1 Two 1' writings on each ¶; strive to increase speed on the second writing.
2 One 3' writing on both ¶s combined; determine *gwam*.

all letters used	LA	1.4 si	5.4 awl	85% hfw

gwam 1' | 3'

As you progress ~~thru~~ *through* school, you may realize quickly ~~much~~ | 4 | 55

on your own how essentia(l) it is to decide what you would like to | 4 | 8 | 59

do in life ~~making~~ *to earn* a living. that way you can consentrate fully | 7 | 12 | 63

on ~~those courses of study~~ *a school curriculum* and develop *all* those character ~~trates~~ *traits* | 50 | 17 | 67

that will prepare you for your chosen career feild. While you | 62 | 21 | 72

may change your mind later, *at least* you will have *gotten started toward* a goal. | 78 | 26 | 77

Become aware of books on carers in your school library ~~too~~ and | 12 | 30 | 81

ready advice from your school Coueilor who will aid you in your | 25 | 34 | 85

decision. ~~Also, interview~~ *Try to chat with* people who have been emplyyed for | 37 | 39 | 90

many years in areas of your career choise. ~~Seek~~ *Examine* what it is | 50 | 43 | 94

that you ~~wish~~ *want* out of ~~your~~ life, and than *just* advance as you best | 62 | 47 | 98

can to acheive what you believe to be your highest potential. | 74 | 51 | 102

SPEED BUILDER 14

14a • Keyboard review

Practice once slowly; a second time for speed; a third time for control.

alphabet 1 Mike Bujnoch excitedly requested verification of the big prize he won.
figures 2 My appointment calendar is full on August 6, 8, 9, 15, 17, 24, and 30.
fig/sym 3 Even with the 10% discount, Model #42-36 will still retail at $598.75.

| 1 | 2 | 3 | 4 | 5 | 6 | 7 | 8 | 9 | 10 | 11 | 12 | 13 | 14 |

14b • Technique builder: manipulative control

(backspace and underline)

Learn to reach for and use the backspace key efficiently as you practice this drill.

1 Caveat emptor is a common Latin term meaning: "Let the buyer beware."
2 Book titles are typed in ALL CAPS or underscored: SEATTLE or Seattle.
3 You should also underscore or CAPITALIZE magazine titles: Fun or FUN.
4 All tax returns must be postmarked by midnight the 15th to be on time.
5 The bold sign read: Absolutely no smokes or drinks in this classroom.
6 Underscore the following misspelled words: recieve, guage, convience.

| 1 | 2 | 3 | 4 | 5 | 6 | 7 | 8 | 9 | 10 | 11 | 12 | 13 | 14 |

CONTROL BUILDER 17

17a • Keyboard review

Practice once slowly; a second time for speed; a third time for control.

alphabet 1 An extra large crowd just blocked my view of a quintet on the trapeze.

figures 2 On May 5, 34,798 attended the home game; on May 1, only 26,502 showed.

fig/sym 3 The MP said that Passes #291 and #486 (3-day) were taken by 10:57 p.m.

| 1 | 2 | 3 | 4 | 5 | 6 | 7 | 8 | 9 | 10 | 11 | 12 | 13 | 14 |

17b • Technique builder

stroking (first finger, both hands)

Make the first-finger reaches without moving the hands as you practice this drill.

1 Three youths are vying for first place in their annual community meet.

2 The officer offered to study our urgent, reoccurring traffic patterns.

3 My judge vouched for the tough youth but withheld further information.

4 In my hurry, I broke a new mirror at the bottom of the corrugated box.

5 Have they referred their irritating staff memo to the comptroller yet?

6 You've just enough time to retype this tariff report for your meeting.

| 1 | 2 | 3 | 4 | 5 | 6 | 7 | 8 | 9 | 10 | 11 | 12 | 13 | 14 |

17c • Basic control builder: one-hand commonly used words

Practice each line of one-hand words 3 or 4 times before keyboarding the sentences. Strive to keep all the action in your fingers.

1 *as my in you saw red few dear upon bed base rate bags aware nylon*

2 *are were only facts safer secrets traded regret union better wage*

3 *after opinion deserves better minimum jolly pump join excavate ad*

4 *As you are aware, my dear, you saw my red nylon bags upon my bed.*

5 *I regret you were safer only after you traded a few secret facts.*

6 *In my opinion, my union deserves a better minimum wage base rate.*

17d • Special control builder: letter drills (j-r)

Practice each sentence at a controlled rate. Work for improved continuity and control of the emphasized letters.

j 1 Julian jetted to Jakarta and joined a jeepload of jittery journalists.

k 2 Kay took much kidding from Kathy for keeping a kitten in her knapsack.

l 3 Lazy lambs lay idle in the lush leaves, living a life of regal luxury.

m 4 Many mothers mailed memorandums mentioning media meetings in Monterey.

n 5 Neighbors neither knew of nor necessarily noticed funny noises nearby.

o 6 Obviously at odds, roving onlookers offered us only opposing opinions.

p 7 Paul painted a happy picture and pocketed the profit from peddling it.

q 8 Qualifying for their quarterfinals, the quartet questioned the quorum.

r 9 That sheriff reorganized recent recruits to dam rapidly rising rivers.

| 1 | 2 | 3 | 4 | 5 | 6 | 7 | 8 | 9 | 10 | 11 | 12 | 13 | 14 |

14c • Basic speed builder:
speed spurts (balanced hand)

Practice each sentence as fast as possible to build stroking speed. Work for continuity of stroking.

1 *Vi is sick, so Iris may go downtown to the social with the girls.*
2 *If and when they do the work right, they may handle the problems.*
3 *The auditor is busy with an angle to aid an amendment for a city.*
4 *If the profit is cut, the firm may halt work for the eight towns.*

14d • Special speed builder:
skill transfer paragraphs

all letters used | LA | 1.4 si | 5.4 awl | 85% hfw

1 Take a 1′ writing on each ¶; compare *gwam*.
2 Practice the numbers only in ¶2.
3 Take a 1′ writing on ¶2; try to improve your speed.
4 Take a 3′ writing on ¶s 1 and 2 combined; determine *gwam*.

gwam 1′ | 3′

Despite the fact that workers in the United States have enhanced their quality of life during the past four decades, they still realize the value of a typical workweek. This point was made in a sequel to a report on the work ethic just off the press.

gwam 1′	3′
12	4 36
26	9 41
40	13 45
49	16 48

For example, the length of the full-time workweek, which did go down between 1900 and 1940, still hovers near 40 hours. In 1981 the typical worker put in 38.1 hours a week; in 1940, 43.7; and in 1900, 53.2. In 1980 the labor force consisted of about 64.3 percent of all Americans.

gwam 1′	3′
12	20 52
26	25 57
39	28 61
46	32 64

gwam 1′ | 1 | 2 | 3 | 4 | 5 | 6 | 7 | 8 | 9 | 10 | 11 | 12 | 13 | 14 |
gwam 3′ | 1 | 2 | 3 | 4 | 5 |

14e • Speed paragraphs
(statistical copy)

all letters used | LA | 1.4 si | 5.4 awl | 85% hfw

1 Two 1′ writings on each ¶; strive to increase speed on the second writing.
2 One 3′ writing on both ¶s combined; determine *gwam*.

gwam 1′ | 3′

A look at many of the exact facts from 324 employers out of 500 who took part in a survey may help you to zero in on ways to tackle usual parts of a data sheet. When asked if they want references, 260 said yes; 16, no; and 48, does not matter. When asked to pick how many, none marked 1; 16, 2; 193, 3; 72, 4; and 43, 5. As to type of reference, 287 prefer former bosses; 37, high school teachers. As many as 252 want college students to list teachers of prime concern.

gwam 1′	3′
13	4 67
26	9 71
40	13 76
55	18 81
69	23 85
83	28 90
95	32 94

When asked if they would prefer to see any part-time work listed, both related and unrelated, 298 said yes; 26, no. As many as 306 would prefer to see full-time summer work listed, even if not related to the type of job the student is seeking; while 18 circled no for this query. As to quoting personal details, 312 said yes; 10, no; and 2 didn't care. Where should these data be given? While 68 opted for the letter, 256 prefer to see such data in the data sheet

gwam 1′	3′
13	36 99
28	41 103
42	46 108
56	50 113
70	55 118
84	60 122
93	63 125

gwam 1′ | 1 | 2 | 3 | 4 | 5 | 6 | 7 | 8 | 9 | 10 | 11 | 12 | 13 | 14 |
gwam 3′ | 1 | 2 | 3 | 4 | 5 |

16c • Basic control builder: one-hand commonly used words

Maintain proper control as you move smoothly from sentence to sentence.

1 *Grace was great cast as a brave star in a secret stage act I saw.*
2 *You were red faced as I reversed a test case on minimum reserves.*
3 *I'm aware my drafted abstracts are safest in a drawer in my safe.*

16d • Special control builder: letter drills (a–i)

Practice each sentence at a controlled rate. Work for improved continuity and control of the emphasized letters.

a 1 An active athlete actually allocated ample time at the acting academy.
b 2 Better books could be bought at Bookland because of buy-back benefits.
c 3 Candy carelessly caused a chain-reaction accident at Carlsbad Caverns.
d 4 Did Don decide he didn't want to drive in the Dallas demolition derby?
e 5 Ellie eventually enlisted every employee to push all three committees.
f 6 Fabulously famous foreigners frequently fly to familiar faraway cafes.
g 7 Guests got the giggles over gag gifts, forgetting to guard their gems.
h 8 Harmless Harry had to handle those hecklers himself at the horse show.
i 9 Idiotic ideas introduced by incoming initiates initially were ignored.

| 1 | 2 | 3 | 4 | 5 | 6 | 7 | 8 | 9 | 10 | 11 | 12 | 13 | 14 |

16e • Control paragraphs

(straight copy)

1 Two 1' writings on each ¶; strive to improve accuracy on the second writing.
2 One 5' writing on both ¶s combined; determine *gwam*.

all letters used | HA | 1.7 si | 6.0 awl | 75% hfw

	gwam 1'	5'
How do you respond when you must take another timed writing? Do	13	3	42
you tense up and experience difficulty performing to the utmost of your	27	5	45
ability? Or do you manage to relax and demonstrate to yourself and	41	8	48
others how adequately you perform at the typewriter? Timed writings pro-	56	11	50
vide both diagnostic and progress checks so your instructor can analyze	70	14	53
whether you need to push for speed, accuracy, or both. Special copy is	84	17	56
prepared to provide both you and your instructor with this information.	99	20	59
After you finish timed writings, look beyond the number of errors	13	22	62
actually typed and consider the kind of errors you made. If you analyze	28	25	65
your errors, at least informally, you may determine patterns in the	41	28	67
various mistakes you continue to create. Perhaps you transpose certain	56	31	70
letters or reach too far for a specific key. After you isolate certain	70	34	73
errors, inquire of your instructor which particular drills you should	84	37	76
just practice on your own to obtain the speed and accuracy you desire.	98	39	79

gwam 1' | 1 | 2 | 3 | 4 | 5 | 6 | 7 | 8 | 9 | 10 | 11 | 12 | 13 | 14 |
5' | 1 | 2 | 3 |

15a • Keyboard review

Practice once slowly; a second time for speed; a third time for control.

alphabet	1	Just as expected, the full moon cast a hazy glow on quiet Beaver Lake.
figures	2	Fire alarms were sounded at 7:48 and 10:25 a.m., and also at 9:36 p.m.
fig/sym	3	Invoice #96480 (36 purses at $8.75 each) totals $315, a markup of 20%.

| 1 | 2 | 3 | 4 | 5 | 6 | 7 | 8 | 9 | 10 | 11 | 12 | 13 | 14 |

15b • Technique builder:
stroking (double letters)

Work for continuity of stroking as you practice these sentences.

1 The staff suggested mailing the new bulletin to all current addresses.

2 An employee assured the annual staff their yearbooks had been shipped.

3 Different offices sent letters expressing the need for added supplies.

4 According to comments on the sheets, the staff meeting was successful.

| 1 | 2 | 3 | 4 | 5 | 6 | 7 | 8 | 9 | 10 | 11 | 12 | 13 | 14 |

15c • Basic speed builder:
speed spurts (balanced hand)

Practice each sentence as fast as possible to build stroking speed. Keep fingers curved and upright; use quick, snappy strokes.

1 The field work did entitle us to cut six bushels of corn and rye.

2 The theory of their firm is to cut the risk and spend the profit.

3 The firm may sign forms to bid with the city to make their signs.

4 The goal of the girls is to form a panel to handle the amendment.

15d • Special speed builder:
skill comparison paragraphs

1 Two 1' writings on ¶1; determine *gwam*.
2 Two 1' writings on ¶2, trying to obtain the same *gwam* as on ¶1.
3 One 3' writing on both ¶s combined.

all letters used ¶ 1 | E | 1.2 si | 5.1 awl | 90% hfw | ¶2 | HA | 1.7 si | 6.0 awl | 75% hfw

	gwam 1'	3'	
Do you recall the first few weeks of class when you began learning	13	4	59
how to type? You may have thought you would never build any speed and	28	9	64
still be able to type accurately. Now, thanks to special speed and	41	14	68
control exercises such as in this book, surely you have increased your	55	18	73
skill in every way. Isn't it fun to be able to put words quickly on	69	23	77
paper and in a form that is easy and neat for all to read?	81	27	81
Knowing how to type well can be extremely important in the future.	14	31	86
The typewriter has long been a tool of communication for both personal	28	36	91
and business use, and keyboarding skill is utilized significantly in	42	41	95
many jobs in business today. For example, if you anticipate seeking a	56	46	100
job using computers or word processing equipment, it is essential that	70	50	105
you be quite familiar with the keyboard and know how to type.	82	54	109

gwam 1' | 1 | 2 | 3 | 4 | 5 | 6 | 7 | 8 | 9 | 10 | 11 | 12 | 13 | 14 |
gwam 3' | 1 | 2 | 3 | 4 | 5 |

15e • Control paragraphs

(straight copy)

1 Two 1' writings on each ¶; strive to improve accuracy on the second writing.

2 One 5' writing on both ¶s combined; determine *gwam*.

all letters used | HA | 1.7 si | 6.0 awl | 75% hfw

	gwam 1'	5'	
How well do you get along with others? A positive response to	13	3	40
this question is extremely crucial if you keenly aspire to work in an	27	5	43
office or relate with others in any kind of career option. Typical	40	8	46
personnel surveys reveal that over eighty percent of those workers who	54	11	48
do lose their jobs often do so because they encounter difficulties in	68	14	51
cooperating with fellow employees. Have you ever taken the time to	82	16	53
discover something about yourself in this regard?	92	18	56
We can all develop many personal traits that really are vital in	13	21	58
our relationships with others if we do not possess them already. Ana-	27	24	61
lyze your own unique traits to determine every factor that appears to	41	27	64
be in your favor. Also, jot down those traits you truly desire to ac-	55	29	67
quire and plan what steps you must take to gain the essential character	69	32	70
traits you have decided you lack. Early evaluation of this aspect in	83	35	73
your employment analysis should result in continuous benefits.	96	38	75

gwam 1' | 1 | 2 | 3 | 4 | 5 | 6 | 7 | 8 | 9 | 10 | 11 | 12 | 13 | 14 |
5' | 1 | 2 | 3 |

CONTROL BUILDER 16

16a • Keyboard review

Practice once slowly; a second time for speed; a third time for control.

alphabet 1 Pam quietly worked five extra hours to analyze the big jar's contents.

figures 2 For further details, call 291-6702, 294-3685, or 295-3729 at any hour.

fig/sym 3 On April 2 at 10:53 a.m., an alarm sounded at 46987 Elm (a toy store).

| 1 | 2 | 3 | 4 | 5 | 6 | 7 | 8 | 9 | 10 | 11 | 12 | 13 | 14 |

16b • Technique builder: stroking

Maintain proper technique and control as you move from row to row.

top row 1 TG&Y sold 86 computers at $247 each (15% discount) easily by 9:30 p.m.

3d row 2 Our two groups were to take your tree tour, too; yet we were too late.

row 3 Two or three youths were to retreat to quiet Roquefort, you were told.

home 4 At Al Hall's garage sale, I saw a Dallas lass sell faded jade glasses.

row 5 As a lass sadly said, Jeff hassled a jaded lad all last fall as a gag.

bottom row 6 Can Cummings and Zornes excavate their bauxite cavern in minimum time?

| 1 | 2 | 3 | 4 | 5 | 6 | 7 | 8 | 9 | 10 | 11 | 12 | 13 | 14 |

15e • Speed paragraphs

(straight copy)

1 Two 1' writings on each ¶; strive to increase speed on the second writing.
2 One 3' writing on both ¶s combined; determine *gwam*.

all letters used | LA | 1.4 si | 5.4 awl | 85% hfw

	gwam 1'	3'
People who try to type but who have never had a course in how	12	4	65
to type correctly often develop several incorrect techniques. They may	27	9	70
have no choice but to look at the keyboard constantly. This, in turn,	41	14	75
may force them to memorize parts of the copy from which they are typing	55	18	79
so that they can then look at the keyboard. Usually, too, those same	69	23	84
people use any finger which seems convenient at the time to strike the	84	28	89
keys quickly.	86	29	90
From the very first day of your beginning typing course, you have	13	33	94
been taught several basic points you are to learn well if you are to be	28	38	99
a successful touch typist. Just how well have you learned these good	42	43	103
habits? Do you always get into a good typing position? Are you really	56	47	108
trying to keep your eyes on your copy? Are your fingers always curved	70	52	113
and both your wrists level and up off the machine in a relaxed position?	85	57	118
Do you make a zealous attempt to type with smooth rhythm?	96	61	122

gwam 1' | 1 | 2 | 3 | 4 | 5 | 6 | 7 | 8 | 9 | 10 | 11 | 12 | 13 | 14 |
gwam 3' | 1 | 2 | 3 | 4 | 5 |

SPEED BUILDER 16

16a • Keyboard review

Practice once slowly; a second time for speed; a third time for control.

alphabet 1 Jebb quickly zeroed in on a moving target, hoping for his sixth award.

figures 2 Runners 598, 602, 731, and 824 have been eliminated from the marathon.

fig/sym 3 Senior rings are $98.50 (less 10% discount) at Mario's at 26347 Josie.

| 1 | 2 | 3 | 4 | 5 | 6 | 7 | 8 | 9 | 10 | 11 | 12 | 13 | 14 |

16b • Technique builder:
stroking (reach strokes)

Reach up to the 3d row and down to the bottom row without moving the hands as you practice this drill.

;-p; j-y 1 ;p; up; top; step; trip; mishap; jyj joy jay jerky jitney year cyclist

s-x; k-, 2 sxs sax sox taxi sixth taxes exotic k,k ask, book, deck, block, knock,

j-m; a-z 3 jmj am jam jump jamb major minimum aza daze dazzle czar zigzag bizarre

4 The yes votes to omit the bylaw was a major step; she is very pleased.

5 For weeks, six boys worked on deck for exotic yacht trips to Zanzibar.

6 The czar sat, dazed after a bizarre mishap; his journey was cancelled.

| 1 | 2 | 3 | 4 | 5 | 6 | 7 | 8 | 9 | 10 | 11 | 12 | 13 | 14 |

CONTROL BUILDER 15

15a • Keyboard review

Practice once slowly; a second time for speed; a third time for control.

alphabet 1 Quinn seemed vexed when he found the lazy pup on top his black Jaguar.

figures 2 Effective March 1, 1983, Box 62-4 on Route 5 should be changed to 207.

fig/sym 3 The savings on Items #36, #37, #38, and #19, (at 40%) amount to $82.95.

| 1 | 2 | 3 | 4 | 5 | 6 | 7 | 8 | 9 | 10 | 11 | 12 | 13 | 14 |

15b • Technique builder: stroking

Concentrate on the words as you practice this drill.

direct 1 My brother, Johnny, ran many races before he believed he was any good.

reaches 2 I believe my Uncle Brent must have misplaced my unlisted phone number.

adjacent 3 As our polls showed, very few people agreed with the union's decision.

keys 4 We may support her for governor if we see her position on oil imports.

| 1 | 2 | 3 | 4 | 5 | 6 | 7 | 8 | 9 | 10 | 11 | 12 | 13 | 14 |

15c • Basic control builder: one-hand commonly used words

Practice the one-hand commonly used words 3 or 4 times. Strive for easy rhythm as you keyboard the sentences.

1 get rate after saw bag pink pool read date my garage opinion base

2 As you are aware, Polly gets a better rate on a car at my garage.

3 My pupil saw a pink nylon bag in my pool at Mullin's Inn in Ohio.

4 In my opinion, a better hymn was read at Easter after you fasted.

15d • Special control builder: guided paragraph writing

1 Take a 1' writing on ¶1; determine *gwam*.

2 Add 4 to 6 *gwam* to this base rate to set a new goal rate.

3 Take two 1' guided writings on ¶1; try to reach your goal rate.

4 Take two 1' guided writings on ¶2 in the same way.

5 Take two 5' writings on ¶s 1 and 2 combined; determine *gwam* on the better writing.

all letters used | HA | 1.7 si | 6.0 awl | 75% hfw

gwam 5'

Certainly by this time you have begun to realize just how useful ⟨3⟩ 30
your ability to keyboard has become to you. While you may have applied ⟨5⟩ 33
your skill primarily to typing assignments for your classes, have you ⟨8⟩ 36
developed much ability in composing at the typewriter? If you approach ⟨11⟩ 39
the development of such a skill properly, success can come easily. ⟨14⟩ 42

An important basic idea is to move from the simple to the complex ⟨16⟩ 44
as you develop your ability to compose. Without looking at any printed ⟨19⟩ 47
or typed copy, keyboard one word: then phrase responses to thoughts that ⟨22⟩ 50
enter your mind. Next, begin to develop complete sentences. Then, at- ⟨25⟩ 53
tempt to create an entire paragraph putting your ideas down quickly. ⟨28⟩ 56

gwam 5' | 1 | 2 | 3 |

Control Builder **15**

67

16c • Basic speed builder: balanced-hand words

Practice the sentences with smooth rhythm; keep hands and arms quiet.

1 *The firms did pay the usual penalty but also did aid the auditor.*
2 *To entitle them to work the land, she got them to sign the forms.*
3 *She may form a panel to air the problem and handle the amendment.*
4 *A pale visitor did slam tight the big door to the ancient chapel.*
5 *If they make their own form, they may make six forms for us, too.*
6 *They may wish a map of their own when they all row to the island.*

16d • Special speed builder: speed spurts

(balanced hand)

Practice each sentence as fast as possible to build stroking speed.

1 She may go to work when I do and also visit the man to sign the forms.
2 When they visit the island, make them sign the forms and pay the duty.
3 Cut the panel to fit the right height and fix the chair and the shelf.
4 I may wish to risk the title and turn pro by the end of the big fight.
5 The visitor may wish to go by air to the island to work for the firms.
6 Turn the map to the right angle to make visible the lay of their land.

| 1 | 2 | 3 | 4 | 5 | 6 | 7 | 8 | 9 | 10 | 11 | 12 | 13 | 14 |

16e • Speed paragraphs

(straight copy)

1 Two 1' writings on each ¶; strive to increase speed on the second writing.
2 One 3' writing on both ¶s combined; determine *gwam*.

all letters used | LA | 1.4 si | 5.4 awl | 85% hfw

gwam 1' | 3'

One basic point in typing which has changed some over the years 13 | 4 | 68
is the amount of effort needed to strike the keys. On the manual 27 | 9 | 73
machine, you certainly must strike each key sharply for the character 41 | 14 | 78
to come out dark enough. On electric and electronic machines, you need 55 | 18 | 82
to use only a light tapping motion. Once you have acquired this type of 69 | 23 | 87
response, you will be amazed at just how much faster you can type with 83 | 28 | 92
much less effort; but it is important to type with control, too. 96 | 32 | 96

As you know, the position of your hands at the machine is also 13 | 36 | 100
important. Both hands should be kept close together in order for the 27 | 41 | 105
fingers to control the keys they are intended to control. When you 40 | 45 | 109
permit your hands to wander out from the center of the keyboard, extra 54 | 50 | 114
motions are required each time the hands reposition themselves to 69 | 55 | 119
strike keys not on the home row. And such motions form habits very 83 | 60 | 124
quickly and may result in an actual loss in both speed and control. 96 | 64 | 128

| 1' | 1 | 2 | 3 | 4 | 5 | 6 | 7 | 8 | 9 | 10 | 11 | 12 | 13 | 14 |

gwam 3' | 1 | 2 | 3 | 4 | 5 |

14c • Basic control builder: one-hand commonly used words

Practice both lines of one-hand words 3 or 4 times. Strive for continuity of stroking as you keyboard the sentences.

1 *in as I my you are cars face debts were at saw red greater tested*
2 *case defer bad aware fewer acts state fare stars created reverses*
3 *In case you face greater reverses, defer stated bad debts faster.*
4 *As you are aware, I regret fewer red cars were tested in my area.*
5 *Grace saw greater stage stars as acts were created at Cedar Hill.*

14d • Special control builder: opposite fingers

Concentrate on each pair of opposite-finger letters as you practice this drill.

1 dk decking darker daybreak disembark kd kidded kindnesses kinds kindle
2 ie ideas idle retrieve imagines believed ei receive deceived sovereign
3 gh height weighted neighbors freight hg huge highlight shortages hedge
4 To be the recipient of an act of kindness kindles further worthy acts.
5 Idle workers tried to deceive me as to the true weight of the freight.
6 My neighbors plan to disembark at daybreak to retrieve their own boat.
7 With obvious kindness, she kidded her boy about his height and weight.

| 1 | 2 | 3 | 4 | 5 | 6 | 7 | 8 | 9 | 10 | 11 | 12 | 13 | 14 |

14e • Control paragraphs

(statistical copy)

1 Two 1' writings on each ¶; strive for improved control rate on the second writing.
2 One 5' writing on both ¶s combined; determine *gwam*.

all letters used | HA | 1.7 si | 6.0 awl | 75% hfw

gwam 1' | 5'

On March 20, 1980, a tremor which recorded at 4.1 on the Richter | 11 | 2 | 38
Scale issued notice that mighty St. Helens was active. This activity | 25 | 5 | 41
took place with increasing intensity until finally on May 18, at exactly | 39 | 8 | 43
8:32 a.m., the volcano erupted with maximum force. Ash was sent almost | 52 | 10 | 46
14 miles into the air. The force decimated an area 8 miles long and 15 | 65 | 13 | 49
miles wide, and one cloud finally reached over 63,000 feet. The vol- | 77 | 15 | 51
cano was actually reduced from its previous 9,677 feet to 8,400 feet. | 89 | 18 | 53

Now, cogent analysis definitely forces the question as to when and | 13 | 20 | 56
which one of the 17 major volcanoes within the Cascade Range will also | 27 | 23 | 59
return to life. Among the 17, 3 have a record of activity resembling | 40 | 26 | 61
that of St. Helens: Mt. Baker (elevation 10,778), Mt. Rainier (14,410), | 52 | 28 | 64
and Mt. Hood (11,235). These 3 were all active between 1840 and 1850, | 62 | 30 | 66
and Baker has demonstrated activity as recently as 1975. New facts now | 76 | 33 | 69
available point out even greater hazards than we have yet to realize. | 90 | 36 | 71

gwam 1' | 1 | 2 | 3 | 4 | 5 | 6 | 7 | 8 | 9 | 10 | 11 | 12 | 13 | 14 |
5' | 1 | 2 | 3 |

17a • Keyboard review

Practice once slowly; a second time for speed; a third time for control.

alphabet 1 Unzipping his heavy jacket, the mover quickly lifted the wooden boxes.

figures 2 On January 13, 1982, the population signs were changed to read 46,057.

fig/sym 3 "Pages 12, 48, 53-67, and 90 of my textbook are soiled," she remarked.

| 1 | 2 | 3 | 4 | 5 | 6 | 7 | 8 | 9 | 10 | 11 | 12 | 13 | 14 |

17b • Technique builder:
stroking (adjacent keys)

Make key reaches smoothly and with confidence as you practice this drill.

1 xc excel excite excerpt exclude oi avoid spoil joint tr try trip train

2 lk elk talk chalk silky ew few knew preview ui quit quite fluid liquid

3 sa sad save sales safari re are more ready return po port post posters

4 Try to post excess posters and preview a talk on the joint train trip.

5 A few quietly quit to avoid the safari and will try to return to port.

6 To save that port, quite a few knew we must chalk up more joint sales.

| 1 | 2 | 3 | 4 | 5 | 6 | 7 | 8 | 9 | 10 | 11 | 12 | 13 | 14 |

17c • Basic speed builder:
balanced-hand words

Work for a more rapid and efficient response as you practice these easy sentences.

1 Goro and Glen may visit the pen pal and then go to the big fight.

2 He may risk a fight if he turns the usual dials of the panel box.

3 May both girls, Sue Ellen and Jana, go to the Haley Civic Social?

4 He is to rush to a downtown firm and do the work for the auditor.

5 I eye a big fight when the rich firm signs for the land downtown.

6 Dudley and Kaye may spend half their pay to go to England by air.

17d • Special speed builder:
speed spurts (double letters)

Practice each sentence as fast as possible to build stroking speed. Try to maintain the same easy rhythm with double-letter combinations.

1 They still need to see the book soon to tell if it will fill the bill.

2 She will fill in for three weeks for employees in those small offices.

3 I cannot attend class in that room today unless I seek staff approval.

4 An officer called to offer immediate support for the community affair.

5 One call will assure us that your firm is shipping sufficient ribbons.

6 Am I to assume they agree with our billing and will correct the error?

7 He announced that congress will discuss the issue during that session.

8 I usually proofread all business letters before they leave the office.

| 1 | 2 | 3 | 4 | 5 | 6 | 7 | 8 | 9 | 10 | 11 | 12 | 13 | 14 |

13e • Control paragraphs

(rough-draft copy)

1 Two 1′ writings on each ¶; strive to increase your control rate on the second writing.

2 One 5′ writing on both ¶s combined; determine *gwam*.

all letters used | HA | 1.7 si | 6.0 awl | 75% hfw

	gwam 1′	5′	

Proof reading is a skill that always will continued to be · 11 · 2 | 30

~considered~
quite vital when you keyboard any kind of work. No one should · 23 · 5 | 33
~material. Do~

~come~
not be lazy as you lookfor all the errors just because it is · 35 · 7 | 35

~ier~ ~electronic~
really easy to correct errors on office equipment for you to- · 47 · 9 | 38

~remains~ ~in~
day. Perfect copy is still the main goal. Errors found fin- · 59 · 12 | 40

~others it is not considered important.~
ished work readily tells time wasn't taken. · 72 · 14 | 43

~whether~
If you take pride in everything you're keyboarding, weather it · 11 · 17 | 45

~ed~ ~certain to~ ~every~
be a draft or finish copy, be sure you look and locate errors. · 24 · 19 | 47

~beyond~ ~break~
Look for any errors you catch when you do experince a pause · 36 · 22 | 50

~keyboarding~
in your typing rhythm. It is simply to allow time to proofread · 48 · 24 | 52

~obvious~
carefully all copy for errors, but then especially try to make · 60 · 26 | 55

~sure the~ ~actually~
certain all finished copy work makes sense. · 69 · 28 | 56

CONTROL BUILDER 14

14a • Keyboard review

Practice once slowly; a second time for speed; a third time for control.

alphabet 1 Jacky performed very well on big quizzes on the textbook and lectures.

figures 2 Please retype pages 5, 18, 25, and 36; 40 and 79 need correcting, too.

fig/sym 3 "Orders #157, #283, #469, and #703 totaled $177.95," he added quickly.

| 1 | 2 | 3 | 4 | 5 | 6 | 7 | 8 | 9 | 10 | 11 | 12 | 13 | 14 |

14b • Technique builder: stroking (rows)

Maintain proper technique and control as you move from row to row.

top row 1 We counted 237 T-shirts (100% cotton) at $9.85 each ($6.40 wholesale).

3d row 2 Quietly try to report to Peter your two or three prior pottery errors.

row 3 Eiko tried to quote their queer wire query to the top-priority people.

home row 4 All last fall as a gag, Jay's dad sold old, odd glass flasks as gifts.

row 5 At last, all Hal Hall's lads had sadly passed all flags at half staff.

bottom row 6 Did the mob nab a zany miner and his box of zinc and mica in the cave?

| 1 | 2 | 3 | 4 | 5 | 6 | 7 | 8 | 9 | 10 | 11 | 12 | 13 | 14 |

17e • Speed paragraphs

(straight copy)

1 Two 1′ writings on each ¶; strive to increase speed on the second writing.
2 One 3′ writing on both ¶s combined; determine *gwam*.

all letters used | LA | 1.4 si | 5.4 awl | 85% hfw

	gwam 1′	3′
Day by day, as you work to increase your ability to strike the keys	13	4	64
more rapidly and accurately, so should you also try to advance in your	28	9	69
ability to use other machine parts. By now you should be aware that	41	14	74
the rate at which you type is determined in part by how effective you	55	18	78
become in using the space bar and the return, backspace, and shift keys	70	23	83
to develop one smooth operation as you type the letters, numbers, and	84	28	88
symbols.	85	28	88
The special drills that should be a part of your daily practice	13	33	93
are unique in their design to help you grow in your ability to type.	27	37	97
As you type these drills, just try to realize that indirectly you are	41	42	102
working on the overall rate at which you type. When you are aware of	55	47	107
areas that cause you difficulty, check to see if some specific exercise	69	52	112
is available to assist you in gaining greater speed. Every effort you	83	56	116
put forth now will certainly pay big dividends later on.	95	60	120

gwam 1′ | 1 | 2 | 3 | 4 | 5 | 6 | 7 | 8 | 9 | 10 | 11 | 12 | 13 | 14 |
3′ | 1 | 2 | 3 | 4 | 5 |

SPEED BUILDER 18

18a • Keyboard review

Practice once slowly; a second time for speed; a third time for control.

alphabet 1 By studying five hours daily, Jack Zornes qualified for two top exams.

figures 2 The final exam will test students over pages 12-35, 49-60, and 87-100.

fig/sym 3 Ad #6857 showed 4-ply, 3-oz. white yarn (reg. $1.29) reduced to $1.09.

| 1 | 2 | 3 | 4 | 5 | 6 | 7 | 8 | 9 | 10 | 11 | 12 | 13 | 14 |

18b • Technique builder:

stroking (direct reaches)

Reach up to the 3d row and down to the bottom row without moving the hands.

b-r; m-u 1 brb brag bribe debris branches abruptly mum must amused number mundane

r-g; u-n 2 rgr urge argued morgue gravy ground unu unable unaware unusual undergo

e-c; n-y 3 ece ace censor ecology receive deck nyn any funny nylon sunny lanyards

4 The man did brag about a bribe but argued he didn't receive any money.

5 You must be unaware of broken branches and unusual debris on the deck.

6 I argued not to spend that much money abruptly on ceiling decorations.

| 1 | 2 | 3 | 4 | 5 | 6 | 7 | 8 | 9 | 10 | 11 | 12 | 13 | 14 |

CONTROL BUILDER 13

13a • Keyboard review

Practice once slowly; a second time for speed; a third time for control.

alphabet 1 The man had just found the prized box when the guards quickly arrived.

figures 2 Senior candidates totaled 1,508; masters, 679; and doctoral, only 234.

fig/sym 3 Ty's Market has Item #9076 on sale for $8.15 (limit 2) through 3/4/88.

| 1 | 2 | 3 | 4 | 5 | 6 | 7 | 8 | 9 | 10 | 11 | 12 | 13 | 14 |

13b • Technique builder: manipulative control (sub and superscripts)

Work for efficient machine manipulation as you practice these sentences.

1 Subscripts must be typed 1/2 space below the line: H_2O, H_2SO_3, $CaCO_3$.

2 Superscripts are typed 1/2 space above the line: 32°, Y^2, Robertson[3].

3 Cortisone ($C_{21}H_{28}O_5$), or its derivative, is well known to my patients.

4 As I pointed out earlier, Breck[3], Dykes[4], and Oates[5] certainly concur.

5 The doctor simply prescribed aspirin ($C_9H_8O_4$) to lower his high fever.

6 References to Roarke[8] and Simmons[9] definitely appear to be incomplete.

| 1 | 2 | 3 | 4 | 5 | 6 | 7 | 8 | 9 | 10 | 11 | 12 | 13 | 14 |

13c • Basic control builder: one-hand commonly used words

Practice each line of one-hand words 3 or 4 times before keyboarding the sentences. Maintain proper control as you move from row to row.

1 I'm you my art on few are in only state acted upon best data read

2 aware saved facts great awards reserves ads traced opinion starts

3 gas we fewer abstracts cases average draft greater treated drawer

4 I'm aware you traced my award; you saved my severe art abstracts.

5 You get my best data only after I read ads on set tax rate cases.

6 I acted on few facts, as gas reserves are great only in my state.

13d • Special control builder (homonym hurdles)

Keyboard each sentence at a controlled rate. Concentrate on these "sound alikes" as you improve control.

1 to too two son sun pair pare for four role roll altar alter seen scene

2 flour flower one won there their bear bare steal steel capital capitol

3 seas sees seize aloud allowed past passed course coarse be bee toe tow

4 We won one game, but the sun was too hot for her son to enjoy himself.

5 He said aloud that only one pair of us was allowed to pare the apples.

6 Four men were seen leaving the scene to raise capital for the capitol.

7 In the past, the two passed the golf course to steal the coarse steel.

8 All the patients showed much patience in making a flower out of flour.

| 1 | 2 | 3 | 4 | 5 | 6 | 7 | 8 | 9 | 10 | 11 | 12 | 13 | 14 |

18c • Basic speed builder: balanced-hand words

Concentrate on continuity as you practice these easy sentences.

1 *Rufus and Enrique wish to do all the signs for the downtown firm.*

2 *Kept too busy to mend them, they got rid of a torn chair and rug.*

3 *The problem with their corps kept Whalen and Henry busy downtown.*

4 *Blanche and Ruby may go by bus to both Kent Lake and Buck Island.*

18d • Special speed builder: speed spurts (common words)

Practice each sentence as fast as possible to build stroking speed. Eliminate pauses between letters and words for greater speed.

1 One of these busy workers might wish to check on the many stock items.

2 Since many of the items are on sale today, be sure to check the price.

3 If I make a final payment on my loan, I can add to my capital reserve.

4 Which of the days do the four wish off to go by car to the big island?

5 If she is able to change her plans, she may loan four items to us now.

6 Prior to today, the cost of supplies and labor made any decision hard.

| 1 | 2 | 3 | 4 | 5 | 6 | 7 | 8 | 9 | 10 | 11 | 12 | 13 | 14 |

18e • Speed paragraphs

(rough-draft copy)

1 Two 1' writings on each ¶; strive to increase speed on the second writing.

2 One 3' writing on both ¶s combined, determine *gwam*.

all letters used | LA | 1.4 si | 5.4 awl | 85% hfw

	gwam 1'	3'
At a state-wide teachers meeting, nine people on a panel were asked to	14	5 | 56
point out those traits they looked for in workers when the	26	9 | 60
firm must decide whom to keep should economic conditions force a cut in	40	13 | 64
its staff. Attitude and loyalty were mentioned quite often.	52	17 | 69
Being excited about working for a firm and showing pride in	64	21 | 73
all work were both very vital.	70	23 | 75
Acting as part of a team by showing respect for those who may	12	28 | 79
rank above or below you on the job gets special merit, one said. A	32	34 | 85
happy workers feel good about them selves and pass this feel-	44	38 | 89
ing along to others. A third advisor said he looks for people	57	42 | 93
who are flexible in their zeal for personal growth within the firm.	71	47 | 98
All agreed that those who try their best can expect the best.	83	51 | 102

second panel member noted that

12c • Basic control builder: one-hand commonly used words

Practice each line of one-hand commonly used words 3 or 4 times. Keyboard the sentences, striving for improved control and continuity.

1 you were in my aware July upon stated exact tests data bad feared
2 we based created taxes severe acreage garage racers wages started
3 abstracts minimum traced award extra ads rate cases aware average
4 We started at a minimum wage based only upon stated average data.
5 Exact tests created bad debts; I fear severe taxes on my acreage.
6 Were you aware my red race car was in my garage in Texas in July?

12d • Special control builder: common word endings

Practice each word ending combination. Concentrate on the combinations as you keyboard the sentences.

1 acquire require reject project finding binding blinding either neither
2 focal local logical form storm perform slight flight might heads leads
3 program telegram diagram inferior superior decision revision provision
4 One provision of that project is that every local decision is binding.
5 He's finding that a storm might cause a slight change in flight plans.
6 Focal point of the local program could be the revision of the diagram.

| 1 | 2 | 3 | 4 | 5 | 6 | 7 | 8 | 9 | 10 | 11 | 12 | 13 | 14 |

12e • Control paragraphs

(straight copy)

1 Two 1' writings on each ¶; strive to improve accuracy on the second writing.

2 One 5' writing on both ¶s combined; determine *gwam*.

all letters used | HA | 1.7 si | 6.0 awl | 75% hfw

	gwam 1'	5'
Very few students enroll in typing courses today simply just to	13	3	40
learn skills to get jobs in offices. Most students now realize that	27	5	42
the typewriter is a tool of communication and that everyone could profit	41	8	45
from even a basic skill in operating a typewriter. While some people	55	11	48
may acquire a greater typing skill than others can ever hope to achieve,	70	14	51
whatever basic skill is obtained will fulfill a very useful purpose for	84	17	54
both personal and career reasons.	91	18	55
Hopefully, your school is providing opportunities for everyone who	13	21	58
yearns to enroll in typing courses to do so. There is ample evidence	27	24	61
that even students in elementary school could profit from knowledge of	42	26	64
the keyboard, especially since many more elementary school students are	56	29	66
gaining access to computers both within the home and their schools.	70	32	69
Many predict that we can expect to see computers become as ordinary as	84	35	72
TV sets in many homes in the not too distant future.	94	37	74

gwam 1' | 1 | 2 | 3 | 4 | 5 | 6 | 7 | 8 | 9 | 10 | 11 | 12 | 13 | 14 |
5' | 1 | 2 | 3 |

SPEED BUILDER 19

19a • Keyboard review

Practice once slowly; a second time for speed; a third time for control.

alphabet 1 Jake examined the quartz carefully before picking two samples to save.

figures 2 Active membership jumped from 25 in 1980 to 41 in 1983 and 67 in 1985.

fig/sym 3 The * refers to Alert (Issues 3-4 and 5-6) and the 1970-82 hurricanes.

| 1 | 2 | 3 | 4 | 5 | 6 | 7 | 8 | 9 | 10 | 11 | 12 | 13 | 14 |

19b • Technique builder: stroking

Compare the ease with which you practice each of these lines.

1 huh hum humid humor hustle hurricane btb but obtain subtle doubts both

2 rtr rut alert ultra return retired rotten opo opt topic tropics opened

3 mym myth myself clammy mystified rvr rave curves swerve revisit review

4 I better revisit the tropics myself before the humid hurricane season.

5 Both topics mystify my students, but I opt to review a hurricane myth.

6 Why hustle to return when at this rate it's better for both to retire?

| 1 | 2 | 3 | 4 | 5 | 6 | 7 | 8 | 9 | 10 | 11 | 12 | 13 | 14 |

19c • Basic speed builder: balanced-hand words

Push for speed with finger-action stroking as you practice these sentences.

1 *If the girls do their work, they may go down to the lake to fish.*

2 *Diana and Tien may fix their gowns and then go to the big social.*

3 *If the auditor is sick, Rodney may wish to sign all of the forms.*

4 *I did make visible by the quay a sign to make a right-angle turn.*

5 *When the problem is too big to handle, hand it to the town panel.*

6 *Did the corps pay for the right box and sign all the usual forms?*

19d • Special speed builder: speed spurt sentences

Practice each sentence as fast as possible to build stroking speed. Work for continuity of stroking as you move from one line to the next.

balanced-hand 1 When she pays for the fur, she may wish to fix it for their sick girl.

2 Visible signs to a lake and downtown dot the handy maps of the island.

double letters 3 All three still feel ill and will need to miss a full week of classes.

4 The cheese was shipped to our current address, and it finally arrived.

common words 5 Figure the total payment for all those items, and mail my check today.

6 Some of the file boxes will be coming to your office early next month.

common words 7 Your agent must cover all the issues at the next meeting in my office.

8 She plans to advise us about our problems with this year's high taxes.

| 1 | 2 | 3 | 4 | 5 | 6 | 7 | 8 | 9 | 10 | 11 | 12 | 13 | 14 |

11e • Control paragraphs

(straight copy)

1 Two 1' writings on each ¶; strive for improved control rate on the second writing.

2 One 5' writing on both ¶s combined; determine *gwam*.

all letters used | HA | 1.7 si | 6.0 awl | 75% hfw

	gwam 1'	5'
Learning how to keyboard efficiently involves more than just ac-	13	3 / 41
quiring the ability to strike the keys rapidly and accurately. As you	27	5 / 44
may well realize, you must also learn how to use several nonkeyboard	41	8 / 47
parts of your typewriter. Since these parts are utilized quite fre-	54	11 / 49
quently, certainly you can understand how the rate at which you keyboard	69	14 / 52
is influenced to some extent by the rate at which you develop in your	83	17 / 55
ability to operate these other typewriter parts.	93	19 / 57
Various typewriter parts necessitate greater practice than others	13	21 / 60
since they are utilized so often. Are you aware that on the average you	28	24 / 63
use the space bar twenty times in every one hundred strokes that you key-	42	27 / 66
board? Also consider how often you utilize the carriage return and both	57	30 / 68
the shift keys. So that your ability to operate typewriter parts will	71	33 / 71
expand at the same rate as your ability to stroke the keys, unique exer-	86	36 / 74
cises are available for daily practice and are included in many lessons.	100	39 / 77

gwam 1' | 1 | 2 | 3 | 4 | 5 | 6 | 7 | 8 | 9 | 10 | 11 | 12 | 13 | 14 |
5' | 1 | 2 | 3 |

CONTROL BUILDER 12

12a • Keyboard review

Practice once slowly; a second time for speed; a third time for control.

alphabet 1 Pat is dazzled by this jovial boxer who fights his main bouts quickly.

figures 2 Apartments 23, 41, and 65 are furnished; 87 and 90, still unfurnished.

fig/sym 3 Inventory Item #K-8329 (tripod) listed on page 406 is now in Room 157.

| 1 | 2 | 3 | 4 | 5 | 6 | 7 | 8 | 9 | 10 | 11 | 12 | 13 | 14 |

12b • Technique builder:

stroking (third and fourth fingers, both hands)

Make these finger reaches without moving the hands or arms as you practice this drill.

1 Your professor opposed the popular pastime of hassling the passengers.

2 Sack the wastepaper and save it on the porch until we're squared away.

3 Sally plans to sail on Saturday, then assist in sweeping the new pool.

4 In my opinion, we should possibly ponder the loan opportunity aspects.

5 We oppose questionable taxes and zealously dissent at wasteful losses.

6 Yoko sat in the sand, satisfied at last with the opportunity to relax.

| 1 | 2 | 3 | 4 | 5 | 6 | 7 | 8 | 9 | 10 | 11 | 12 | 13 | 14 |

19e • Speed paragraphs

(statistical copy)

1 Two 1' writings on each ¶; strive to increase speed on the second writing.
2 One 3' writing on both ¶s combined; determine *gwam*.

all letters used | LA | 1.4 si | 5.4 awl | 85% hfw

	gwam 1'	3'	
Did you know that New York City has more high buildings than any	13	4	60
other city in this country? That large city has 3 edifices over 1,000	26	9	64
feet high, 3 between 900-999, and 3 between 800-899. One major trade	36	12	67
center is 1,350 feet high and has 110 stories. Yet another well-known	48	16	71
building, the Empire State, is 1,250 feet high and has 102 stories. But	60	20	75
when the tower on top is included, the new figure does reach 1,472 feet.	74	25	80
A third very high edifice is 1,046 feet high and has 77 floors.	84	28	83
You would just be amazed at the view from the top of one edifice	13	32	88
in Chicago. It is 1,454 feet high and has 110 stories. Not quite as	25	36	92
high is another big building at 1,136 feet with 80 stories. A third	37	40	96
building extends to 1,127 feet with 100 stories. Two others measure	49	44	100
859 feet with 74 stories and 850 with 60. In 1981, the highest build-	59	48	103
ing in Houston was one at 1,002 feet with 75 stories. Second place	71	52	107
may go to an edifice under way which will measure 970 feet.	82	55	111

gwam 1' | 1 | 2 | 3 | 4 | 5 | 6 | 7 | 8 | 9 | 10 | 11 | 12 | 13 | 14 |
3' | 1 | 2 | 3 | 4 | 5 |

SPEED BUILDER 20

20a • Keyboard review

Practice once slowly; a second time for speed; a third time for control.

alphabet 1 Several fans exited quickly when the jazz performers had said goodbye.

figures 2 The tenants had already vacated Apartments 5, 17, 38, 60, 84, and 129.

fig/sym 3 Those remnants--reduced 40%--measured 16 2/3" x 45" and 17 1/8" x 90".

| 1 | 2 | 3 | 4 | 5 | 6 | 7 | 8 | 9 | 10 | 11 | 12 | 13 | 14 |

20b • Technique builder: manipulative control (space bar)

Space quickly between words; use down-and-in motion of the right thumb as you practice these sentences.

1 The four women plan to go to the city with the girls if I can go, too.

2 Of all the work they need to do, this job must be done with most care.

3 If I may do so, I wish to pay for the work when I sign for both forms.

4 Six men from the firm cut the oak and now wish to be paid for the job.

5 That woman and my son may run in a key race if they can make the team.

6 Many in the city do own land by the lake and may plan to bid for more.

| 1 | 2 | 3 | 4 | 5 | 6 | 7 | 8 | 9 | 10 | 11 | 12 | 13 | 14 |

CONTROL BUILDER 11

11a • Keyboard review

Practice once slowly; a second time for speed; a third time for control.

alphabet 1 Amazingly, Rex became the first picker to quit work and join the Navy.

figures 2 Room keys 103, 325, and 406 were turned in; 784 and 921 are still out.

fig/sym 3 Item #40-92 was back ordered; #31-58 (old #67-42) was sent last month.

| 1 | 2 | 3 | 4 | 5 | 6 | 7 | 8 | 9 | 10 | 11 | 12 | 13 | 14 |

11b • Technique builder: stroking (second finger, both hands)

Make the second-finger reaches without moving the other fingers out of position as you practice this drill.

1 Haru did go deer hunting, deciding to hike indirectly to the airfield.

2 Mike likes to hike, but he decided to ride a bike to the new airstrip.

3 Five identical kittens kept the individual kennel keepers busy indeed.

4 Nine cadets kindly kidded the kicker before the kickoff at Kyle Field.

5 The editors decided to edit the article identifying the two hijackers.

6 Dede decided to dictate a decision to her clients following her edict.

| 1 | 2 | 3 | 4 | 5 | 6 | 7 | 8 | 9 | 10 | 11 | 12 | 13 | 14 |

11c • Basic control builder: one-hand commonly used words

Practice each line of one-hand words 3 or 4 times before keyboarding the sentences. Work for continuity of stroking.

1 we in are few were upon read best only acted extra regret drafted

2 eager average taxes readers acreage decrease rewarded estate fact

3 opinion abstract stated water reversed states reserve save served

4 In my opinion, water rates are best based only upon stated facts.

5 After we read extra facts, we regretted Johnny acted on my draft.

6 Only a few taxes were decreased; Brad regretted we were defeated.

11d • Special control builder: word building

Practice each line at a controlled rate. As you keyboard each line, concentrate on the word endings.

1 indicate indicates indicated indicators indication economic economical

2 economists economically edit editor edition editorial enclose enclosed

3 enclosures enclosing plan planned planning rejects rejected rejections

4 quest question questioning questionnaire possible possibly possibility

5 A few economists question and even reject certain economic indicators.

6 Please edit my enclosed questionnaire and reject questionable figures.

7 Possibly the plan I am enclosing will be economically feasible to you.

8 He indicated that he plans to print his editorial in the next edition.

| 1 | 2 | 3 | 4 | 5 | 6 | 7 | 8 | 9 | 10 | 11 | 12 | 13 | 14 |

20c • Basic speed builder: balanced-hand words

As you practice these sentences, keep your hands and arms quiet, with action entirely in the fingers.

1 Their work may entitle the girls to name a theme for the socials.
2 With problems to air for the audit, the firm kept the panel busy.
3 The work for the downtown firms kept them both too busy to visit.
4 Ruth kept the auto, so Elena may go to the island by bus to work.

20d • Special speed builder: skill comparison sentences

Practice each sentence as fast as possible to build stroking speed. Compare your stroking continuity with each type of sentence.

balanced-hand	1	Name six good firms, and I may pay them to handle all the work for us.
one-hand	2	As you are aware, my taxes are based in my case on stated estate data.
combination	3	When you go to pump the gas and oil my car, do the work in the garage.
	4	The tax auditor may make me pay for an extra opinion in my rate cases.
3d row	5	Two or three were there with our group who tried to quiet our protest.
adjacent keys	6	As we walked, hands in pockets, she quietly responded to our opinions.
direct reaches	7	Recently, a number of great musicians agreed to organize a fund drive.
	8	Bright skies often bring a number of girls out onto my large sun deck.

| 1 | 2 | 3 | 4 | 5 | 6 | 7 | 8 | 9 | 10 | 11 | 12 | 13 | 14 |

20e • Speed paragraphs

(straight copy)

1 Two 1' writings on each ¶; strive to increase speed on the second writing.
2 One 3' writing on both ¶s combined; determine *gwam*.

all letters used | LA | 1.4 si | 5.4 awl | 85% hfw

gwam 1' | 3'

Every college student usually has a chance to join one or more   13   4 | 68
groups between the first and last years of schooling. If you should   26   9 | 73
go to college, you may become eligible to join certain clubs on the   40   13 | 78
basis of your grade point average or your area of study. Before you   54   18 | 82
agree to become a member of any group, you should weigh certain key   67   22 | 87
factors rather than join just because all your friends are joining.   81   27 | 91
For one thing, you should realize what you will gain as a member.   94   31 | 96

If you earn the right to become a member of an honor society as   13   36 | 100
a result of your grades and do join, that fact will look good on your   27   40 | 105
resume. So that you can reveal to any prospective employer that you did   41   45 | 109
more than attend required classes, you should examine the goals of the   56   50 | 114
various professional clubs and consider joining those groups that would   70   55 | 119
aid your personal growth. But keep in mind that you gain from being a   84   59 | 124
member of a group according to how much you give to that organization.   98   64 | 128

gwam 1' | 1 | 2 | 3 | 4 | 5 | 6 | 7 | 8 | 9 | 10 | 11 | 12 | 13 | 14 |
3' | 1 | 2 | 3 | 4 | 5 |

10c • Basic control builder: one-hand two-letter combinations (digraphs)

Practice each two-letter combination 3 or 4 times before keyboarding the words which follow each combination. *Think* the two-letter combinations.

1 on one only once noon upon nylon person iron wonder auction bonus
2 re rare were share aware admire where review revise great foreign
3 te ten rate vote water enter after protest later often term tempt
4 Only one person bid on our stamp collection at the auction today.
5 Were you aware that they revised your review of the foreign film?
6 Tenile will protest if the water rate is tempered by ten percent.

10d • Special control builder: guided paragraph writing

1 Take a 1' writing on the ¶; determine *gwam*. This is your base rate.
2 Add 4-6 words to your base rate to determine your goal rate. Find ¼' goals for new writings at your goal rate.
3 Take 1' writings as ¼' guides are called until you reach your goal rate.

all letters used | A | 1.5 si | 5.7 awl | 80% hfw

I am glad to answer your question about our January 18 bill of
account to Kent Corporation for $950.88. The bill covers two purchases
of $205.20 on December 20 (your invoice #2489 minus 10% trade discount
plus 7% sales tax) and $745.68 on January 11 (your invoice #3762 minus
20% trade discount plus 7% sales tax).

10e • Control paragraphs

(straight copy)

1 Two 1' writings on each ¶; strive to improve accuracy on the second writing.
2 One 5' writing on both ¶s combined; determine *gwam*.

all letters used | A | 1.5 si | 5.7 awl | 80% hfw

	gwam 1'	5'	
You will be wise to establish exemplary work habits from the very	13	3	40
beginning of your first job. Several of the outstanding work habits you	28	6	43
need to develop involve the proper usage of your time. You must arrive	42	8	46
at work on time every day. Punctuality indicates that you value your	56	11	49
job. Being punctual also has a positive effect on you. When you are	70	14	52
late for work, you fall behind, hurry to catch up, and make mistakes.	84	17	55
If you are prompt, you are relaxed and work more accurately.	96	19	57
Efficient office workers must possess an ability to organize their	13	22	60
everyday assignments. They must be able to make decisions quickly and	28	25	63
have a high work output. They must be accurate in their work and meet	42	28	65
the work standards of the office. They tend to keep things always orga-	56	31	68
nized so that they will not waste time searching for them as they begin	70	33	71
each job. They organize their work by writing down the due dates and	84	36	74
then dividing the jobs into categories.	92	38	75

gwam 1' | 1 | 2 | 3 | 4 | 5 | 6 | 7 | 8 | 9 | 10 | 11 | 12 | 13 | 14
5' | 1 | 2 | 3

SPEED BUILDER 21

21a • Keyboard review

Practice once slowly; a second time for speed; a third time for control.

alphabet 1 The prized vase was just a mixture of grey, aqua, and sky blue colors.

figures 2 On August 4, they served 387 breakfasts, 592 lunches, and 610 dinners.

fig/sym 3 The item (#670-081) sells for $15 each; 2/$28; 3/$39; 4/$48; or 5/$55.

| 1 | 2 | 3 | 4 | 5 | 6 | 7 | 8 | 9 | 10 | 11 | 12 | 13 | 14 |

21b • Technique builder: stroking (double letters)

Try to maintain the same even rhythm as you practice these sentences.

1 They all happily cheered the winning football team on a cool fall day.

2 The queen bee buzzed as she collected the pollen from the yellow rose.

3 Jeff was feeling quite ill before he was called into the meeting room.

4 She planned a speech on office careers for the class meeting tomorrow.

5 She bagged all the good apples in the barrel for the sale at the mall.

6 The old gutters on the roof fell off during the sleet storm last week.

| 1 | 2 | 3 | 4 | 5 | 6 | 7 | 8 | 9 | 10 | 11 | 12 | 13 | 14 |

21c • Basic skill builder: easy trigraphs

Practice each three-letter combination 3 or 4 times before keyboarding the words which follow each combination.

1 anc ranch insurance fir first fire firm ans answer transportation

2 ake make taken fake ang arrange change tangle hen when then henna

3 She wanted a chance to make transportation arrangements for them.

4 When should she make arrangements to change their fire insurance?

21d • Special speed builder: guided paragraph writing

1 Take a 1' writing on ¶1; determine *gwam*.
2 Add 5 *gwam* to base rate to set a new goal rate.
3 Take two 1' guided writings on ¶1; try to reach your goal rate.
4 Take two 1' guided writings on ¶2 in the same way.
5 Take two 3' writings on ¶s 1 and 2 combined; determine *gwam* on the better writing.

all letters used | A | 1.5 si | 5.7 awl | 80% hfw

gwam 1' | 3'

You will learn a great deal about your job by reading. Every cler- 14 | 5 | 49
ical job requires reading skill. You must be able to read instructions 28 | 9 | 54
and verify data in a variety of reference sources. You also must be able 42 | 14 | 59
to comprehend or understand what you have read in order to effectively 56 | 19 | 63
utilize what you have gained by reading. 65 | 22 | 66

In order to read information so that you comprehend it, you should 13 | 26 | 71
initially determine the overall topic of the text and why it is impor- 27 | 31 | 75
tant. Then rapidly read through the text to get an overview. Read the 42 | 36 | 80
text a second time and give attention to details. Lastly, ask yourself 56 | 40 | 85
some questions to verify that you comprehend what you have read. 69 | 45 | 89

gwam 1' | 1 | 2 | 3 | 4 | 5 | 6 | 7 | 8 | 9 | 10 | 11 | 12 | 13 | 14 |
gwam 3' | 1 | 2 | 3 | 4 | 5 |

9e • Control paragraphs

(statistical copy)

1 Two 1' writings on each ¶; strive to increase your control rate on the second writing.
2 One 5' writing on both ¶s combined; determine *gwam*.

all letters used | A | 1.5 si | 5.7 awl | 80% hfw

gwam 1' | 5'

Before April 15 of each year, you and millions of others are re- | 12 | 2 | 36
quired by the Internal Revenue Service to submit an income tax return. | 27 | 5 | 39
By January 31, you will receive your W-2 form (Wage and Tax Statement) | 39 | 8 | 41
from your employer. You will enclose Copy B of the W-2 form with your | 53 | 11 | 44
tax return. You must ascertain which tax form to use--1040EZ, 1040A, | 64 | 13 | 46
or 1040. Your gross amount of income and filing status ascertain which | 78 | 16 | 49
tax form will aptly satisfy your requirements. | 87 | 17 | 51

There are numerous items (deductions) that you may subtract from | 13 | 20 | 53
your total gross income to make up your taxable income. You may use a | 27 | 23 | 56
deduction of 25% of the first $100 you give to charity ($100 x 25% = | 36 | 25 | 58
$25). For example, if you donated $50 to your church, your deduction | 49 | 27 | 60
would be $12.50 ($50 x 25%). However, if you donated $150, your deduc- | 59 | 29 | 63
tion would be only $25 since $25 is the limit for this item. Consult | 71 | 32 | 65
your tax book for a list of other deductions. | 80 | 33 | 67

gwam 1' | 1 | 2 | 3 | 4 | 5 | 6 | 7 | 8 | 9 | 10 | 11 | 12 | 13 | 14 |
5' | 1 | | 2 | | 3 | |

CONTROL BUILDER 10

10a • Keyboard review

Practice once slowly; a second time for speed; a third time for control.

alphabet 1 V. Bick's group was the fifth jazz quartet listed on the Roxy program.

figures 2 I leave at 9:45 a.m. on Flight 630; I return at 2:18 p.m. on Flight 7.

fig/sym 3 We ordered 65 copies of Book #90-3 at $13 each and 82 copies of #84-7.

| 1 | 2 | 3 | 4 | 5 | 6 | 7 | 8 | 9 | 10 | 11 | 12 | 13 | 14 |

10b • Technique builder:
stroking (first finger, **both hands**)

Make the first-finger reaches without moving the hands as you practice this drill.

1 After the jury found the person guilty, Judge Jaffe gave the judgment.

2 For good nutrition, I included many fruits and vegetables on the menu.

3 Greta gave Bob a hat at his birthday party on Monday, the seventeenth.

4 It is obvious that Beth Cummings ought to study nursing in the future.

5 Our neighbor, Yvonne, has had a minimum of four job offers this month.

6 Betty was very thirsty after sunbathing in the bright summer sunshine.

| 1 | 2 | 3 | 4 | 5 | 6 | 7 | 8 | 9 | 10 | 11 | 12 | 13 | 14 |

21e • Speed paragraphs

(straight copy)

1 Two 1' writings on each ¶; strive to increase speed on the second writing.
2 One 3' writing on both ¶s combined; determine *gwam*.

all letters used	A	1.5 si	5.7 awl	80% hfw

	gwam 1'		3'

When you finish your business courses in school, you should have 13 4 64
the basic preparation to enter an office job. However, your learning 27 9 69
is not finished. In many ways, it is just starting. Every day you will 42 14 74
learn something new on the job. Procedures and technology are changing 56 19 79
rapidly, and you must keep up with new advances. You will learn from 70 23 83
individuals employed in the office with you as well as from the people 84 28 88
who supervise you. 88 29 89

There are ample opportunities to continue your learning once you 13 34 94
are working. Your company may sponsor courses or seminars within the 27 38 98
company. Be sure to inquire about courses which are available in your 41 43 103
own area at the colleges or adult learning centers. You may want to 55 48 108
enroll in a college program on a part-time basis. Think about further- 69 52 112
ing your education. In a changing and amazingly complex business world, 84 57 117
this may be the only way to keep up to date. 93 60 120

```
gwam  1' | 1 | 2 | 3 | 4 | 5 | 6 | 7 | 8 | 9 | 10 | 11 | 12 | 13 | 14 |
      3' |     1     |     2     |     3     |     4     |     5     |
```

SPEED BUILDER 22

22a • Keyboard review

Practice once slowly; a second time for speed; a third time for control.

alphabet 1 Fred Kante was proven to be lazy just because he quit the boxing team.

figures 2 We need 12 copies of all the pictures numbered 18, 29, 30, 47, and 56.

fig/sym 3 We received a 40% discount ($138.96) on Stock Item #257 (walnut desk).

```
| 1 | 2 | 3 | 4 | 5 | 6 | 7 | 8 | 9 | 10 | 11 | 12 | 13 | 14 |
```

22b • Technique builder: manipulative control

(element return)

Set the left margin at 30 (pica) or 36 (elite); set a tab stop at the center *plus 10*. Practice the lines as directed

	tab → Typewriting
has become	tab → the major
means	tab → of written
communication	tab → in business and
is becoming	tab → increasingly so in
our personal and	tab → professional lives.

CONTROL BUILDER 9

9a • Keyboard review

Practice once slowly; a second time for speed; a third time for control.

alphabet 1 Jim G. Ortez lived in quiet luxury in the back part of a Welsh castle.

figures 2 Annie had scores of 75, 65, 80, 91, 72, and 63 for an average of 74.2.

fig/sym 3 Our note (#196) for $72,580.40 is due on March 30 (plus 14% interest).

| 1 | 2 | 3 | 4 | 5 | 6 | 7 | 8 | 9 | 10 | 11 | 12 | 13 | 14 |

9b • Technique builder: stroking (rows)

Maintain proper technique and control as you move from row to row.

top row 1 My payment of $194.80 for a calculator (Model #2573) is due on 9/6/85.

3d row 2 We were quite upset as two of your reporters were rude to our writers.

3 You were required to prepare three quarterly reports for Peter Pruitt.

home row 4 As Kass said, dad's glass of fake daffodils adds a gala look all fall.

bottom row 5 Zoe minimized my concern for the six victims involved in a bomb scare.

6 My sabbatical leave enables me to visit the Zapotec Indians in Mexico.

| 1 | 2 | 3 | 4 | 5 | 6 | 7 | 8 | 9 | 10 | 11 | 12 | 13 | 14 |

9c • Basic control builder: one-hand two-letter combinations (digraphs)

Practice each two-letter combination 3 or 4 times before keyboarding the words which follow each combination. Work for greater control as you practice these sentences.

1 as cash ask fast assure base pass purchase please glass passenger

2 st most test staff last state mistake artist estate start request

3 pl plan place plot please apply plaza explain employ reply simple

4 I was pleased when Asa assured me the purchaser paid him in cash.

5 Most of my mistakes on the real estate test are on the last page.

6 I am pleased that she plans to apply for employment at the plaza.

9d • Special control builder: transition traps

Work for smooth stroking transition between words of each two-word pair as you keyboard these lines.

words 1 tourist told every young maintaining good grades since jet took at two

2 the eager about the am maintaining began new yesterday you two o'clock

3 streetcar ride many yachts good daily academic courses Atlanta Airport

sentences 4 I am maintaining good daily grades since I began new academic courses.

5 The Estana Airlines jet took off from Atlanta Airport at two o'clock.

6 The eager tourist told Katie about the many yachts seen in Naples Bay

| 1 | 2 | 3 | 4 | 5 | 6 | 7 | 8 | 9 | 10 | 11 | 12 | 13 | 14 |

22c • Basic skill builder: common phrases

Keyboard the phrases and sentences as fast as possible to build keystroking speed.

1 *I would | thank you | very much | have a | copy of | like to | have a | we will*
2 *to have | of the | that you | to our | like to | your letter | to be | for your*
3 *I would very much like to have a copy of the book that you wrote.*
4 *Thank you for your letter which we will forward to our treasurer.*

22d • Special speed builder: skill transfer paragraphs

1 One 1' writing on ¶1; determine *gwam.*
2 Take 1' writings on ¶2 until you equal or exceed your gwam on ¶1.

all letters used	A	1.5 si	5.7 awl	80% hfw

gwam 1'

Maybe you, like most people, do not take the time to sit down 13
and analyze your attitude about yourself. But, a self-analysis is 27
often an enormous part of knowing yourself and your abilities. 41
You need to ask yourself questions about your assets, your lia- 55
bilities, and your goals in life. 58

You need to ~~have~~ *maintain* a positive approach, ~~to~~ *about* the mistakes you 13
have made ~~along the way.~~ *in your past* Someone once stated that a mistake is 25
not a failure, ~~if~~ *when* you *have* learned something from ~~it.~~ *the experience* Just because 40
you have made ~~mistakes before~~ *errors in your past* is not evidence you *#* will continue 55
to do so. Concentrate upon the successes*!* ~~you have had!~~ 64

22e • Speed paragraphs (straight copy)

1 Two 1' writings on each ¶; strive to increase speed on the second writing.
2 One 3' writing on both ¶s combined; determine *gwam.*

all letters used	A	1.5 si	5.7 awl	80% hfw

gwam 1' | 3'

Success in business is based on your attitude toward your work as 13 | 4 | 67
well as your abilities and how you work. A positive attitude toward 27 | 9 | 72
your work can be the difference between success and failure. If you 41 | 14 | 76
enjoy your work experience, you will have a positive attitude. If you 55 | 18 | 81
dislike your work, you will no doubt have a negative attitude. Nobody 69 | 23 | 86
likes to be around a negative person. Every beginner has a lot to learn. 84 | 28 | 91
But if your attitude is favorable, you will learn faster. 96 | 32 | 95

A quiet sense of self-confidence and a belief in yourself are essen- 14 | 36 | 99
tial to a good attitude and success. Another important factor in a 27 | 41 | 104
positive work attitude is getting along with people. A good attitude 41 | 46 | 108
also includes enthusiasm for your work and for the company that employs 56 | 50 | 113
you. The beginning worker must be willing to learn. You need to be 69 | 55 | 118
dependable and do what you say you will do. You need to be an organized 84 | 60 | 123
worker and be able to follow instructions. 92 | 63 | 125

gwam 1' | 1 | 2 | 3 | 4 | 5 | 6 | 7 | 8 | 9 | 10 | 11 | 12 | 13 | 14 |
3' | 1 | 2 | 3 | 4 | 5 |

8c • Basic control builder: one-hand two-letter combinations (digraphs)

Practice each two-letter combination 3 or 4 times before keyboarding the words which follow each combination. Strive for accuracy and control.

1 io radio violin patio union lion senior motion junior iodine iota
2 es best these impress tests requests salesperson estate yesterday
3 hi him his hire high think while hill history behind machine hide
4 A senior sat on the patio listening to violin music on the radio.
5 Yesterday my best salesperson impressed me with her pleasantness.
6 I hired him because I was highly impressed with his work history.

8d • Special control builder

(long words)

Work for continuity of stroking while still maintaining control as you keyboard these long words.

10-12 letters
1 management organizing government headquarters stockholders immediately
2 individuals supervisor considerable reimbursed overpayments department

12-14 letters
3 representative comprehensive responsibility distribution possibilities
4 satisfactorily clarification qualifications construction approximately

sentences
5 The management has responsibility for organizing the new headquarters.
6 Four individuals satisfactorily met the qualifications for supervisor.

sentences
7 Their representative reimbursed the stockholders for the overpayments.
8 The comprehensive government report needed considerable clarification.

| 1 | 2 | 3 | 4 | 5 | 6 | 7 | 8 | 9 | 10 | 11 | 12 | 13 | 14 |

8e • Control paragraphs

(rough-draft copy)

1 Two 1' writings on each ¶; strive to increase your control rate on the second writing.

2 One 5' writing on both ¶s combined; determine *gwam*.

all letters used | A | 1.5 si | 5.7 awl | 80% hfw

	gwam 1'	5'
Do you know ^that a successful ^tele phone call begins ~~when~~ ^prior to answer-	14	3	29
ing the ^tele phone? Your desk must be organized with ~~all~~ ^some necessary	27	5	32
~~things~~ ^supplies such as pens, notepads, message forms, ^& pads and useful refer-	41	8	34
ence books. Then you ~~won't~~ ^will not have to transfer a caller ^to hold as you	55	11	37
will be able to ^handle answer a call quick ^ly and efficient ^ly.	66	13	39
You will make a ^favorable good impression on callers if you ~~reply to~~ ^answer the	13	16	42
tele phone promptly. A prompt answer is courteous ~~ly given~~ ^and effective. A	27	19	45
slow answer is extremely rude no matter ~~what you may be doing~~ ^to callers. how busy you are	41	21	47
At your job you must be prepared to give ~~all~~ ^your full attention to a	54	24	50
^caller person. Other wise, you ~~make them feel unimportant.~~ ^may make a bad impression.	64	26	52

SPEED BUILDER 23

23a • Keyboard review

Practice once slowly; a second time for speed; a third time for control.

alphabet 1 A prize was awarded to Virj as the quickest and most flexible gymnast.

figures 2 The facts in Footnote 46 are on page 2730 in the book written in 1895.

fig/sym 3 They gave us the usual 2% discount on our order #45-86 for $19,102.37.

| 1 | 2 | 3 | 4 | 5 | 6 | 7 | 8 | 9 | 10 | 11 | 12 | 13 | 14 |

23b • Technique builder:
stroking (reach strokes)

Make each reach without moving the other fingers out of position as you practice this drill.

a-z; j-u 1 aza amazing dazed plaza Elizabeth juj jungle July judge justified June

f-r; d-e 2 frf Frank for from furious prefer ded Edward debates agreed desk sedan

l-o; g-r 3 lol Louise Olga losing cold gold low grg Grant grateful progress Greta

4 In July, Edward and Olivia Grant will visit the amazing Amazon jungle.

5 Frank was grateful that Olga agreed to judge the debates at the plaza.

6 Greta was justified in her fury at Elizabeth for losing the June file.

| 1 | 2 | 3 | 4 | 5 | 6 | 7 | 8 | 9 | 10 | 11 | 12 | 13 | 14 |

23c • Basic skill builder:
easy trigraphs

Practice each three-letter combination 3 or 4 times before keyboarding the words which follow each combination.

1 *tic notice article fic certificate official ity quality authority*

2 *lan balance land plan isi visitor decision for formal performance*

3 *men commend payment man manage human many ign sign foreign design*

4 *I signed his quality performance certificate and recommended him.*

5 *He has authority to visit foreign lands for official information.*

6 *Just send the payment for the balance due along with this notice.*

23d • Special speed builder:
speed spurts (balanced hand)

Practice each sentence as fast as possible to build stroking speed.

1 The usual city audit problems kept both Andy and Dorian busy downtown.

2 The busy firms work to embody the civic and social goals of the towns.

3 When shall I turn to the bid for the title to the rich land and field?

4 The firms may wish aid when they augment their fight for an amendment.

5 Doris and Blanche Towlen wish to visit the chapels of an ancient city.

6 The fuel profit and coal quantity problems also kept all the men busy.

| 1 | 2 | 3 | 4 | 5 | 6 | 7 | 8 | 9 | 10 | 11 | 12 | 13 | 14 |

7e • Control paragraphs

(straight copy)

1 Two 1' writings on each ¶; strive to improve accuracy on the second writing.

2 One 5' writing on both ¶s combined; determine *gwam*.

all letters used	A	1.5 si	5.7 awl	80% hfw

gwam 1' | 5'

A lot of your everyday contact with people involves conversation. 13 | 3 | 41
You need to recognize the fact that a good deal of your enjoyment and 27 | 5 | 44
prosperity in life will depend on your ability to converse with people. 42 | 8 | 47
If you are able to converse with people, you will be more apt to get 56 | 11 | 50
along with them. Attempt to make the other person feel important. Make 70 | 14 | 53
your conversation a two-way process. If you display a friendly interest 85 | 17 | 55
in other people, they will be friendly to you. 94 | 19 | 57

In improving communicating skills, the most troublesome task you 13 | 21 | 60
will undertake is to remain quiet and listen to others. Give others the 28 | 24 | 63
opportunity to express their opinions. Think of a group of people as a 42 | 27 | 66
sports team and remember to give every player the chance to play. An- 56 | 30 | 68
other essential part of talking in a group is having good eye contact. 70 | 33 | 71
Look at every person as they converse and as you speak to them. Looking 85 | 36 | 74
at them reassures people that you are interested in what they say. 98 | 38 | 77

gwam 1' | 1 | 2 | 3 | 4 | 5 | 6 | 7 | 8 | 9 | 10 | 11 | 12 | 13 | 14 |
     5' | 1 | | 2 | | 3 |

CONTROL BUILDER 8

8a • Keyboard review

Practice once slowly; a second time for speed; a third time for control.

alphabet 1 Vince Gephard took an excursion to Mozambique for crystals and jewels.

figures 2 Job 89 consists of 137 pages; Job 90, 452 pages; and Job 91, 60 pages.

fig/sym 3 The terms of Invoice #57-319 from J-6 Co. (dated 4/18) are 2/10, n/30.

| 1 | 2 | 3 | 4 | 5 | 6 | 7 | 8 | 9 | 10 | 11 | 12 | 13 | 14 |

8b • Technique builder: stroking

(combination sentences)

Maintain correct home row position as you practice this drill.

3d row 1 We were upset Terrie Troutt was required to quit work at your request.

2 Porter tried to rewrite your quarterly reports prior to your pep talk.

home row 3 Hal Hall shall wash glasses; Sal Asalke's dad shall also wash glasses.

4 Kass Falk saw a glass fall off a shelf; jagged glass slashed his legs.

bottom row 5 On Monday, convicts escaped by the cave next to the zoological garden.

6 Did six men vacate a live animal exhibit at a zoo near Kennedy Center?

| 1 | 2 | 3 | 4 | 5 | 6 | 7 | 8 | 9 | 10 | 11 | 12 | 13 | 14 |

23e • Speed paragraphs
(rough draft)

1 Two 1' writings on each ¶; strive to increase speed on the second writing.

2 One 3' writing on both ¶s combined; determine *gwam*

all letters used	A	1.5 si	5.7 awl	80% hfw		gwam 1'	3'

	1'	3'
An important skill for ~~every~~ *a good* leader to ~~learn~~ *develop* is that of	12	4 | 48
bringing about change success‿fully. By nature, people tend to	24	8 | 52
resist *change just* because they are happy, *with the status quo* and want to stay with the ~~way~~	42	14 | 58
things ~~are and leave it the same~~ *same situation*. As a good leader ~~you should~~	48	16 | 60
realize that this resistance ex~~si~~ts and work to over‿come it	60	20 | 64
~~fear~~ when the change is necessary.	66	22 | 66
A good leader will implement change that ~~e~~ffects people in *a*	12	26 | 70
~~an unusual~~ *the following* ways: First, ~~introduce~~ *propose* the ~~very~~ idea ~~of change~~ to	21	29 | 73
the people by stating that the change is needed; next ask for	34	33 | 78
~~lists of~~ suggestions for bringing about the ~~new~~ *pending* change; And,	45	37 | 81
after the change has been made, time from *to* time review ~~all of~~	57	41 | 85
the ~~effects~~ *results* with the people most closely affected.	67	44 | 89

SPEED BUILDER 24

24a • Keyboard review

Practice once slowly; a second time for speed; a third time for control.

alphabet	1	Frank P. Vogeler acquired two bronze boxes from the jolly auctioneers.
figures	2	Over 1300 medals were purchased--258 gold, 479 silver, and 632 bronze.
fig/sym	3	The new tax (.5%) was passed with 38,274 votes for and 29,106 against.

| 1 | 2 | 3 | 4 | 5 | 6 | 7 | 8 | 9 | 10 | 11 | 12 | 13 | 14 |

24b • Technique builder:
stroking (adjacent keys)

Keep fingers curved and upright as you practice this drill.

1 re here before receive revise as ask last purchase we were weeks lower

2 er order here after other po propose policy op option copy oi join oil

3 sa saw Sally necessary io union options question ew new few knew threw

4 Vera Weber asked to join the union when the new credits were proposed.

5 Lew saw a copy of the proposed policy before the options were revised.

6 Sally received twelve purchase orders from Ohio Oil and Gas last week.

| 1 | 2 | 3 | 4 | 5 | 6 | 7 | 8 | 9 | 10 | 11 | 12 | 13 | 14 |

7a • Keyboard review

Practice once slowly; a second time for speed; a third time for control.

alphabet 1 Jake D. Gomez is anxious about his quest for review of a one-act play.

figures 2 Project 64890-1 will employ 1,257 people for at least 30 to 36 months.

fig/sym 3 The insurance policy (#46972) for $58,000 will mature on June 3, 2001.

| 1 | 2 | 3 | 4 | 5 | 6 | 7 | 8 | 9 | 10 | 11 | 12 | 13 | 14 |

7b • Technique builder: manipulative control

(sub and superscripts)

Use automatic line finder when keyboarding sub and superscripts. Work for efficient machine manipulation.

1 Carbon dioxide, CO_2, is a gas; and carbon disulfide, CS_2, is a liquid.

2 The theory has been studied by people such as Cavannaugh[4] and Dolger[5].

3 Formulas for hydrogen sulfide and sodium carbonate are H_2S and Na_2CO_3.

4 Wasn't vitamin A_1, $C_{20}H_{30}O$, a compound extracted from fish-liver oils?

5 A good definition of vitamin B_6 is found on page 320 of Megavitamins[8].

6 I checked her sources (Phillips[5] and Harkin[6]) and found them accurate.

| 1 | 2 | 3 | 4 | 5 | 6 | 7 | 8 | 9 | 10 | 11 | 12 | 13 | 14 |

7c • Basic control builder: one-hand two-letter combinations (digraphs)

Practice each two-letter combination 3 or 4 times before keyboarding the words which follow each combination. Concentrate on the digraphs in the words.

1 de made decrease desk dividend indeed order debate leader provide

2 at sat that rate estate water state date later operate anticipate

3 ac act acquire fact place actor space acclaim pack achieves teach

4 Dean and Della debated about deciding to decrease their dividend.

5 Does Nate anticipate that water meters will be operational later?

6 In fact, the actor actually acquired talent and achieved acclaim.

7d • Special control builder:

(direct reaches)

Practice each line at a controlled rate. Make long reaches with minimum hand movement.

1 jumped neck many must musical decorated minimum received summary debts

2 numbers muscles concert broken brightly collected umbrella hymn prices

3 curb special symphony ceremony nerve gymnasium conference direct doubt

4 Brad must have hurt a muscle in his neck after falling on an umbrella.

5 Their conferences included symphony concert numbers at minimum prices.

6 Ace Gymnasium was decorated and brightly lit for the special ceremony.

| 1 | 2 | 3 | 4 | 5 | 6 | 7 | 8 | 9 | 10 | 11 | 12 | 13 | 14 |

24c • Basic skill builder: common phrases

Keyboard the phrases and sentences as fast as possible to build keystroking speed.

1 should be | if you | we would | with you | do not | would like | in your | to a
2 you and | have a | like to | of our | I will | you to | to you | one of | of your
3 for this | I would | very much | the enclosed | should be | appreciate your
4 I should be able to meet with you and Chi in your office at five.
5 If you do not have a copy of our catalog, I will send one to you.
6 We would like to invite you to attend one of our college classes.

24d • Special speed builder: speed spurts (double letters)

Practice each sentence as fast as possible to build stroking speed.

1 All office employees will soon attend business letter writing classes.
2 All college bulletins suggest an early application for fall admission.
3 We will arrange to have dinner following the weekly committee meeting.
4 Jill will need three different books for her college accounting class.
5 Phillip offered to supply food for the afternoon association meetings.
6 She assumes the attending officers will discuss the issue of accruals.

| 1 | 2 | 3 | 4 | 5 | 6 | 7 | 8 | 9 | 10 | 11 | 12 | 13 | 14 |

24e • Speed paragraphs

(statistical)

1 Two 1' writings on each ¶; strive to increase speed on the second writing.
2 One 3' writing on both ¶s combined; determine *gwam*.

all letters used | A | 1.5 si | 5.7 awl | 80% hfw

	gwam 1'	3'
In the last quarter report for this year, it was stated that a	12	4	54
weighted average yield realized on the total investment as of June 30	26	9	59
grew from 8.35% to 8.67%. The total benefit payments were $493,952,630.	36	12	62
Total assets rose over the 12 months from $4.9 billion to nearly $6.4	47	16	66
billion. The cash reserves on hand were reduced from 7.2% to 6.3%.	59	20	70
Average bond maturity (excluding cash) was reduced from 12.8 years to	72	24	74
10.3 years.	73	24	75
In the stock package, 22 new companies were picked up and 18 were	12	28	79
let go. Fixed loans grew during the fiscal year to reach nearly $1.8	25	33	83
billion with average yields of 17.7%. Real estate values (16% of the	36	36	87
total package) totaled $832 million. Due to the rent increases and	49	41	91
a rising cost of living, the real estate program has become a major	64	46	96
effort to protect our total investments picture until the fiscal year	78	50	101
1990.	78	50	101

| gwam | 1' | 1 | 2 | 3 | 4 | 5 | 6 | 7 | 8 | 9 | 10 | 11 | 12 | 13 | 14 |
| 3' | | 1 | | 2 | | 3 | | 4 | | 5 |

6c • Basic control builder: one-hand two-letter combinations (digraphs)

Practice each two-letter combination 3 or 4 times before keyboarding the words which follow each combination. Work for greater control as you practice these sentences.

1 *ou you four south enough ouch ought sour ounces hour thought loud*
2 *se see set seem sell case second send ease please secret base sew*
3 *in into intend fine inject join king insert again train pine main*
4 *Harold thought that four ounces of sour cream ought to be enough.*
5 *It seemed to please Cassey when she passed second base with ease.*
6 *I injected an insert into a training plan we intend to institute.*

6d • Special control builder: word building

Practice each line at a controlled rate. As you keyboard each line, concentrate on the word endings with each new word.

1 consider considered considering considerable consideration book booked
2 bookkeeper bookkeeping age agent agency contract contracts contracting
3 contractual public publicity publicize publicizing arrange arrangement
4 employ employer employing employees manage manager managing management
5 The agent has made contractual arrangements for publicizing that book.
6 Our bookkeeper wishes us to consider using a public employment agency.
7 The employees showed a great deal of consideration to the new manager.
8 The management is arranging to have a new employment contract written.

| 1 | 2 | 3 | 4 | 5 | 6 | 7 | 8 | 9 | 10 | 11 | 12 | 13 | 14 |

6e • Control paragraphs
(straight copy)

all letters used | A | 1.5 si | 5.7 awl | 80% hfw

1 Two 1' writings on each ¶; strive to increase your accuracy on the second writing.
2 One 5' writing on both ¶s combined; determine *gwam*.

	gwam 1'	5'
Facts and figures are frequently processed by computers; however,	13	3	42
it is people who keep an office running smoothly. Think of yourself as	28	6	45
playing one certain position on your office team. Play this position to	42	8	48
the utmost of your abilities. If it is your duty to maintain office rec-	57	11	51
ords, be absolutely certain that these records are as exact and accurate	71	14	54
as you can make them. If you are assigned a report, do your utmost to	86	17	57
be sure that the report is written as well as you can possibly write it.	100	20	59
As an office team player, you will undoubtedly be held accountable	13	23	62
for performing the tasks assigned to you. When you are assigned a job	28	26	65
to complete, it is necessary for you to organize your working habits and	42	28	68
duties so the job is completed on time. Resist the inclination to put	56	31	71
off until tomorrow what should be done today. Work hard at each assign-	71	34	74
ment and do the most outstanding work that you are capable of doing.	85	37	76
Then you will be able to take pride in your finished product.	97	39	79

gwam 1' | 1 | 2 | 3 | 4 | 5 | 6 | 7 | 8 | 9 | 10 | 11 | 12 | 13 | 14 |
5' | 1 | 2 | 3 |

25a • Keyboard review

Practice once slowly; a second time for speed; a third time for control.

alphabet	1	Jack B. Maxey studied with zeal to improve his final math quiz grades.
figures	2	Flight 786 leaves Chicago at 12:49 and arrives in New Orleans at 3:50.
fig/sym	3	Our newest stationery (Executive Bond, #670-958) is 7 1/2" by 10 3/4".

| 1 | 2 | 3 | 4 | 5 | 6 | 7 | 8 | 9 | 10 | 11 | 12 | 13 | 14 |

25b • Technique builder: stroking
(direct reaches)

Make the direct reaches without returning to the home row as you practice this drill.

b-r; u-m	1	brb Bruce abroad bridges brilliant umu summer volumes aluminum columns
n-y; n-u	2	nyn canyon many penny rainy sunny nun thunder annual bonus ounce until
e-c; b-t	3	ece place grace office receive effect btb doubt obtain debt tabulation
	4	No doubt, Bruce Bradley will travel abroad during his summer vacation.
	5	New aluminum columns are being placed on the bridge at Thunder Canyon.
	6	Grace Brye will obtain an annual bonus for her many brilliant volumes.

| 1 | 2 | 3 | 4 | 5 | 6 | 7 | 8 | 9 | 10 | 11 | 12 | 13 | 14 |

25c • Basic skill builder: easy trigraphs

Practice each three-letter combination 3 or 4 times before keyboarding the words which follow each combination.

1 ene benefit general tiv effective executive ish publish establish
2 enc conference reference dis discuss district dit credit addition
3 pri price private prior ugh enough thought ial special industrial
4 There was a general discussion in reference to industrial credit.
5 We published a price list for the benefit of the representatives.
6 The district executive thought the special conference was enough.

25d • Special speed builder: speed spurts
(common words)

Practice each sentence as fast as possible to build stroking speed. Eliminate pauses between letters and words for greater speed.

1 The work orders for your sales office should not take much of my time.
2 They will be glad to send you complete information before the meeting.
3 We are making the offer because we really believe in our fine product.
4 The dealer will not supply the materials without your written request.
5 They would like to thank you for your reports to the credit committee.
6 Please look over the enclosed information about our complete programs.
7 A manager of that department has just become president of the company.
8 Their special prices are part of their sales plan to get new business.

| 1 | 2 | 3 | 4 | 5 | 6 | 7 | 8 | 9 | 10 | 11 | 12 | 13 | 14 |

5e • Control paragraphs

(straight copy)

1 Two 1′ writings on each ¶; strive to increase accuracy on the second writing.
2 One 5′ writing on both ¶s combined; determine *gwam*.

all letters used | A | 1.5 si | 5.7 awl | 80% hfw

	gwam 1′		5′

If the occasion arises that you are offered two comparable jobs, how do you decide which offer to accept? There are many factors to think about when comparing the two jobs. The distance you will be traveling to and from each job is a prime consideration for you. The size of the company is another factor. Only you know if you would prefer working in a large firm or a small business. Of course, one extremely important deciding factor would be the salary you have been offered.

13	3	41
27	5	43
41	8	46
55	11	49
69	14	52
83	17	55
97	19	57

Before deciding which job you wish to choose, other data should be contemplated. These include the fringe benefits each job is offering. Parking can be an added expenditure if the company does not have ample parking for its employees. Be sure to find out if the medical insurance is paid by you or by the company. Is the company required to help pay your tuition if you decide to further your schooling? What type of pension or retirement plans are available?

13	22	60
28	25	63
42	28	66
56	31	69
71	34	71
84	36	74
93	38	76

gwam 1′ | 1 | 2 | 3 | 4 | 5 | 6 | 7 | 8 | 9 | 10 | 11 | 12 | 13 | 14 |
5′ | 1 | | 2 | | 3 | |

CONTROL BUILDER 6

6a • Keyboard review

Practice once slowly; a second time for speed; a third time for control.

alphabet 1 Winona Zimmer excels at five skills required to get a high-paying job.
figures 2 Errors were found on pages 12, 35, 46, 77, 180, and 195 of the report.
fig/sym 3 Her hourly wage (Time Card #4293-16) is $5.80 with $8.70 for overtime.

| 1 | 2 | 3 | 4 | 5 | 6 | 7 | 8 | 9 | 10 | 11 | 12 | 13 | 14 |

6b • Technique builder:
stroking (rows)

Make each reach without moving the other fingers out of position as you practice this drill.

top row 1 They sold 2 kegs of #6 nails at $4.73 and 1,800 feet of rope at $1.95.
3d row 2 Roy Witt wrote the story of proper etiquette for your quarterly paper.
row 3 We were without power to your two typewriters due to faulty wet wires.
home 4 Al Lask shall add a dash of salt to a slaw salad; Kass shall add dill.
row 5 Jaffa's gag glass shall add a spark at a gala fall affair for Al Hall.
bottom row 6 The zinc box that vanished was some six or seven cubic inches in size.

| 1 | 2 | 3 | 4 | 5 | 6 | 7 | 8 | 9 | 10 | 11 | 12 | 13 | 14 |

25e • Speed paragraphs

(straight copy)

1 Two 1' writings on each ¶; strive to increase speed on the second writing.
2 One 3' writing on both ¶s combined; determine *gwam*.

all letters used | A | 1.5 si | 5.7 awl | 80% hfw

gwam 1' | 3'

In order to improve your communication skills, you need to realize | 13 | 4 | 66
that communicating is a process of sending and receiving messages. When | 28 | 9 | 71
you speak or write, you are the sender. When you listen or read, you | 42 | 14 | 76
are the receiver. You will send messages more expertly if you speak or | 56 | 19 | 81
write in specific terms rather than just general terms. Your listener | 71 | 24 | 86
or reader will get your message if you make your statement or request | 85 | 28 | 90
so clear that it will not be misunderstood. | 93 | 31 | 93

The communication message you send will be clearer if you make it | 13 | 35 | 97
brief. Your readers or listeners will understand five words better than | 28 | 40 | 102
they will understand fifteen words. Avoid using the same words over and | 42 | 45 | 107
over. Use variety in your words and in the length of your sentences. | 57 | 50 | 112
Also, remember to be positive in the tone of your message. Say what you | 71 | 55 | 117
can do rather than what you cannot do. Choose words that will not be | 85 | 59 | 121
easily misunderstood by your receiver. | 93 | 62 | 124

gwam 1' | 1 | 2 | 3 | 4 | 5 | 6 | 7 | 8 | 9 | 10 | 11 | 12 | 13 | 14 |
gwam 3' | 1 | | 2 | | 3 | | 4 | | 5 | |

SPEED BUILDER 26

26a • Keyboard review

Practice once slowly; a second time for speed; a third time for control.

alphabet 1 Mick put the antique gold and bronze jeweled vase in a box for safety.
figures 2 The test on Chapter 27 covers Topics 8 and 9 on pages 543 through 601.
fig/sym 3 Course #7980-2 ("Advanced Typing") is offered during Term 3 (1/5-4/6).

| 1 | 2 | 3 | 4 | 5 | 6 | 7 | 8 | 9 | 10 | 11 | 12 | 13 | 14 |

26b • Technique builder: stroking

Concentrate on the words as you practice these sentences.

adjacent keys
1 Pomeroy's case was referred to a policy board for opinions and action.
2 We knew last week that it was necessary to acquire more new milk cans.
3 Did Polly try a toasted poppyseed croissant with milk at the new deli?

direct reaches
4 Sunny doubted my music recital would bring in a large paying audience.
5 Our secretary, Herbert, recently placed his finances in a mutual fund.
6 We spent the rainy autumn days playing music and reading many volumes.

| 1 | 2 | 3 | 4 | 5 | 6 | 7 | 8 | 9 | 10 | 11 | 12 | 13 | 14 |

CONTROL BUILDER 5

5a • Keyboard review

Practice once slowly; a second time for speed; a third time for control.

alphabet 1 Pamela gave Jack a quartz watch and a fine onyx ring for his birthday.

figures 2 Their baseball games should be held on 5/3, 5/28, 6/4, 6/19, and 7/10.

fig/sym 3 Our check for $297.38 (dated 1/4) covers Invoice #506 (less 3% disc.).

| 1 | 2 | 3 | 4 | 5 | 6 | 7 | 8 | 9 | 10 | 11 | 12 | 13 | 14 |

5b • Technique builder: manipulative control

(backspace)

Learn to reach for and use the backspace key efficiently as you practice these sentences.

1 Bryan is looking for Wildflowers of Kentucky, not Wildflowers of Ohio.

2 Does Bob Sampson live at 409 Twentieth Street or 409 Thirtieth Street?

3 Did Osami and Billy really enjoy Tecumseh! when they saw it last week?

4 I should have added two teaspoons of salt rather than two tablespoons!

| 1 | 2 | 3 | 4 | 5 | 6 | 7 | 8 | 9 | 10 | 11 | 12 | 13 | 14 |

5c • Basic control builder: one-hand two-letter combinations (digraphs)

Practice each two-letter combination 3 or 4 times before keyboarding the words which follow each combination. Work for continuity of stroking.

1 ra ray rare rate brass erase rage rather practice extra brag wrap

2 rs first ours teachers course answers hears worst dangers runners

3 Radine would rather pay the extra rate for the rare brass statue.

4 Ours were the worst answers the first course teachers ever heard.

5d • Special control builder: guided paragraph writing

1 Take a 1' writing at a controlled pace; determine *gwam* for base rate.

2 Add 4-6 words to your base rate to set a new goal rate.

3 Take two 1' guided writings on each ¶; try to reach your goal rate.

4 Take one 5' writing on both ¶s combined; determine *gwam*.

all letters used | A | 1.5 si | 5.7 awl | 80% hfw

	gwam 1'	5'
There is no standard attire for most offices. However, some firms	13	3	31
do specify what type of clothing they prefer employees wear. If your	27	5	33
job requires that you meet the public, your firm will want you to pro-	41	8	36
ject a favorable image to the public. You should realize that your em-	56	11	39
ployer is interested in what you wear to the office.	66	13	41
If you work for a company that does not enforce a dress code, how	13	16	44
can you discover what is appropriate to wear to the office? One of the	28	19	47
best methods is to examine the people around you and observe what they	42	22	50
customarily wear. Another method is to discuss the problem with your	56	24	52
supervisor. If you are not certain what is appropriate, request your	70	27	55
supervisor's advice.	74	28	56

gwam 1' | 1 | 2 | 3 | 4 | 5 | 6 | 7 | 8 | 9 | 10 | 11 | 12 | 13 | 14 |
5' | 1 | 2 | 3 |

Control Builder **5**

52

26c • Basic skill builder: common phrases

Keyboard the phrases and sentences as fast as possible to build keystroking speed.

1 there is | one of | we are | is a | of our | for you | that we | will be | may be
2 to be | pleased to | one of | to you | of our | be of | would like | forward to
3 thank you | for your | would like to | there is | have been | has a | and the
4 There is a chance that we may be able to be of assistance to you.
5 One of our people will be pleased to be of help to you next week.
6 We are happy to enclose a ticket for you to see one of our shows.

26d • Special speed builder: speed spurt sentences

Practice each sentence as fast as possible to build stroking speed. Work for smooth, quick stroking.

balanced-hand	1	The panel did lend us a map to make the problem visible to an auditor.
	2	Did the six men cut down the big oak and the bush, and may I pay them?
double letters	3	If possible, I will discuss her comments at the noon meeting tomorrow.
	4	Terry is currently planning to enroll in business college in the fall.
common words	5	I most sincerely wish to thank you for your business during this year.
	6	The total payment was received last week before the order was shipped.
common words	7	They will send the articles and books to you as soon as they are done.
	8	The paper and forms which you ordered will be mailed to you this week.

| 1 | 2 | 3 | 4 | 5 | 6 | 7 | 8 | 9 | 10 | 11 | 12 | 13 | 14 |

26e • Speed paragraphs

(straight copy)

1 Two 1' writings on each ¶; strive to increase speed on the second writing.
2 One 3' writing on both ¶s combined; determine *gwam*.

| all letters used | A | 1.5 si | 5.7 awl | 80% hfw |

gwam 1' 3'

As you begin your first office job, you will be working with people — 14 | 5 | 63
with a varied mixture of ideas and beliefs. Some will be very strict — 28 | 9 | 68
about their standards of conduct. Others will have much looser stan- — 41 | 14 | 72
dards of what is proper behavior. You are going to have to develop — 55 | 18 | 77
your own set of standards regarding what is right and wrong in terms — 69 | 23 | 81
of business behavior. Your personal behavior will reflect the moral — 83 | 28 | 86
standards that you prize. — 88 | 29 | 88

Some of the moral standards of conduct have become overall rules — 13 | 34 | 92
of behavior for all office employees. A basic rule is to always respect — 28 | 38 | 97
the rights and feelings of other people. A second rule requires that — 42 | 43 | 102
you keep confidential any information heard in the office which must — 55 | 48 | 106
not be shared with other people. A third overall concept is that you — 69 | 52 | 111
should not use the time, supplies, or information of an employer for — 83 | 57 | 115
your own gain or profit. — 88 | 59 | 117

gwam 1' | 1 | 2 | 3 | 4 | 5 | 6 | 7 | 8 | 9 | 10 | 11 | 12 | 13 | 14 |
gwam 3' | 1 | 2 | 3 | 4 | 5 |

4c • Basic control builder: one-hand two-letter combinations (digraphs)

Practice each two-letter combination 3 or 4 times before keyboarding the words which follow each combination. Keep the hands and arms quiet; use *finger* action.

1 *et metal basket greet regret athlete forget cadet letter competes*
2 *li like limit light quality lively violin files list policy slice*
3 *ho hope hotel host shop hour who school holiday horse how thought*
4 *Don't let me forget to place your letter of regret in the basket.*
5 *Olive says she likes to watch the lights of the lively fireflies.*
6 *The Hopkins Hotel hosted a happy hour for all the holiday guests.*

4d • Special control builder: one-hand sentences

Practice each sentence at a controlled rate; strive for accuracy and continuity as you type.

1 As Barbara was aware, we regretted Webster was awarded a better grade.
2 My red setter was a plump, jolly puppy after we fed him my sweet milk.
3 I agree a sweet, red onion creates a great taste in Julio's beef stew.
4 At a Warsaw cafe, we were served tea in a carafe after we ate dessert.
5 At a debate at East Texas State, Eva regretted we were graded average.
6 Holly was aware Cesar created average minimum rates at my trade union.
7 On my estate, Junko grew a few plum trees on a knoll at a pool's edge.
8 After we saw a few test grades, we were aware Dee Dee deserved awards.

| 1 | 2 | 3 | 4 | 5 | 6 | 7 | 8 | 9 | 10 | 11 | 12 | 13 | 14 |

4e • Control paragraphs

(statistical copy)

1 Two 1' writings on each ¶; strive for improved control rate on the second writing.
2 One 5' writing on both ¶s combined; determine *gwam*.

all letters used | A | 1.5 si | 5.7 awl | 80% hfw

	gwam 1'	5'

When offering cash discounts, sellers encourage buyers in settling [13] [3] [37]
their debts within a short time period after receiving invoices. The [27] [5] [40]
discount usually applies up to 10 days from the date of the sales in- [41] [8] [43]
voice. The buyer who pays after day 10 (up to day 30) pays the net [53] [11] [45]
amount of the invoice. A 2% discount would be expressed "2/10, net [65] [13] [48]
30." If an invoice of $9,000, dated July 25, with terms of 2/10, net 30, [77] [15] [50]
is remitted on or before August 4, there would be a savings of $180. [89] [18] [53]

Yet, when the invoice is not remitted within the 10 days, the full [13] [20] [55]
amount of $9,000 would have to be remitted within 30 days--on or before [25] [23] [58]
August 24. It is, therefore, quite imperative that a buyer analyze each [39] [26] [60]
invoice to ascertain the date by which this discount saving may be real- [54] [29] [63]
ized. For example: Invoice #678 marked February 13 with terms of 2/10, [66] [31] [66]
net 30 for $450 worth of goods must be paid by February 23 in order to [79] [34] [68]
acquire the cash discount of $9. [85] [35] [70]

| gwam 1' | 1 | 2 | 3 | 4 | 5 | 6 | 7 | 8 | 9 | 10 | 11 | 12 | 13 | 14 |
| 5' | | 1 | | | 2 | | | 3 | |

SPEED BUILDER 27

27a • Keyboard review

Practice once slowly; a second time for speed; a third time for control.

alphabet	1	Jacqueline asked a boy from Venezuela to judge the water polo exhibit.
figures	2	We received 12,865,720 responses to Questionnaire 493 sent out on 9/4.
fig/sym	3	If you add 1/4, 3/8, and 5/6 (Question 50, page 279), you get 1 11/24.

| 1 | 2 | 3 | 4 | 5 | 6 | 7 | 8 | 9 | 10 | 11 | 12 | 13 | 14 |

27b • Technique builder: manipulative control

(shift keys and lock)

Improve control of these important service mechanisms as you practice these sentences.

	1	Tom and Ana Rios met Paul and Joann O'Neal at Mario's on Tenth Street.
shift keys	2	Pam is taking Managerial Finance and Economic Theory at Grant College.
	3	The Harth Company store on Broadway has been sold to Amalgamated, Inc.
	4	The THASCO and FOSTCO merger was reported in THE ENQUIRER and on WKPR.
shift lock	5	GRAND OPENING SPECIAL! This week only! Buy two shirts, GET ONE FREE!
	6	NEWSFLASH! The Buckeyes OVERWHELM the Royals! Thirty-two to NOTHING!

| 1 | 2 | 3 | 4 | 5 | 6 | 7 | 8 | 9 | 10 | 11 | 12 | 13 | 14 |

27c • Basic skill builder: easy trigraphs

Practice each three-letter combination 3 or 4 times before keyboarding the words which follow each combination.

1 nal final original personal wor worth work worry tor factor storm
2 pro project prompt profit ent sent agent entire oth other nothing
3 the then they there sur insure pressure ive given active delivery
4 The factory was given a final project worth more than the others.
5 The doctor says Kathy has personal problems and pressure at work.
6 The director originally approved of both of the insurance agents.

27d • Special speed builder: skill comparison sentences

Practice each sentence for 30″ or 1′. Strive to achieve the same rate on Sentences 2-6 as on the first sentence.

balanced-hand	1	The city auditor paid a formal visit to all six of the town officials.
one hand	2	We regret no federal tax rate case was acted upon in my state in July.
combination	3	We took care as we undid a box of authentic war mementos for my shelf.
3d row	4	Pat hurried up to her territory to try to speak with two other people.
adjacent keys	5	Our top director was sure her proposal would be welcomed by the group.
direct reaches	6	Myra announced that the county will soon break ground for the library.

| 1 | 2 | 3 | 4 | 5 | 6 | 7 | 8 | 9 | 10 | 11 | 12 | 13 | 14 |

3e • Control paragraphs:

(rough-draft copy)

1 Two 1' writings on each ¶; strive to increase your control rate on the second writing.

2 One 5' writing on both ¶s combined; determine *gwam*.

| all letters used | A | 1.5 si | 5.7 awl | 80% hfw |

gwam 1' | 5'

Progressing in jobs means that you establish goals your-   13 | 3 | 32
self. Without goals, your advancement may be aimless. Ask   27 | 5 | 35
the following: how can I accelerate in terms of my present   40 | 8 | 37
job? Who can give me the help most in my present job? Can I   54 | 11 | 40
prepare myself? Should I embark on these efforts? I am cap-   67 | 13 | 43
able of succeeding?   77 | 15 | 45

To realize gains from any of these answers will necessitate an   12 | 18 | 47
extra effort on your part. Putting extra attention on those   26 | 21 | 50
answers will help you best improve your skills and abilities   39 | 23 | 52
in what you are doing. Don't be afraid to find help where you   52 | 26 | 55
needed. And, most of all, you develop compelling desires to   66 | 29 | 58
be success ful in whatever you do.   69 | 29 | 58

CONTROL BUILDER 4

4a • Keyboard review

Practice once slowly; a second time for speed; a third time for control.

alphabet 1   Jim's quartet sang six ballads in the key of C and won several prizes.

figures 2   Please place an order for Item 8140529 on page 673 of the new catalog.

fig/sym 3   He traded Items #891, #267, and #354 for new ones at a cost of $1,400.

| 1 | 2 | 3 | 4 | 5 | 6 | 7 | 8 | 9 | 10 | 11 | 12 | 13 | 14 |

4b • Technique builder:

stroking (third and fourth fingers, both hands)

Make these finger reaches without moving the hands or arms as you practice the sentences.

1   Hazel was dazzled by all the topaz and quartz sold at the town bazaar.

2   The happy boy ripped the paper wrapping from the package at the party.

3   The paragraph contained quotations from books about woodworking tools.

4   Lois Ortez spoke to six people who were anxious about the sales award.

5   Does Paul Wohl actually want only two copies of his school photograph?

6   Those willow trees outside my window were swaying wildly in the storm.

| 1 | 2 | 3 | 4 | 5 | 6 | 7 | 8 | 9 | 10 | 11 | 12 | 13 | 14 |

27e • Speed paragraphs

(straight copy)

1 Two 1' writings on each ¶; strive to increase speed on the second writing.
2 One 3' writing on both ¶s combined; determine *gwam*.

all letters used | A | 1.5 si | 5.7 awl | 80% hfw

	gwam 1'	3'	
It is almost imperative that we all maintain a learning attitude.	13	4	67
In other words, we must remain alert to the possibilities and oppor-	27	9	71
tunities for learning and growing in our jobs. Many large firms recog-	41	14	76
nize the need for additional training for their employees. This may be	56	19	81
the result of updated knowledge or technology in our field of exper-	69	23	85
tise. No matter how much we currently know or how excellent our skills	84	28	90
are, we all can learn new things if we are required to do so.	96	32	94
Take advantage of every chance to learn that comes your way. Ini-	13	36	98
tial training is often given to all new employees. You may also be	27	41	103
allowed training if you are lacking in a skill, assigned to a new depart-	41	46	108
ment, or given new duties. If your employer puts in new equipment, you	36	51	113
may be trained in its proper use. Employees are often trained before	70	55	117
they are promoted to any new responsibilities. Welcome all chances to	84	60	122
learn new information or skills.	90	62	124

gwam 1' | 1 | 2 | 3 | 4 | 5 | 6 | 7 | 8 | 9 | 10 | 11 | 12 | 13 | 14 |
3' | 1 | 2 | 3 | 4 | 5 |

SPEED BUILDER 28

28a • Keyboard review

Practice once slowly; a second time for speed; a third time for control.

alphabet 1 The squad recognized that Bob J. Vox was an extremely fine key player.

figures 2 On 10/16, the temperature dropped 37 degrees from 89 to 52 in 4 hours.

fig/sym 3 The 10% tax ($287.56) was paid "in full" by check dated March 3, 1984.

| 1 | 2 | 3 | 4 | 5 | 6 | 7 | 8 | 9 | 10 | 11 | 12 | 13 | 14 |

28b • Technique builder:

stroking (double letters)

Try to maintain the same even rhythm as you practice these sentences.

1 Molly Green was sorry that her summer trip to Savannah was called off.

2 When Jon won the million-dollar lottery, he soon sailed off to Hawaii.

3 I scuffed a heel on my boot as I stepped on a loose board in my attic.

4 Their accountant keeps accurate books for the annual college expenses.

5 She hurriedly shipped the necessary supplies for those at the meeting.

6 Todd was puzzled by the matter discussed in the class on good manners.

7 Their trustee will soon supply us with the three missing installments.

8 Jeff's attorney dismissed the witness following the court proceedings.

| 1 | 2 | 3 | 4 | 5 | 6 | 7 | 8 | 9 | 10 | 11 | 12 | 13 | 14 |

3a • Keyboard review

Practice once slowly; a second time for speed; a third time for control.

alphabet	1	Peggy gladly baked an extra quiche for the women at the jazz festival.
figures	2	Six students earned the following grades: 62, 85, 91, 73, 80, and 94.
fig/sym	3	I will have up-to-date data (in $ and %) on 3/15, 4/27, 6/9, and 8/30.

| 1 | 2 | 3 | 4 | 5 | 6 | 7 | 8 | 9 | 10 | 11 | 12 | 13 | 14 |

3b • Technique builder: stroking (second finger, both hands)

Make the second-finger reaches without moving the other fingers out of position as you practice this drill.

1 The concerned citizens considered the inefficient economic indicators.
2 Did the chief editor dedicate the second edition to his niece Lucinda?
3 The chicken, pickles, and cheeses we took to the picnic were inedible.
4 Our clerk initialed the invoice and we received the order in December.
5 Ms. Dickson was elected to serve on the city civic activities council.
6 They received a certificate identifying an eligibility for a dividend.

| 1 | 2 | 3 | 4 | 5 | 6 | 7 | 8 | 9 | 10 | 11 | 12 | 13 | 14 |

3c • Basic control builder: one-hand two-letter combinations (digraphs)

Practice each two-letter combination 3 or 4 times before keyboarding the words which follow each combination. Strive for accuracy and control.

1 be beater better beam obey believe behind behaves below bee beach
2 ar tarry artist arrive card part share aware dollar various start
3 ec deck record expect special reject erect decrease decide secret
4 Bea believes the dog will behave better after an obedience class.
5 Bert hopes Arthur's flight arrived in Aruba earlier than Marta's.
6 I expect we may decide to erect a new deck when we inspect yours.

3d • Special control builder: letter drills (s-z)

Keyboard each sentence at a controlled rate. Concentrate on the emphasized letters and accuracy as you practice each sentence.

s	1	Sara said the sales situation is serious and should be discussed soon.
t	2	Tom Tate thanked them for attempting to settle their outstanding debt.
u	3	Ursula undoubtedly will understand the urgency of the union situation.
v	4	Verna had to give the voters evidence of her active civic involvement.
w	5	When Wendy's written work was reviewed, two of her answers were wrong.
x	6	Mitsugu paid my expenses to the excellent xylophone concert at Xavier.
y	7	Yes, the factory generally lays off over seventy employees every year.
z	8	Zachary amazingly can memorize several dozen different city ZIP codes.

| 1 | 2 | 3 | 4 | 5 | 6 | 7 | 8 | 9 | 10 | 11 | 12 | 13 | 14 |

28c • Basic skill builder: common phrases

Keyboard the phrases and sentences as fast as possible to build keystroking speed.

1 we do | we would | you are | appreciate your | would like | to be | the above

2 in our | like to | on the | to have | from the | have a | you have | would like

3 to be | you to | you can | you are | you will | with your | in the | I am | is to

4 We do appreciate your help in our efforts to have a good meeting.

5 We would like to invite you to pick any gift from the above list.

6 You are to be commended on the efforts you have made to be mayor.

28d • Special speed builder: guided paragraph writing

1 Take a 1' writing on the ¶; determine *gwam*.
2 Add 5 *gwam* to this base rate to set a new goal rate.
3 Take two 1' guided writings on the ¶; try to reach your goal rate.

all letters used | A | 1.5 si | 5.7 awl | 80% hfw

gwam 1'

In any clerical job, you will frequently need to depend upon oral   13
communications. You must be able to listen extremely carefully to hear   28
what the other person is saying. Give your full attention to the person   42
who is talking. Listen for facts and organize these facts as you listen   57
in order to have a clear comprehension of what was said.   68

| 1 | 2 | 3 | 4 | 5 | 6 | 7 | 8 | 9 | 10 | 11 | 12 | 13 | 14 |

28e • Speed paragraphs

(rough draft)

1 Two 1' writings on each ¶; strive to increase speed on the second writing.
2 One 3' writing on both ¶s combined; determine *gwam*.

all letters used | A | 1.5 si | 5.7 awl | 80% hfw

gwam 1'   3'

Since some part of a very large per cent of all business   11   4 | 51
transactions
deals is conducted by the tele phone, we all ~~must make ourselves~~   23   8 | 55
need to *to refresh* *our*
occassionally stop our techniques for dealing with callers.   38   13 | 60
in our habits *treat*
Very often we become lazy and tend to ~~use~~ an office telephone   54   18 | 65
should always strive to
like ~~we handle~~ the one at home, so we ~~work hard to overcome the~~   64   21 | 68
telephone
~~developments of~~ our office techniques.   72   24 | 71
each a
Remember that we are representatives of our ~~company~~ offices   11   28 | 75
communicate *Our*
and our company when we ~~talk~~ with our callers. Words and tone   26   33 | 80
be emphasized because
of voice must ~~count since~~ our callers can not see our gestures   41   37 | 85
ial *our*
or face expressions. we just have our speech and attitude to   54   42 | 89
want to be efficient
convey the idea that we ~~are businesslike~~ and co-operative during   68   46 | 94
every
~~each~~ call.   70   47 | 94

2c • Basic control builder: one-hand two-letter combinations (digraphs)

Practice each two-letter combination 3 or 4 times before keyboarding the words which follow each combination. *Think* the two-letter combinations.

1 *ta tax start tame tan state entertain stand estate station taught*
2 *ea each defeat beach team bear learn idea great wear appear steam*
3 *She taught a taxing class at State about starting in real estate.*
4 *We each had the idea that our team would easily defeat the Bears.*

2d • Special control builder: letter drills (j-r)

Keyboard each sentence at a controlled rate. Concentrate on the emphasized letters and improved control as you repeat this drill.

j 1 When Joan was just a junior, she judged her major would be journalism.

k 2 Last week Kenneth asked the bank to check the mistake in his bankbook.

l 3 It is likely that Lillian will apply for law school later in the fall.

m 4 The management might send Marge to the membership meetings in Memphis.

n 5 Elena announced that neither she nor Nelson won the national contests.

o 6 Mr. Ortez occasionally orders overstocked books from the organization.

p 7 The person who apparently planned the procedure was very professional.

q 8 They quickly acquired the quantity of quarters required for the quota.

r 9 Robert arranged to return the records regarding the radar regulations.

| 1 | 2 | 3 | 4 | 5 | 6 | 7 | 8 | 9 | 10 | 11 | 12 | 13 | 14 |

2e • Control paragraphs

(straight copy)

1 Two 1' writings on each ¶; strive to improve accuracy on the second writing.
2 One 5' writing on both ¶s combined; determine *gwam*.

| all letters used | A | 1.5 si | 5.7 awl | 80% hfw |

	gwam 1'	5'

As you prepare to work in an office, one of the most essential — 13 / 3 / 39

skills you need to acquire is knowing how to utilize the business tele- — 27 / 5 / 41

phone. When you communicate with people on the telephone, you convey — 41 / 8 / 44

an attitude about yourself, your job, and other people. The people you — 55 / 11 / 47

speak to form impressions of you and your firm depending solely on how — 69 / 14 / 50

you speak to them. It is essential that you realize the importance of — 84 / 17 / 53

your telephone voice. — 88 / 18 / 54

You can have an effective telephone voice if you communicate with — 13 / 20 / 56

people in a pleasant manner. A pleasant voice is much easier to listen — 28 / 23 / 59

to than one which is loud, harsh, or grating. You can improve your — 41 / 26 / 62

voice if you think and talk with a smile. Try to think of the caller — 55 / 29 / 65

as a person who needs your help. Remember to enunciate clearly and — 69 / 31 / 67

carefully. Correct speech is necessary since the person cannot read — 83 / 34 / 70

your lips or see your expression over the telephone. — 93 / 36 / 72

gwam 1' | 1 | 2 | 3 | 4 | 5 | 6 | 7 | 8 | 9 | 10 | 11 | 12 | 13 | 14 |
gwam 5' | 1 | 2 | 3 |

SPEED BUILDER 29

29a • Keyboard review

Practice once slowly; a second time for speed; a third time for control.

alphabet 1   Dot Jackson and Felipe Vazquez were lazing on a sunny beach in Mexico.

figures 2   The new bowling scores are: Joe 246, Van 157, Sally 198, and Kay 203.

fig/sym 3   Yang's Bookstore (phone: 631-928-6743) has 50% off on all paperbacks.

| 1 | 2 | 3 | 4 | 5 | 6 | 7 | 8 | 9 | 10 | 11 | 12 | 13 | 14 |

29b • Technique builder: Manipulative control

(backspace)

Learn to reach for and use the backspace key efficiently as you practice these sentences.

1   The book Remembering was reviewed in The Washington Post and Newsweek.

2   Foster and William Company published the book Just the Facts! in 1983.

3   We must be complete, clear, and concise when writing business letters.

4   Two rules to follow in the fire drill are: no running and no talking.

5   He needs the merchandise now; not next week, next month, or next year.

6   Did Marcy say the meetings start on the seventeenth or the nineteenth?

| 1 | 2 | 3 | 4 | 5 | 6 | 7 | 8 | 9 | 10 | 11 | 12 | 13 | 14 |

29c • Basic skill builder: easy trigraphs

Practice each three-letter combination 3 or 4 times before keyboarding the words which follow each combination.

1   and understand thousand own town down known sit deposit positions

2   sid consider president tur turn natural ual usual actual annually

3   I understand the town may reconsider its position on natural gas.

4   The president returned a one thousand dollar deposit to the town.

29d • Special speed builder: skill transfer paragraphs

all letters used   A   1.5 si   5.7 awl   80% hfw

1 Take a 1' writing on each ¶; compare *gwam*.
2 Practice the numbers only in ¶2.
3 Take a 1' writing on ¶2; try to improve your speed.
4 Take a 3' writing on ¶s 1 and 2 combined; determine *gwam*.

	gwam 1'	3'
Throughout history, a state has had the right to justly impose	13	4 / 41
taxes. The common types of taxes that the states impose are personal	27	9 / 46
income tax, sales tax, and real-estate tax. These taxes, plus fees	40	13 / 51
and licenses, give a state the needed revenue to sustain its various	54	18 / 55
functions.	56	19 / 56
Five states have what is labelled flat-rate personal income tax.	13	23 / 60
For example, if a state requires that 3% of all taxable income (gross	27	28 / 65
income minus itemized deductions) be paid to the state, a person having	41	32 / 70
$6,000 in taxable income would pay $180 (3% x $6,000) while a person	50	35 / 73
having $4,000 taxable income would pay $120 (3% x $4,000).	56	37 / 75

gwam 1' | 1 | 2 | 3 | 4 | 5 | 6 | 7 | 8 | 9 | 10 | 11 | 12 | 13 | 14 |
gwam 3' | 1 | 2 | 3 | 4 | 5 |

1e • Control paragraphs

(straight copy)

1 Two 1' writings on each ¶; strive to improve accuracy on the second writing.
2 One 5' writing on both ¶s combined; determine *gwam*.

all letters used	A	1.5 si	5.7 awl	80% hfw

	gwam 1'	5'	
You will discover that there are ample chances for a job if you	13	3	40
possess good typing skills. Clerical people are usually needed in all	27	5	43
sizes of firms. Both large and small firms are always seeking new	40	8	45
people with good basic skills and positive attitudes about work. Good	55	11	48
workers are needed in all areas. If you have a substantial interest	68	14	51
in a special field of work or a special city, look into the jobs avail-	83	17	54
able in those areas.	87	17	55
If you are to be successful in finding employment, you must possess	14	20	57
foresight. Foresight is looking ahead or planning for the future. It	28	23	60
indicates you understand what is required in order to get a job as well	42	26	63
as how to prepare for the next job up the ladder. You will show fore-	56	29	66
sight if you continuously strive to improve your English. The higher in	71	32	67
a job you go, the more important English will become to you. You will	85	34	72
also need to demonstrate foresight by staying current in business trends.	100	37	75

gwam 1' | 1 | 2 | 3 | 4 | 5 | 6 | 7 | 8 | 9 | 10 | 11 | 12 | 13 | 14 |
5' | 1 | 2 | 3 |

CONTROL BUILDER 2

2a • Keyboard review

Practice once slowly; a second time for speed; a third time for control.

alphabet 1   Rex quickly emphasized the goals of the various new jobs in the store.

figures 2   The answers to items 20, 31, 47, and 65 are in Chapter 48 on page 679.

fig/sym 3   Apartment 2094 in Bldg. 38 has bedrooms 22.5' x 16.7' and 17.5' x 15'.

| 1 | 2 | 3 | 4 | 5 | 6 | 7 | 8 | 9 | 10 | 11 | 12 | 13 | 14 |

2b • Technique builder:

stroking (first finger, both hands)

Make the first-finger reaches without moving the hands as you practice this drill.

1   Meg Grant brought a group of forty buyers into this store on Thursday.

2   Did the teacher give Lin some very urgent typing to do for Mr. Graves?

3   Greg just grinned when we asked him if he was enjoying his new stereo.

4   The travel group will journey into the jungle on their tour this year.

5   Frank was very curt with your brother Timothy at the studio yesterday.

6   Mrs. Jay wants Jeff to become a member of the youth management bureau.

| 1 | 2 | 3 | 4 | 5 | 6 | 7 | 8 | 9 | 10 | 11 | 12 | 13 | 14 |

29e • Speed paragraphs

(statistical)

1 Two 1' writings on each ¶; strive to increase speed on the second writing.
2 One 3' writing on both ¶s combined; determine *gwam.*

all letters used	A	1.5 si	5.7 awl	80% hfw

	gwam 1'	3'
Do you realize that if you are a bookkeeping clerk, one of your	13	4 | 65
duties may be to verify each purchase invoice your employer receives?	27	9 | 69
Initially, you will compare an invoice with what your employer ordered.	42	14 | 74
For example: If you verify Purchase Invoice #8642, dated June 17, you	54	18 | 78
will check to see that the quantities and amounts agree with what you	68	23 | 83
specified in your Purchase Order #5309. Then you will need to check to	81	27 | 88
see if the goods have actually been received.	90	30 | 91
You will then verify the document by "extending" or multiplying the	14	35 | 95
unit amounts (cost of one unit) by the quantities (number of units pur-	28	39 | 100
chased). For example: If you ordered 16 items at $15.12, you multiply	40	44 | 104
these amounts to see if the price on the invoice ($241.92) is accurate.	53	48 | 108
You will add all the amounts to see if the total of the invoice is accu-	67	53 | 113
rate. If you verify that the whole document is accurate, you will stamp	82	57 | 118
"Approved" on the form and sign your name.	91	60 | 121

gwam 1' | 1 | 2 | 3 | 4 | 5 | 6 | 7 | 8 | 9 | 10 | 11 | 12 | 13 | 14 |
3' | 1 | 2 | 3 | 4 | 5 |

SPEED BUILDER 30

30a • Keyboard review

Practice once slowly; a second time for speed; a third time for control.

alphabet 1 Wilcox got five dollars for my "antique" ring at the July park bazaar.

figures 2 The final score of game 8 was 63 to 57; the game 9 score was 40 to 21.

fig/sym 3 She earned interest this year of $1,347.50 (7 7/8%) on Account #26419.

| 1 | 2 | 3 | 4 | 5 | 6 | 7 | 8 | 9 | 10 | 11 | 12 | 13 | 14 |

30b • Technique builder:

stroking (double letters)

Try to maintain the same even rhythm as you practice these sentences.

1 The winners took the official pennant in the annual college ball game.

2 Sam dragged our soggy baggage across the street and around the puddle.

3 Jeffery discussed all the good books he had seen on bottle collecting.

4 Due to a traffic stoppage, all the staff arrived late for the meeting.

5 It took a good deal of effort to struggle up the grassy, narrow cliff.

6 Wendall now has the added worry of a loose muffler on his classic car.

| 1 | 2 | 3 | 4 | 5 | 6 | 7 | 8 | 9 | 10 | 11 | 12 | 13 | 14 |

CONTROL BUILDER 1

1a • Keyboard review

Practice once slowly; a second time for speed; a third time for control.

alphabet 1 If he is six payments overdue, Juan Vacquez might as well go bankrupt.

figures 2 They mailed out 125,980 survey forms and received only 73,467 answers.

fig/sym 3 I gave discounts of $54 (6.7%) on May 23 and $91.50 (8.4%) on June 15.

| 1 | 2 | 3 | 4 | 5 | 6 | 7 | 8 | 9 | 10 | 11 | 12 | 13 | 14 |

1b • Technique builder: stroking (rows)

Maintain proper technique and control as you move from row to row.

top row 1 Invoice #4892-637 from J. Rohner & Co. was for $508 less 10% discount.

3d row 2 Pete reported it is true two or three of your reporters tried to quit.

row 3 We wrote your letter to request two typewriters with a quire of paper.

home row 4 Kass has the glass flask his dad had at Hajah's gala affair at Dallas.

row 5 Ladd had a glass of soda as Ada had a salad with half a glass of soda.

bottom row 6 During vacations, Bonny Zimmerman manages their box office at the zoo.

| 1 | 2 | 3 | 4 | 5 | 6 | 7 | 8 | 9 | 10 | 11 | 12 | 13 | 14 |

1c • Basic control builder: one-hand two-letter combinations (digraphs)

Practice each two-letter combination 3 or 4 times before keyboarding the words which follow each combination. Concentrate on the digraphs in the words.

1 ca can case card cargo carry cash camera vacation medical carried

2 ce place cement dance lace certain census central service balance

3 er paper better deliver person order several quarter later ledger

4 On our vacation, Cathy carried her spare cash in her camera case.

5 I am certain my niece is invited to a dance at the Central Hotel.

6 Your order for ledger paper will be delivered later this quarter.

1d • Special control builder: letter drills (a-i)

Practice each sentence at a controlled rate. Work for improved continuity and control of the emphasized letters.

a 1 I have taken action against the association regarding the application.

b 2 Bob Gibbon was able to obtain a buyer for both his boat and his cabin.

c 3 Calvin was accepted because of his specific technical accomplishments.

d 4 Cindy did find a decisive method for dealing with the delivery delays.

e 5 Each editor evaluated the pre-existing economic education requirement.

f 6 Jeff refers most families to funds with fairly safe financial futures.

g 7 Eiko was glad to give the group suggestions for bringing about change.

h 8 Hannah thought Mr. Hahn was through checking off the history homework.

i 9 Indeed, I did think Iris had an incredible idea for increasing income.

| 1 | 2 | 3 | 4 | 5 | 6 | 7 | 8 | 9 | 10 | 11 | 12 | 13 | 14 |

30c • Basic skill builder: common phrases

Keyboard the phrases and sentences as fast as possible to build keystroking speed.

1 *if you | may need | you may | you have | to have | with you | or the | you will*
2 *am sure | I am | for the | you for | need to | have the | will enjoy | the time*
3 *If you have the time, I am sure you will enjoy reading that book.*
4 *You may need to have all your records with you for the tax audit.*

30d • Special speed builder: skill comparison paragraphs

1 One 1' writing on ¶1; determine *gwam*.
2 Take 1' writings on ¶2 until you equal or exceed your *gwam* on ¶1.
3 One 3' writing on both ¶s combined; determine *gwam*.

all letters used ¶1 | E | 1.2 si | 5.1 awl | 90% hfw | ¶2 HA | 1.7 si | 6.0 awl | 75% hfw

	gwam 1'	3'
People work for many different motives. Some people toil only	13	4 | 55
for the money they earn. Some people work just for the pursuit of a	26	9 | 59
job well done. Others work so that they can be with other people rather	41	14 | 64
than be alone. In order to get people to do a job well, leaders need	55	18 | 69
to know why these people work. Only then can leaders get the best work	69	23 | 74
from their people.	73	24 | 75
Good leaders are individuals who understand other people. They	13	29 | 79
comprehend what motivates people to do a good job. They can communi-	27	33 | 84
cate well and have the ability to deal with human relations problems.	41	38 | 88
They exhibit patience in dealing with people and realize that everyone	55	43 | 93
is unique with varying wants and needs. A good leader is able	69	47 | 98
to gain the cooperation of all the team members.	78	50 | 101

gwam 1' | 1 | 2 | 3 | 4 | 5 | 6 | 7 | 8 | 9 | 10 | 11 | 12 | 13 | 14 |
gwam 3' | 1 | 2 | 3 | 4 | 5 |

30e • Speed paragraphs
(straight copy)

1 Two 1' writings on each ¶; strive to increase speed on the second writing.
2 One 3' writing on both ¶s combined; determine *gwam*.

all letters used | A | 1.5 si | 5.7 awl | 80% hfw

	gwam 1'	3'
The need for office workers is expected to increase faster than all	14	5 | 66
other occupations during the next decade. This growth is mostly an out-	28	9 | 71
come of an increase in paperwork in most kinds of organizations. The	42	14 | 76
computer will control much of the paperwork and may have a strong im-	56	19 | 80
pact on work procedures. However, the computer will not affect all	69	23 | 85
office jobs. Demand for office workers will continue to be strong in	83	28 | 89
the firms that offer a service to the public.	92	31 | 92
It is imperative for you to keep up to date on what technology and	13	35 | 97
procedures are being used in business even if you are not working full	28	40 | 102
time. There are often openings for temporary jobs since most busi-	41	44 | 106
nesses use extra help during peak work loads. If you wish to work in	55	49 | 111
temporary positions, you will be required to be familiar with what is	69	54 | 115
happening in the business world in general. Take every chance to dis-	83	58 | 120
cover what is happening in the business world.	92	62 | 123

gwam 1' | 1 | 2 | 3 | 4 | 5 | 6 | 7 | 8 | 9 | 10 | 11 | 12 | 13 | 14 |
gwam 3' | 1 | 2 | 3 | 4 | 5 |

PART 2: CONTROL BUILDERS 1-30

Each Control Builder in Part 2 contains the following sections: (1) a keyboard review, (2) a technique builder, (3) a basic control builder, (4) a special control builder, and (5) a set of paragraphs for control development. In order that these lessons provide an appropriate blending of emphasis on techniques and keyboarding control, the following suggestions are given for intensive, repetitive practice.

Keyboard review. As in Part 1, each *Keyboard review* in Part 2 consists of an alphabetic sentence, a figure sentence, and a figure/symbol sentence. Keyboarding these sentences slowly the first time, pushing for greater fluency with the first repetition, then dropping back for control will set the stage, both mentally and physically, for practicing the control builders that follow.

Technique builder. Each *Technique builder* is designed to reinforce basic keyboarding techniques through concentration on typical areas of weakness: stroking, responding with accuracy and control to certain reach patterns, and operating the manipulative parts of the keyboard.

As the *stroking* and *response pattern* drills are keyboarded, concentrate on the marginal cues which point out correct finger-action reaches, desired stroking responses, and proper finger and hand alignment. Try to maintain keyboardng continuity without sacrificing proper technique and control.

While keyboarding the *manipulative control* drills, work for refinement and control in operating the manipulative parts of the keyboard appropriate to overall growth in keyboarding facility. Techniques emphasized involve using the backspacer, keyboarding subscripts and superscripts, constructing special symbols, operating the tabulator and return, and aligning on lines.

Basic control builder. The *Basic control builders* provide concentrated practice on one-hand 2-letter combinations and commonly used words, difficult 3-letter stroking patterns, and common phrases. Similar to Part 1, these drills in Part 2 also provide an opportunity to practice keyboarding from script. In striving for improved control and continuity while keying these exercises, practice the one-hand 2-letter combinations and words and also the trigraphs and phrases in isolation before keyboarding the sentences that follow. Responding to these sentence elements first *as units* should facilitate achieving smooth rhythm and control.

Special control builder. Each *Special control builder* emphasizes a stroking combination drill designed specifically for developing keyboarding continuity and accuracy. After a series of drills on specific letters of the alphabet, intensive practice is provided on (1) one-hand sentences; (2) word building, long reaches, and long words; (3) two-word combinations, the first of which ends with the same letter with which the second word begins; (4) common word endings; (5) two- and three-word sound alikes; and (6) awkward and opposite finger stroking combinations—all of which contribute to uneven, inaccurate keyboarding. The primary goal of these types of drills is the sound development of appropriate response patterns both in *reading* and *keying* copy of varying difficulty.

Triple-controlled straight- and statistical-copy guided writings in Special Control Builders 5, 10, 15, 20, and 30 provide challenging opportunities for achieving appropriate speed-forced rates through self-paced or teacher-paced practice on progressively more difficult copy.

Control paragraphs. The *Control paragraphs* in Part 2 consist of straight-copy, rough-draft, and statistical timed writings progressing from average to high average to difficult levels of difficulty by design through the use of the triple-control indices. Base rates established through repeated 1-minute attempts on each paragraph help guide the student in achieving realistic 5' *gwam* goals. Successful attainment of individual goals in keyboarding these control paragraphs should come as a culmination of intensive differentiated practice for refinement of technique patterns, conscientious speed-forcing attempts, and the development of appropriate keystroking response—continuity with control—according to the level of copy difficulty.

Empowering S
Teaching Information Li
Hands-on and
Activit

Active Learning

Carol Anne
and
Deborah B.......
Editors

Library Instruction Publications

ISBN: 0-9652711-9-6

Preface

As with the previous titles in the Active Learning Series published by Library Instruction Publications, this book strives to provide librarians and other teachers with innovative lessons plans to better educate our students. These exercises are intended to provide creative instructional methods for teaching the information literacy competencies set forth by the Association of College and Research Libraries. In Information Literacy: Competency Standards for Higher Education, published in 2000, ACRL identified six key characteristics that an information literate individual should be able to perform. These are the ability to:

- determine the extent of information needed;
- access the needed information effectively and efficiently;
- evaluate information and its sources critically;
- incorporate selected information into one's knowledge base;
- use information effectively to accomplish a specific purpose; and
- understand the economic, legal, and social issues surrounding the use of information, and access and use information ethically and legally. (1)

In this publication, we highlight activities that foster and encourage critical thinking as it relates to information literacy. We believe critical thinking is an essential element in information literacy. In order to negotiate the world around us, it is important to take a discerning view of the abundant amount of information available. These activities focus on teaching conceptual and transferable information literacy abilities. The instructional lesson plans focus on library activities that provide hands-on as well as minds-on experiences.

As the information age continues to expand, an essential component of a librarian's job is to teach students lifelong skills to access and assess information. To accomplish this task, library instruction sessions need to include a hands-on component, which allows students to use specific resources, and a minds-on element, which ensures that students think about the tools' process so that these acquired skills may easily be transferred to other applications.

The book includes classroom activities, out-of-class or homework activities, and distance learning activities. It is divided into five sections that focus on, or fit the following categories:

1. **Group Activities**—These are exercises designed to be completed by groups of two or more students. A group activity is one in which each student is responsible for one or more aspects of the exercise and in which students must work collaboratively in order to successfully complete the exercise.

2. **Case-based Activities**—In this type of activity, a story or narrative is used to help students develop information literacy skills. The narrative may be based on fact or it may be a fictionalized account. Students are asked to solve problems posed by the narrative. However, they won't be able to solve the problem without identifying, locating and using information. These activities allow students to work at their own pace and tend to underscore real world applications for information literacy.

3. **Librarian-led Activities**—These are activities in which a librarian guides a large percentage of the learning activity. The librarian will provide the parameters of the activity, materials for students to work on, guidance during the activity, and any wrap up or closure. Librarian led learning activities can serve as scaffolding for students just beginning to use the library or to do research.

4. **Debunking Activities**—In this type of activity, preconceived notions and firmly held opinions about information are challenged. Any learning activity in which students examine why they think in a certain way is a debunking activity. Ethical questions about privacy, copyright, intellectual freedom and plagiarism can be explored thoroughly in a debunking activity. Activities that involve evaluating the World Wide Web also fit into this category.

5. **Empowering through Assessment**—The assessment activities integral in these lessons generate student learning. Through many of these activities students articulate and process their acquired knowledge of information literacy concepts.

Each lesson plan is organized into five categories:
   a. Circumstances of the Instruction;
   b. Objectives of the Instruction;
   c. Components of the Instruction;
   d. Evaluation; and
   e. Supplementary Materials.
The Supplementary Materials, which include handouts and guides, can be found in digital format on disk in order to facilitate reproduction.

The editors wish to thank all contributors to this endeavor. We appreciate the wide range of experience shared in these lesson plans. We are confident that readers will be able to use them in their own classrooms to enhance their information literacy curriculum.

Carol Anne Germain
Deborah Bernnard
University Libraries, University at Albany
September 14, 2004

1. ACRL Task Force on Information Literacy Standards, Information Literacy: Competency Standards for Higher Education, *College & Research Libraries News* 61.3 (March 2000): 207.

Table of Contents

Meet the Contributing Authors

Jeanine M. Akers (jmakers@memphis.edu) is Instructional Service Librarian at the University of Memphis. She received her MLS from the University of Kentucky and is currently pursuing a master's degree in English with a concentration on Composition Studies from the University of Memphis.

Virginia Bailey (baileyv@acu.edu) is a Reference Librarian at Abilene Christian University where she is liaison to the sociology and psychology departments. Virginia holds a Bachelor of Science in Human Services from University of Oregon and a MLIS from Louisiana State University.

Laura Baker (bakerl@acu.edu) is the Government Documents Librarian at Abilene Christian University. She is the liaison to the campus freshman library instruction program and to the music, political science/law, and agriculture departments. She holds a B.B.A in computer information systems from ACU and a MLIS from the University of Texas at Austin.

Cheryl A. Bartel (cbartel@library.ucla.edu) is a reference and instruction librarian at the Louise M. Darling Biomedical Library at UCLA. She received her MLIS from UCLA and her BA in English and Education from Valparaiso University. Cheryl is the liaison to the Schools of Nursing and Public Health as well as a number of departments in the School of Medicine, and does instruction to these areas in particular.

Eloise Bellard (bellard@adelphi.edu) is an Assistant Professor and Reference Librarian/Coordinator of Instructional Services for the Library at Adelphi University. She received her MLS from St. Johns University in New York and a BA in Communications and Education from Marymount Manhattan College. Eloise is an active member in ACRL and recent Past President of the Greater New York Metropolitan Area Chapter. Her extensive teaching experience spans over 25 years and includes both credit and non-credit bearing library research and information literacy classes. In addition, she is currently responsible for developing and implementing the curricula for Information Literacy Modules used in the Graduate School of Social Work and in the Freshman Experience course at Adelphi. She is actively researching ways to infuse Information Literacy throughout the curriculum employing student based /active learning techniques.

Deborah Bernnard (dbernnard@uamail.albany.edu) is the User Education Librarian and Information Science Bibliographer at the University at Albany. She holds a BA in Politics from Fairfield University and an MLS from the University at Albany. Her responsibilities include providing reference services, managing the information science collection, and scheduling and teaching library workshops. She is also an instructor for UNL 205, Information Literacy, a one-credit undergraduate course. Deborah presents and publishes on a variety of Information Literacy topics. She is a member of the American Library Association, serving as chair of the 2003 Conference Program Committee of the Library Instruction Roundtable. Deborah also serves on the Continuing Education Committee of the Capital District Library Council and she is a member of the Eastern New York Chapter of the Association of College and Research Libraries (ENY/ACRL).

Stephanie Sterling Brasley (sbrasley@library.ucla.edu) is the Information Literacy Coordinator at UCLA's College Library the undergraduate library. She coordinates instructional improvement, departmental outreach, and other general aspects of the information literacy program. Currently, Stephanie serves on the development team for the Educational Testing Services' Information, Communication, and Technology Literacy assessment project. As a member of the UCLA Library's Information Literacy Initiative, she is leader of the Measuring group which is responsible for developing program evaluation and classroom assessment tools for information literacy. Stephanie holds an MLS and a BA in Spanish literature from UCLA.

Gerald T. Burke (gburke@uamail.albany.edu) is a Bibliographer of Humanities at the University at Albany. He has taught UNL–205, an information literacy course offered at the University. He has an MLS and MA in English, both from the University at Albany.

David Ettinger (dettingr@gwu.edu) is an instruction, reference, and collection development librarian at the Gelman Library, George Washington University. Part of the Education and Instruction Group, he is also an adjunct professor at the Elliott School of International Affairs where he teaches a one-credit course on international relations research. A Princeton graduate, he has a PhD in political science from Columbia University and earned his MLS from Rutgers.

Allison Faix (afaix@coastal.edu) is Reference/Interlibrary Loan Librarian at Kimbel Library, Coastal Carolina University, in Conway, South Carolina. She received her MLIS degree from the University of Pittsburgh.

Christopher Frasier (cfrasier@wsc.ma.edu) is a Reference/Instruction Librarian at Ely Library, Westfield State College, Westfield, MA. He holds the MLS from the University at Albany, and a Bachelor of Business Administration from Siena College.

Dorothy Glew (medfg01@moravian.edu) is a Reference/Public Services Librarian and Coordinator of Instruction at Reeves Library, Moravian College in Bethlehem, PA. In addition to a BA and MLS, she holds an MA and PhD in English. She has served as

Chairperson of the Lehigh Valley Chapter of the Pennsylvania Library Association. She is active in Reeves's Friends of the Library and has just been awarded a grant to fund a Friends-sponsored program to mark the centennial of Isaac Bashevis Singer.

Carol Anne Germain (cg219@albany.edu) is the Networked Resources Education Librarian at the University at Albany. In this position, she teaches UNL 205 (the Libraries' credit-based information literacy course) and other course-related sessions, develops web-based instruction, and provides reference services at the University Library. Her research interests include the persistence of URLs in academic resources, marketing and instruction.

Jill Gremmels (jill.gremmels@wartburg.edu) is College Librarian at Wartburg College in Waverly, Iowa, one of ten institutions invited to the Best Practices in Information Literacy Conference in 2002. A longtime promoter of information literacy, she and her colleagues have established Information Literacy Across the Curriculum as a component of Wartburg's general education program. Their library-wide mission of educating information-literate lifelong learners guides all library activities and services. Jill holds the MLS from the University of Maryland.

Benjamin R. Harris (Benjamin.Harris@Trinity.edu) holds an MLIS and an MA in Composition/Rhetoric/Literacy from the University of Oklahoma. He is currently a Reference/Instruction Librarian at Trinity University. His most recent work is related to making connections between information literacy instruction and archival research methods, as well as examining how various library/information environments are including direct and indirect instruction methods through web sites and other electronic services.

Holly Heller-Ross (holly.hellerross@plattsburgh.edu) is a member of the Library Faculty in instruction services at the Feinberg Library at Plattsburgh State University. In 2002–2003 she studied the topic of academic integrity and plagiarism as a Fellow in the Plattsburgh State University Institute for Ethics in Public Life. Holly received the SUNY Chancellors Award, holds an MLS from SUNY Albany, and a BA in Environmental Science from Plattsburgh State.

Karen Hendrick (hendrick@acu.edu) is Head of Public Services at Abilene Christian University and liaison to the communication and history departments. She holds a BA in history from ACU and a MLS from Texas Woman's University.

Mary K. Hill (hillmar@gvsu.edu) is the Circulation/Inter-Library Loan Librarian at Grand Valley State University. Mary received her MLS from Western Michigan University. Mary's career over 30 years has covered special, public, as well as academic libraries.

Cinthya Ippoliti (cippolit@library.ucla.edu) is a Reference Librarian at the UCLA Biomedical Library. She received her MLIS from the UCLA Graduate School of Education and Information Studies. She works with a variety of faculty, staff, students and departments within the Center for Health Sciences and provides reference and instruction services. Her interests include technology based instruction and collection development.

Pamela A. Jackson (pjackson@sjsu.edu) is Reference Librarian and Library Liaison to Math and Computer Science at San José State University in California. She is active in the development of interactive online library instruction tutorials and outreach to international students. Pamela has given conference presentations on aspects of library instruction, including plagiarism, active student learning, and the use of hands-on assignments in library instruction sessions. She holds an MA in Library and Information Studies from the University of Wisconsin-Madison and an MA in English from Sonoma State University.

Anna Marie Johnson (annamarie@louisville.edu) is a Reference Librarian and Team Leader for Information Literacy at the University of Louisville. She holds an MLS and an MA in comparative literature from Indiana University and has taught both beginning and intermediate composition at the local community college and the University of Louisville. Her current research interests include prevention of plagiarism, the use of citation management software in the writing classroom, and the use of primary sources as components of information literacy instruction.

Susan L. Kendall (susan.kendall@sjsu.edu) is Reference Librarian and Government Publications Coordinator at San José State University's Dr. Martin Luther King, Jr. Library. She is also an adjunct professor in Reference Services in the Graduate School of Library and Information Sciences at San José State University. In conferences where Sue has presented sessions, the main themes have been government publications and information competence, and business competencies. She holds an MA in Library Science from the University of Denver and an MA in American History from the University of Nevada, Las Vegas.

Deborah M. LaFond (dlafonde@albany.edu) is Social Sciences Bibliographer for the departments of Women's Studies, Africana Studies, Communication, Psychology and Educational and Counseling Psychology at the University at Albany, SUNY. As liaison for these departments, she is responsible for collection development, instruction, and research process assistance to students and faculty affiliated with these departments. She works on the University's Main Library Reference Desk and develops a variety of discipline specific electronic and print guides which take into account interdisciplinary studies. Prior to her joining the University Libraries at the University at Albany, she received her MLIS from the University of California at Berkeley and served as reference librarian at the Doe and Moffitt Libraries for 10 years. She also worked at the California School of Professional Psychology (Alameda, CA) for three years.

Kate Manuel (kmanuel@lib.nmsu.edu) is the Library Instruction Coordinator at New Mexico State University. She has taught a number of library instruction courses (full and partial credit, full and partial term, general and discipline specific), as well as courses on the First Year Experience, Introductory English Composition, Latin, Greek, and Classical Studies. She has an MS in Library and Information Science from Catholic University and an MA in Classical Studies from Duke University.

Michelle S. Millet (michelle.millet@trinity.edu) is the Information Literacy Coordinator at Trinity University in San Antonio, TX. She has an MA in History and an MA in Library and Information Science. Her research interests include assessment of information literacy skills, librarians as teachers, and the challenges facing new librarians.

Kari Nyren Mofford (parkerk@wit.edu) is the Instruction Coordinator/Information Technology Librarian at the Wentworth Institute of Technology in Boston, MA. She earned her BA at Wheaton College and her Masters degree at Simmons College. She also is a Track 1 graduate of Immersion '02.

Kim Ranger (rangerk@gvsu.edu) is the Information Literacy Coordinator at Grand Valley State University. She spent her half-year sabbatical in 1999 at the Queensland University of Technology in Brisbane, Australia. She has a strong interest in active learning incorporating various learning styles, and received the GVSU Pew Teaching Excellence Award from the Library. Kim holds an MILS degree.

Debbi Renfrow (debbir@ucr.edu) is currently the Instruction Coordinator in the Rivera Library at the University of California, Riverside. She holds a BA in History from the University of California, Riverside, and an MLIS from San Jose State University.

Patti Ryan (pryan@yorku.ca) is a reference librarian at Scott Library, York University. She holds a BA from York University and an MLIS from The University of Western Ontario. She is a member of the Information Literacy Committee at York University Libraries, and serves as the library liaison for the campus Centre for the Support of Teaching. Her research interests include critical pedagogy in information literacy instruction, and the role of technology in teaching. She has presented on these themes at several conferences, including the Workshop on Instruction in Library Use (WILU) and the Association for Library and Information Science Education.

Barbara Shaffer (bshaffer@oswego.edu) is currently Education Librarian at Penfield Library, State University of New York at Oswego. As such she is responsible for instruction at both undergraduate and graduate levels, primarily focused on Teaching Resource Center orientation or ERIC database research. She holds an MLS from Syracuse University and an MS in Curriculum & Instruction from University of Wisconsin-Madison.

Dominique Turnbow (dturnbow@library.ucla.edu) is a reference librarian at the University of California, Los Angeles Louise M. Darling Biomedical Library. She graduated with a BA in Women's Studies from California State University, San Marcos and she received her MLIS form the University of California, Los Angeles. She provides reference and instruction services to a variety of departments serving undergraduate, graduate, and professional students, as well as clinical faculty and staff in the School of Medicine and the Center for Health Sciences at UCLA. Her research interests include Information Architecture and Information Literacy.

Section 1——Group Activities

Processing Information: Understanding the How, Where, and Why of Information Resources

Learning Library Resources: Discovering and Comparing Your Choices

Dissecting a Database

Brainstorming Keywords for Research Topics in Psychology

Indexes for Psychology: How to Choose Them, How to Use Them

Western Music to 1750

Integrating Citation Method into Information Literacy Instruction

Finding Eighteenth and Nineteenth-Century Periodicals

Critical Exploration of Periodical Indexes: A Lesson Plan for Active Learning

"The Flow of Information:" Understanding How Scholarly Information Is Created and Organized

First-Year Web Searching

Notes:

Processing Information: Understanding the How, Where, and Why of Information Resources

Jeanine Akers
Instructional Services Librarian
The University of Memphis
jmakers@memphis.edu

Circumstances of the Instruction

Insight into the ways that information is produced and disseminated will help students
determine the extent of their information needs,
understand what potential sources exist to meet those needs, and
demonstrate the need to consider information resources critically.
An introduction to and discussion about the process of how information about a
newsworthy event is spread, as well as how information from the scientific/scholarly
world makes its way to the popular press, can help students understand the various types
and purposes of information resources.

The following exercise can be used in a credit-bearing information literacy class, taking
up one class period. However, portions of the exercise can also be adapted for one-shot
instructional sessions taking no longer than twenty minutes. Finally, the events/topics
used in the exercise can be substituted with events/topics relevant to a specific discipline
and used as an introduction to the literature of a particular field.

Objectives of the Instruction

Students will be able to:
- understand the framework of the various types, purposes, and scope of
  information resources;
- identify how information is produced, organized, and disseminated; and
- evaluate information resources and know the value of doing so.

Components of the Instruction

Preparation
- Before class, arrange the room for discussion and group activity.
- Choose events/topics for each group.
- Gather a variety of publications about each event/topic (see Supplementary
  Materials).

- Photocopy the Information Process Timeline (see Supplementary Materials).
- Plan for groups to present their timelines.

Presentation

Open a class discussion by asking the students where/when they first heard about a specific major event. You might consider using the *Facts on File Yearbook, American Decades* or *The Pew Research Center's Survey Reports* web site at—http://people-press.org/reports/ —to help identify major events. Ask students to think about the "information source" from which they learned about this event (parent, friend, teacher, journalist, scholar, professional, etc.) and ask them how reliable this source is (knowledgeable, accurate, or biased).

Now, use this same topic to demonstrate the process of information from the time immediately following the event through the days, months, weeks, and years following the event. Several academic libraries have developed excellent tutorials and worksheets on this process. You might consider having your students view:

- Pennsylvania State University's *Information Cycle* Flash tutorial at— http://www.libraries.psu.edu/instruction/infocyle.htm

- UCLA's *Flow of Information Guide* at— http://www.library.ucla.edu/libraries/college/help/flow/ or the

- Five Colleges of Ohio's *Flow of Information* at— http://www.denison.edu/collaborations/ohio5/infolit/a1flow/

As you move through each step of the information production and dissemination process, be sure to point out various aspects of the information resources used, including format, audience, purpose, length, language, scholarly/popular, and bias.

Hands-on Activity:

- Now that the students should have grasped an understanding of the process and types of information resources, give them an opportunity to demonstrate this new knowledge.
- Break the students into groups and assign each group a particular event.
- Give each group various articles and books on that topic that were published at varying times and for varying purposes.
- Ask the students to list these resources in chronological order from oldest to newest on the **Information Process Timeline** appended to this lesson plan and included on the disk. Each student can be given a timeline individually, but you

might consider ways that students can present their timelines to the class (transparency/opaque projections, whiteboard/chalkboard, or poster board).

Evaluation

Evaluation of this exercise can be done as the groups present the **Information Process Timelines** to the class. The individual timelines can also be collected so that you can provide feedback to the students. As a means of assessing the students' understanding of the topic, they could be asked to write a brief summary or to sketch a diagram of the information process.

Supplementary Materials

The materials in this section have been placed on the accompanying disk so they can easily be copied and/or modified to fit the needs of individual libraries and instructors.

- **Example Topics and Resources for Information Process Group Exercise**

- **Timeline of Information Resources**

Timeline of Information Resources on the Topic of _____

(Developed by Jeanine Akers, The University of Memphis)

Citation	Type of Resource (book, book chapter, newspaper article, magazine article, scholarly journal article, conference proceeding)	Audience (general, scholars, professionals)	Purpose (persuade, inform, sell, offer an opinion)	Length	Language (easy to understand, complex, specialized)	Author (journalist, scholar, professional, other)	Bias
Year: Title: Author(s):							
Year: Title: Author(s):							
Year: Title: Author(s):							
Year: Title: Author(s):							
Year: Title: Author(s):							
Year: Title: Author(s):							

Please briefly describe the process by which information on this topic was produced and disseminated:

20 Processing Information...

Learning Library Resources: Discovering and Comparing Your Choices

VIRGINIA BAILEY

Reference Librarian
ABILENE CHRISTIAN UNIVERSITY, ABILENE TX
baileyv@acu.edu

LAURA BAKER

Government Documents Librarian
ABILENE CHRISTIAN UNIVERSITY, ABILENE TX
bakerl@acu.edu

KAREN HENDRICK

Head of Public Services
ABILENE CHRISTIAN UNIVERSITY, ABILENE TX
hendrick@acu.edu

Circumstances of the Instruction

This active learning lesson uses a group activity to acquaint students with a variety of library resources relevant to their research needs. It enables students to become more effective researchers by informing them of what sources are available (selection) and how to choose among them (evaluation). It can be adapted for undergraduate students or graduate students, using either print or electronic sources, and can be tailored to the specific subject needs of the class. This method supports the goal of introducing a large number of library resources in a short amount of time. We use this technique at Abilene Christian University when instructors request that the class be introduced to a wide variety of information sources.

Librarians divide the class into groups. Each group examines one or more databases/books and completes a worksheet (see Supplementary Materials) that helps group members learn about their resource. Groups take turns sharing their findings with the rest of the class while the librarian fills in a comparative chart (see Supplementary Materials) based on the group reports. At the end of class, students will see a list of pertinent resources with evaluative features that help them select the sources appropriate for their interests.

Objectives of the Instruction

Students will be able to:
- select appropriate library resources;

- utilize resources skillfully and knowledgeably;

- identify distinguishing features of sources;

- apply evaluation criteria to library resources; and

- devise effective research strategies.

Components of the Instruction

Preparation

The librarian prepares the following materials in advance (see Supplementary Materials):
1. Worksheet with sample topics and selected resources
2. Comparative chart
3. Session evaluation

The worksheet specifies a library resource and a sample research topic for each group to explore along with a list of questions about the resource itself. The librarian collaborates with the professor to determine the topics, and the library resources, appropriate for the level and research needs of the students. If general subjects are appropriate, hot topics in the news or from popular culture should be used to generate student interest.

The librarian will also need to prepare the comparative chart for class discussion. The chart summarizes the worksheet answers in tabular form to facilitate comparison across the various resources covered. A blank chart should be used showing only the list of databases/books and the comparative criteria headings. The chart will be filled in as group responses are presented. The librarian may want to have a completed chart that he or she can refer to as a prompt for the factual elements of the resources.

If databases are being taught, it is necessary to schedule the class in a computer lab so that groups can have hands-on time with the databases. If books or printed indexes are being taught, the librarian should gather these print resources in the classroom. A chalkboard, flip chart, smart board, or similar tool should be available to summarize the results of the group work.

Presentation

Welcome students, and explain the purpose and format of the class period. Many students, even graduate students, may not be familiar with the library home page, so the librarian may need to present an overview of basic features and highlight key databases.

Divide the class into groups of 3–4 people. Give each group a worksheet (see Supplementary Materials). The worksheet specifies a database/book and a research topic to explore along with a list of questions about the resource itself. Explain that the purpose is not to learn about the research topic but to learn about the resource. Each group answers the worksheet questions and then reports back to the class. Allow 20 minutes or so for groups to work on their own before beginning the reports. The librarian can circulate to provide help as needed.

After all groups have completed the worksheet, they report their findings. Someone from the group demonstrates the database for the class, while the librarian or another student fills in the comparative chart based on group reports. A free-flowing discussion during the reporting is essential for effective instruction. Comments and further questions from the librarian contribute to a more meaningful learning experience. For example, asking questions such as, "What is the difference between a magazine article and a journal article?" or "When would you want a topic overview as opposed to something specific?" or "If I need something current, what types of sources would I look for?" will help students make connections between the library resource and their information need.

As groups report, the comparison chart becomes more complete. By the end of class, students see a list of appropriate research tools with comparative, evaluative notes that will help them choose a relevant source. The librarian concludes by summarizing the chart verbally.

Evaluation

The class discussion and completed comparison chart provide evidence of the students' understanding of their assigned resource and their ability to compare that knowledge across other resources.

An optional class evaluation assesses the professor's and the students' impressions of the session. The librarian hands out the evaluation sheets during the last five minutes of class and collects them as students leave.

After students complete their research project, the librarian seeks professorial input again regarding the quality of the student product and the value of the library session.

Supplementary Materials

The materials in this section have been placed on the accompanying disk so they can easily be copied and/or modified to fit the needs of individual libraries and instructors.

- **Library Resources Worksheet**

- **Sample Topics**

- **Comparative Chart**

- **Evaluation**

Notes:

Dissecting a Database

CHERYL A. BARTEL
> *Reference Librarian, Research, Instruction and Collection Services Dept.*
> UCLA LOUISE DARLING BIOMEDICAL LIBRARY
> *cbartel@library.ucla.edu*

CINTHYA IPPOLITI
> *Reference Librarian, Research, Instruction and Collection Services Dept.*
> UCLA LOUISE DARLING BIOMEDICAL LIBRARY
> *cippoliti@library.ucla.edu*

DOMINIQUE TURNBOW
> *Reference Librarian, Research, Instruction and Collection Services Dept.*
> UCLA LOUISE DARLING BIOMEDICAL LIBRARY
> *dturnbow@library.ucla.edu*

Circumstances of the Instruction

"Dissecting a Database" (see Supplementary Materials) is a tool that was developed by the librarians in the Reference Division of the UCLA Biomedical Library to assist students in navigating new database interfaces. We use this tool as an in-class activity in many of our courses to foster student engagement and retention of general database concepts. Students are challenged with identifying key elements, which range from default search features to truncation symbols, across a variety of databases. The goal of this activity is to provide students with the tools to utilize any kind of database, rather than to focus on the specific features of each database they encounter.

The implementation of this tool supports discovery-based learning by encouraging students to use a resource they have never used before without any guidance on how to do so. The class is divided into groups—the number of groups and students in each group will vary according to class size. Each group answers several questions about utilizing the resource. When the time is up, one person from each group reports the group's findings to the class. This encourages a full class discussion, led by the student and librarian together, about the most effective way to use the resources. *"Dissecting a Database"* is unique in that it is an incredibly flexible way to teach multiple resources to a class and has successfully been implemented across diverse subject areas and information literacy levels.

Theories of Instruction and Learning in Nursing

The Theories of Instruction and Learning in Nursing Health Information Literacy Lab portrays a wonderful example if its application in the classroom environment. This lab supports a graduate nursing class and assists students in finding information about the role of the nurse as educator. This involves not only teaching patients, but other staff as well and would focus on utilizing such concepts as nursing outcomes.

Information literacy concepts and activities are an integral part of the course, thereby allowing students to create a learning framework that they could later apply to their own teaching environment. The active learning session of the class includes "*Dissecting a Database*," which guides students not only to identify the various elements of each resource they are examining, but also to understand the cognitive and didactic processes involved in approaching these resources from a perspective that emphasizes general concepts rather than specific details.

Objectives of the Instruction

At the end of this class, students will be able to:

- locate the UCLA Biomedical library and have a general sense of where to locate books, journals, and online resources in order to facilitate future visits to the library;

- recognize *PubMed (MEDLINE), CINAHL, PsycINFO* and *Web of Science* as key databases relevant to nursing in order to locate journal articles for research assignments;

- recognize *MEDLINEPlus* as a key source of patient information in order to support their role as patient educator;

- locate additional patient information materials in resources such as *MD Consult* and *MICROMEDEX* in order to support their role as patient educator;

- construct a simple, effective search strategy, using synonyms if needed, in a variety of databases in order to effectively do research; and

- refine their searches using limits or keywords based on their results in order to effectively do research.

Components of the Instruction

Preparation

Prior to the class, select the most relevant databases/resources for the particular class. For example, for the graduate nursing education class of approximately 20 students, the librarians identified *PubMed* (Medline), *CINAHL, PsycINFO,* and *Web of Science* as the key databases and *MEDLINEPlus, MD Consult* and *MICROMEDEX* as three key resources with patient education materials. We paired each database with a patient education resource for the students to compare. This can be done with any alternative resource, or the databases can be analyzed individually.

Additionally, identify a sample search topic relevant to the class. Write the topic on the board for students to start identifying key words as they wait for the class to start. You will use the key words they generate in the brief keywords exercise. We selected "Does educating patients improve outcomes by increasing compliance with the treatment plan?" as the topic.

Presentation

Begin by doing a general overview of the library and library resources. Introduce yourself and describe the class, making sure that the students understand that they will be actively participating and that they know what will be expected of them. Introduce the concept of an article database and explain how it differs from a library catalog. Explain how to get help in the future. Give a general introduction to the resources you will be using in the activity, largely covering how to find them and why to use them.

Next, do a warm-up activity using the key words generated by the students before the class began. Ask them to identify the main concepts given in the research question. Write each of the concepts on the board. Have the students give you the keywords they came up with for each of the concepts. Use this as the basis of a discussion of Boolean operators and perform a sample search in one of your databases.

Hands-on Activity

The primary part of the class is the hands-on activity, which is based on *"Dissecting a Database"* (see Supplementary Materials). Split the class into groups. Explain to the students that they will be exploring a new resource and attempting to answer a list of questions in 15 minutes. If they have trouble with a question, they should skip it and move on. They should also be prepared to both discuss the questions and do a brief demo of their resource. This can be done either with a single database for each group, or, as we did for this class, by having each group compare two different resources.

Be sure to allow enough time for the group presentations. It can take 15 minutes per group, depending on the level of detail you expect them to cover. During the presentation, you can also ask questions to stimulate conversation and direct their presentation (e.g., "What did you think of *x* feature?" or "Did you find *x* easy to use?). You may need to tactfully step in and redirect if a group provides incorrect or misleading information. At the end of each presentation, if there are any critical features that were not covered, you can do a brief demo.

Examples are given here of both the generic *"Dissecting a Database"* questions and the questions as they were modified for the Theories of Instruction and Learning in Nursing course. One of the primary differences is that *"Dissecting a Database"* is designed for each group to look at a single database, while in the nursing class each group compares a database to a specialty resource that contains patient education materials.

Evaluation

One of the useful aspects about *"Dissecting a Database"* is that assessment is built into the activity. The assessment process occurs when students are asked to report their findings to the class, allowing the librarian to appraise whether or not the groups have achieved the learning outcomes of the activity. If a student answers a question in a way that does not demonstrate he/she has attained mastery of the learning outcome, an educational opportunity arises for the entire class. The librarian is then able to demonstrate and/or discuss the issue with the class. If further assessment is desired, one can choose from a variety of techniques including the One-Minute Paper, Muddiest Point, or 3-2-1 Cards. Please refer to our resources list at the end of this lesson plan for information.

Supplementary Materials

The materials in this section have been placed on the accompanying disk so they can easily be copied and/or modified to fit the needs of individual libraries and instructors.

- **Theories of Instruction and Learning in Nursing Activity Grid**

- **Life Sciences Class Grid**

Resources

Angelo, Thomas A., and K. Patricia Cross. *Classroom Assessment Techniques: A Handbook for College Teachers.* Second Edition. 1993.

UCLA Louise M. Darling Biomedical Library. "Dissecting a Database: Teaching Yourself How to Search." 19 February 2004. http://www.library.ucla.edu/biomed/quickguides/dissectingdb.html. [Web site accessed: 25 March 2004].

UCLA Louise M. Darling Biomedical Library. "Comparing Database Features." 26 February 2004. http://www.library.ucla.edu/libraries/biomed/tutorials/db_compare.html. [Web site accessed: 25 March 2004].

Brainstorming Keywords for Research Topics in Psychology

ALLISON FAIX

Reference / Interlibrary Loan Librarian
COASTAL CAROLINA UNIVERSITY, CONWAY SC
afaix@coastal.edu

Circumstances of Instruction

This exercise is designed to help students in an upper-level psychology class prepare to search online periodical indexes. Students work together in small groups to brainstorm keywords on the same sample research topic. Working together in groups gives the students a chance to learn from one another. By having everyone work on a sample topic instead of their chosen topics, the students are able to practice thinking about search strategies before they begin working with their own topic. At Kimbel Library, this exercise is used as a transition into another exercise that deals with searching and comparing online periodical indexes.

The librarian carefully chooses the topic in advance of the class session. Ideally it is a topic that will engage the students' interest without being a topic that any students in the class have already chosen. The topic should also be one that the librarian knows will contain good examples of synonyms, related concepts, alternate spellings, and truncation possibilities. In this exercise, the librarian serves as a facilitator.

The exercise lasts about 20 minutes and can be done successfully with classes as large as 35 students.

Objectives of the Instruction

After the instructional session, the student will be able to:
- determine alternate terms, spellings, and related concepts that might improve the search results;
- identify keywords to use for searching a specific topic; and
- distinguish ways to use truncation when searching databases to improve search results.

Components of the Instruction

Preparation

Before class, arrange tables in the room to create six separate group tables. Have copies of the exercise (see Supplementary Materials) on hand to distribute to students at the right time. Bring dry erase markers or chalk to write on the board.

Presentation (5 minutes)

Set up the exercise by asking the question "How many people have tried to do a search and have gotten zero results, even though you know there probably should be at least one result for your topic?" Discuss student comments and then briefly explain the objectives of the exercise to the students.

Group activity (15 minutes)

Introduce the chosen topic to students and hand out an exercise sheet to each student. The exercise sheet (see Supplementary Materials) should have the topic written at the top and should be divided into a few logical categories based on the topic. At Kimbel Library, the topic "Attitudes of college students towards sun tanning as a risky behavior: a preliminary investigation" is used and the exercise sheet is divided into three categories—

- one for keywords related to attitudes,
- one for keywords related to sun tanning, and
- one for any other related concepts.

Start students off with general suggestions like, "Are there any medical or scientific terms for any of these words?" Ask the students to work with the others at their table for the next five minutes to come up with as many different terms as possible for each category. Walk around the room and visit each group to see how they are doing, then write the topic and categories on the board.

Stop the groups after five minutes (more or less time can be given to the groups if needed). Ask the first group for the keywords they produced for the first worksheet category. Write the terms on the board and point out helpful information as necessary, which may include useful ways of truncating terms.

Continue with each group until no new terms are offered, then provide any important terms that the students didn't generate (make your own list of terms before the class). For example, with the sun tanning topic, student groups might not always realize that sun tanning is more commonly called sunbathing in Great Britain and several other countries; this is important because indexes are often international in coverage.

By the time you get to the last category of keywords, there should be a very large list of useful keywords and variations listed on the board. This list should illustrate to students the importance of brainstorming topics before they begin searching. Finish up the exercise by pointing out that generating lists like this, before starting a search, will produce better search results and fewer zero hits. This can be a good transition to other exercises about how to search online periodical indexes and OPACS.

Evaluation

During the session, check with each group as they are working to answer questions and see how they are doing. If students don't seem to be on track with what they should be doing, try to offer suggestions that will get them thinking in the right direction.

An informal evaluation can be done by noticing whether or not students in the class seem to be using the skills they learned in the session when they come back to ask for help with their research later in the semester. The professor could also be asked at the end of the semester if they think coming to the library seemed to help their students or not. For a more formal evaluation, the librarian could create a worksheet on which students record their keyword choices for their research topic. The librarian can ask the professor to collect these so librarians could evaluate student performance.

Supplementary Materials

The materials in this section have been placed on the accompanying disk so they can easily be copied and/or modified to fit the needs of individual libraries and instructors.

- **Sample Keywords**

- **Brainstorming Keyword Exercise**

Notes:

Indexes for Psychology: How to Choose Them, How to Use Them

ALLISON FAIX
Reference / Interlibrary Loan Librarian
COASTAL CAROLINA UNIVERSITY, CONWAY SC
afaix@coastal.edu

Circumstances of Instruction

This exercise is designed to help students in an upper-level psychology course begin searching online periodical indexes for journal articles. The exercise can be used immediately following "Brainstorming Keywords about Research Topics in Psychology" (see p. 29 of this volume) or separately.

Students are instructed to run the same search in four different online periodical indexes that are commonly used in psychological research and to compare the results that they find in each database. They work in small groups so they have the opportunity to learn from one another. The librarian's role in this exercise is primarily that of a facilitator.

The exercise lasts about 25 minutes and can be done successfully with classes as large as 35 students.

Objectives of Instruction

The objectives of this library instruction exercise are to:
- familiarize students with the library's indexes that contain citations and/or articles in psychology and related disciplines;

- give students hands-on experience searching four of the library's online periodical indexes;

- help students realize that thorough research involves searching in more than one index; and

- demonstrate that some search terms will work well in one index but not in another and that trying different keywords in different indexes can help them achieve better results.

Components of the Instruction

Part 1—Preparation

Before class, arrange the tables in the classroom to create six separate group tables. Make sure each group has access to at least one computer that they can use to search the online periodical indexes. A laptop and projection unit can be used by the librarian if available.

Prepare slips of paper with different combinations of keywords on the same topic. Each group will get one set of keywords to search. If you are doing this exercise after an exercise on brainstorming, it can be helpful to continue using the topic the students have just brainstormed keywords on and to choose keywords related to that topic. Keywords can be tested in advance to make sure they produce different results in each of the four databases. There are two handouts (see Supplementary Materials) necessary for this exercise. One is a list of the library's indexes that will be especially helpful to psychology majors and the other is the worksheet for the exercise that lists the four indexes the students will be asked to search. Space is provided on the worksheets in which to record the results of their searches.

Part 2—Presentation (5 minutes)

Provide each student with a list of online periodical indexes available through the library that index articles related to psychology. This list should include the web address where the indexes are available as well as a very short description of each.

Go through the list and ask how many students have used each index before. As you are going through the list, note which indexes everyone in the class will use and which indexes are more specialized and might be more useful to some people than others.

Part 3—Hands-on Activity (20 minutes)

Use the laptop and projection unit to show the class where to find the indexes they will be using on the library's web page.

Give each group a copy of the exercise and a list of keywords they have been assigned to search. Each group is allotted about 10 minutes to search each of the four indexes on the exercise sheet for their keywords. While they are searching, they are instructed to record the number of hits they get for their keywords in each index, as well as any interesting features of the search results. For example, are the hits for magazine or journal articles? Are all of the articles in English, or are some in other languages? Do they have any questions about the indexes?

While the groups are searching, the librarian should visit each group to answer any questions that they have and to encourage them to pay special attention to how the indexes work instead of just rushing through to get done as fast as possible. If some groups seem to finish faster than others, the librarian can give them more keywords to search or ask them to also try their terms in another index that is not listed on the sheet.

When all of the groups have finished, call on each group and ask for a volunteer to share with the class the terms that group searched and the number of articles they found in the first index on the list. Ask which group found the most articles in that index, and which group found the least articles and compare the differences in the terms that they each searched. In this way students will hopefully notice that even though they are all searching for the same topic, different keywords will get different results in different indexes. After going through each index, ask the groups which index they thought worked best for the terms they were assigned, and why they think their terms worked well in that index. If the group had an index in which their term didn't work well, ask them what terms they think might work better and why.

If time allows, the librarian can use the laptop and projection unit to demonstrate some of the advanced features of each of the indexes that the students have just searched. This would include how to determine if the library owns a particular journal and how to print or e-mail articles or lists of citations.

Evaluation

During the session, check with each group as they are working to answer questions and see how they are doing. If students don't seem to be on track with what they should be doing, try to offer suggestions that will get them thinking in the right direction.

An informal evaluation can be done by noticing whether or not students in the class seem to be using the skills they learned in the session when they ask for help with their research later in the semester. The professor could also be asked at the end of the semester if they think that coming to the library session seemed to help their students or not.

Supplementary Materials

The materials in this section have been placed on the accompanying disk so they can easily be copied and/or modified to fit the needs of individual libraries and instructors.

- **Indexes for Psychology**

- **Keyword Worksheet**

- **Index Worksheet**

Notes:

Western Music to 1750

Dorothy Glew

Reference /Public Services Librarian and Coordinator of Instruction
Moravian College, Bethlehem PA.
medfg01@moravian.edu

Circumstances of the Instruction

The exercise described was developed for students enrolled in the course Western Music to 1750 at Moravian College. The course covers such topics as music in antiquity, Roman Catholic liturgical forms, the rise of the Baroque, the origins of opera, the ascendancy of instrumental music, etc. Students taking the course are music majors or minors and are typically sophomores. There were approximately 22 students in the class, and it was a 70-minute period.

This was the second library instructional session for the students in this course. The two library instruction classes provide the basics of music research. The first class covered searching for books on the online catalog and journal articles on *RILM* (see note under Supplementary Material) to prepare students for their first paper. In the second class, the librarian reviews and reinforces what students learned in the first class and teaches them about additional sources (besides books in the stacks and journal articles) and how to think critically about them, in preparation for a second required paper.

Objectives of the Instruction

After this instructional session, students will be able to:
- understand the rigors of research and plan a research strategy;
- recognize the nature and purpose of various kinds of sources for music research (reference, primary/secondary, etc.);
- distinguish the advantages and disadvantages of those sources;
- effectively evaluate web sources; and
- size up the results of doing music research on the fee-based web and the free web and choose searching tools accordingly.

Components of the Instruction

Preparation

Prior to this session, students were assigned several sections of the library's online research tutorial that highlight different library-related resources. The tutorial is at—
http://home.moravian.edu/public/reevestutorial/pages/index.htm

The assigned sections included:
- reference sources;
- primary vs. secondary sources;
- how to do precision searching on the web; and
- how to evaluate web sources.

In addition, students critique these parts of the tutorial by filling out an evaluation form (see Supplementary Materials). This ensures that they do the assignment and that improvements are made to the tutorial based on student responses.

The class is held in a computer lab so that every student can work at a terminal. Since one activity involves working in teams, the ideal setting would be one in which students can work in clusters.

Presentation and Hands-on Activity

The class started with an announcement that students would be studying the various kinds of music sources and that they would engage in group research on the sample topic—"Handel's Writing of Italian Operas for the English Stage." Students were asked why it might be useful for them to begin their research by consulting encyclopedia articles on their topic. Discussions followed about the ways that encyclopedias can be useful and the reasons why encyclopedia articles typically don't "count" as sources. In this way students developed an understanding of the strengths and limitations of encyclopedia articles. They did a search on the online catalog for a music encyclopedia in the reference collection and agreed on the most promising ones for a paper on their sample topic.

In addition, the assignment required students to find one primary source on their own topic. To prepare them for this, their professor had assigned a section of the library tutorial that explains and illustrates primary sources. In class, they were asked for examples of primary sources on the group topic. Suggestions included an opera or other musical composition by Handel.

The students then searched the online catalog for primary sources on their collective topic and discussed what they found. While they had identified numerous musical compositions by Handel, they were unable to find other kinds of primary sources, correspondence, interviews, etc. A discussion followed as to why this was the case and why, in general, primary sources are more plentiful for some topics than for others. They also talked about why primary sources are important for some kinds of papers and essential for this paper.

Students were asked to define a good source, and they generated a list of characteristics. Since not a single student in the class knew, they were told the difference between the fee-based web and the free web and were given examples of each. Then they were divided into four teams, two fee-based web teams and two free web teams. Each team consisted of four students, and each had to find one good source on the group topic. Each group needed a reporter who would justify their choice in light of the criteria. To prepare them for this activity, they had been assigned a section of the library tutorial on evaluating web sites. While they searched, the professor and librarian circulated to see how each group was progressing.

At the end of the searching period, each team described the source they found and the rest of the class viewed the source the team was describing. In this way, students not on the team could evaluate the source and challenge or concur with the team's assessment. One of the fee-based teams found an excellent article; another team found one that was unsatisfactory. Students volunteered reasons why one was good and the other was not.

One of the free web teams found a site with a good bibliography on Handel; the other team was unable to find any good source. The latter team complained about all the commercial sites (on which Handel CDs were being sold, for example) or sites with .edu domains that turned out to be course syllabi that mentioned Handel. The class ended with a discussion of the limitations of the free web and the strengths of the fee-based web for doing music research.

Evaluation

Time didn't permit a formal assessment of the session but there were ample opportunities for informal assessment since there was a great deal of online searching and verbal participation by the students. Each time students conducted online searches, the professor and librarian circulated, checking to see how they were doing. The presentation by each team (fee-based and free web) allowed the professor and librarian to assess students' ability to define a good source and support their definition with an example. In the case of one of the free web teams, the librarian and professor articulated the shortcomings of the sources they had found and of the free web as a tool for doing music research.

Supplementary Material

The material in this section has been placed on the accompanying disk so it can easily be copied and/or modified to fit the needs of individual libraries and instructors.

- **Tutorial evaluation form**

Note:
RILM Abstracts of Music Literature is an international guide to literature about music. *RILM* indexes a variety of document types including periodical articles, books, commentaries, dissertations, reviews, etc. and covers the period from 1967 to the present. It is widely considered the premiere source for academic research on music.

Integrating Citation Method into Information Literacy Instruction

BENJAMIN R. HARRIS
Reference/Instruction Librarian
TRINITY UNIVERSITY
Benjamin.Harris@Trinity.edu

Circumstances of the Instruction

Citation method is rather like solving a puzzle. One has an idea of how the pieces go together, but the pieces may not be neatly laid out and ready for application. Students must understand that the citation process is challenging work and that it is best to use available guidelines and resources to insure accuracy and integrity.

This instruction session will give students some basic information on the philosophy of citation before putting this philosophy into practice by constructing bibliographic citations and in-text citations. In addition, the activity will give instructors an opportunity to reinforce previous library and online catalog orientation. While almost any grade level could benefit from instruction in citation methodology, it is assumed that most students seeking this assistance will be first-year college or university students.

The following activity is appropriate for class sizes of 12 to 24 individuals, although accommodations could be made for smaller/larger classes. With adequate preparation by the course instructor, the following session will require 60 to 75 minutes.

Objectives of the Instruction

Upon completion of this instructional session, students should be able to:
- comprehend the importance of accurate citation method;
- construct a number of different bibliographic citations using a print/electronic style guide; and
- demonstrate knowledge of library resources learned in a prior instruction session.

Components of the Instruction

Preparation

Prior to this instruction session, students should have attended a library and online catalog orientation. The course instructor should have selected a specific citation style for use in the course (i.e., *MLA, APA*, etc.), and should also select a resource offering assistance in using the citation style. Since one class may use a handbook on citing sources, and another may use an excerpt from a course textbook, and yet another may use handouts or online sources, the information literacy instructor should be familiar with the specific resource being used by a class as these resources may differ in scope.

Presentation

The information literacy instructor should give a brief presentation reviewing the questions listed in this section.

Why is citation an important part of academic work?
- To keep track of your research.
- To give credit to the intellectual property of others.
- To show your credibility as a writer/researcher on a particular topic.
- To allow your readers the opportunity to extend their reading on the topic.

What does an accurate citation say about the author?
- The writer is credible and has taken the time and effort to be certain that his/her work is accurate. This also benefits the writer's authority and his/her ability to persuade.

Why are citation styles different?
- Citation styles have been designed and established by specific groups for use within a certain community. Differences between one style and another will usually depend on the needs and interests of the original organization.
- For example, the full author name is very important to writers in the Modern Language Association. The American Psychological Association puts less emphasis on the full name, and makes the date more predominant. The content and the arrangement of a citation relates directly to the interests of the group for whom the citation style has been constructed.

What are the basic components of a citation?
- While there are some consistencies between citation styles and between the citations for various sources, each is different. (This would offer the information literacy instructor an opportunity to look at a single citation, a single-author book for example, in a variety of different citation styles.)
- Punctuation is also an issue in citation construction. Just as in any written document, a comma means one thing while a period means another. The use of underlining or italicizing is also designed to tell the reader something about the source. Punctuation is also a sign of an author's accuracy; failure to follow established guidelines suggests a lack of care or interest in providing accurate and appropriate source documentation.

What is the most efficient method for preparing to cite sources?
- Make notes immediately when you find and as you use a source.

- If possible, create citations and complete a "working" bibliography during the information location and gathering process.
- Update the "working" bibliography after the final draft is completed. This will help a writer to refrain from completing a bibliography in a rushed manner at the end of the writing process.

What are in-text citations?
- In-text citations are notations within a piece of writing that denote which source was used in providing a quotation or piece of information. For every bibliographic citation, there should be an in-text citation within the text.
- Just as bibliographic citations are different depending on the citation style in use, in-text citations also differ in format and content. (This offers an opportunity to show an in-text citation for the same source using two or three different citation styles.)

Hands-on Activity

Split the students into groups of two. Each group will receive a list of three texts—an anthology of scholarly essays, a journal, and a topical web site. To simulate an actual research experience, it is suggested that these three texts relate to similar topics. It is suggested that each group receive a different list of texts. (See the sample activity in the Supplementary Materials.)

Each group will:
- locate the print items in the library (using the online catalog to find the call number);
- locate the web site using the Internet;
- construct a bibliographic citation for each item; and
- construct the appropriate in-text citation for each item.

After completing the citations, one group will trade citations with another group and check each for accuracy.

Class Discussion
Several groups may be asked to share their account of locating the item and citing the item. Their bibliographic and in-text citation may be placed on an overhead projector for the benefit of the entire class.

Evaluation

The success of this learning experience can be evaluated in several ways.

First, the ability of students to construct correct citations in groups can be evaluated by reviewing their written examples of cited materials.

Second, a short quiz provided at the end of the instruction session would help to evaluate students' understanding of the session and their success in achieving the course objectives.

Third, the information literacy instructor may wish to follow up the instruction session with an e-mail or short meeting with the course instructor to determine the accuracy of students' use of citation method in their class assignments. The information literacy instructor may then alter or adapt the current lesson to enhance this component of instruction for particular classes, academic disciplines, or grade levels.

Supplementary Material

The material in this section has been placed on the accompanying disk so it can easily be copied and/or modified to fit the needs of individual libraries and instructors.

- **Sample activity sheet**

Finding Eighteenth and Nineteenth-Century Periodicals

MICHELLE S. MILLET

Information Literacy Coordinator
TRINITY UNIVERSITY, SAN ANTONIO TX
Michelle.Millet@Trinity.edu

Circumstances of the Instruction

This information literacy lesson targets students in a humanities class and teaches them how to find eighteenth and nineteenth-century periodicals. Students in the class will learn how to locate periodicals through print indexes and digital collections. In the current research environment, undergraduate students are learning how to access periodicals through databases and most articles they locate are in electronic format. This class will stress the importance of finding information specifically using print indexes and then locating that article regardless of format—print, microform, digital, or interlibrary loan.

Learning how to use a print index and locate articles in formats other than electronic remains an important skill, especially for students studying the humanities. While more and more periodicals and primary source materials are being digitized, not every institution has access to these resources and students should still be using print indexes to locate periodical citations. Understanding a print index and how it works will often help students learn to better utilize electronic abstracts and indexes. The exercises designed for this class work to help students appreciate research and de-emphasize the need for only full-text resources. Alternatively, including digital collections of primary sources or even microfilm collections makes the class more complex, but also sheds light on the variety of information available to students and helps them grasp a variety of different resources in one class.

This information literacy activity works best with upper level undergraduate students or any class where the instructor would like them to locate primary source periodicals. A class size of 20 or fewer students works best; however, the class can function with a larger number of students if additional sources are available. This lesson plan can be used in a 50-minute instruction period or adjusted for longer classes by using more resources and prompting more discussion and questions.

Objectives of the Instruction

At the conclusion of this lesson, students will be able to:
- locate sources in the online library catalog and in the building;
- effectively use a periodical index, including the use of subject searching;

- identify parts of a citation and determine the difference between author, article title, and title of periodical;

- know how to locate a copy of a periodical article regardless of format;

- recognize that primary source materials come in a variety of formats; and

- use research skills to build search strategies and use subject headings.

Components of the Instruction

Preparation

Bring the chosen resources, including indexes, finding aids, and/or other materials that you will refer to during class, into the classroom and be prepared to demonstrate how to use them. If using multiple volumes and you cannot temporarily relocate them, choose a select few for the class to use. The number of resources you will need depends on class and/or group sizes. Ideally, every group should use a different source. However, if you do not have enough types of sources for each group to have a unique title, use different volumes of the same source for separate groups.

The four sources used in this class were the *Poole's Index to Periodical Literature, 1802–1907*, *Wellesley Index to Victorian Periodicals, 1824–1900*, *Index to Early American Periodical Literature*, and the *Making of America*, a digital library of primary source documents. Choose sources that will work best for your specific class and library. Any indexes, bibliographies, guides, or electronic collections that focus on 18th or 19th century materials and primary sources will work well.

Prepare worksheets for each group and each resource (print or electronic resource). The example worksheet contains generic questions, but can be modified if you would like students to answer questions specific to resources you use (see Supplementary Materials). Copy the handout, "Finding 18th and 19th Century Periodicals," making adjustments for your institution.

Introduction to the sources

Give students an overview of the tools they will be using in class so that they are somewhat comfortable with these sources. Stress that these print sources were the precursors to the online databases that students often use. If possible, you may want to use an overhead of a page from an index to show them what pages will look like and how to identify subject headings and interpret a citation.

An alternative strategy is to do this part of your instruction after you pass out a volume of the index to each group and then have them walk through the index with you. It is also important to explain how to find the full periodical titles, as they are not always listed in every volume of an index. Pointing out these key print-resource tools will help students' transition to electronic databases. You may also want to show students how they would find an index in the catalog and tell them where these specific indexes are normally located.

For online resources, instruct students on how to access them. Some background information about an electronic source can also be helpful. Demonstrate any key features that you think students will find necessary and those they might overlook.

If using a guide or bibliography to a microfilm collection, explain the collection's holdings and refer students to the guide. Often librarians find that students have not yet ventured into the microforms area of the library; alert them to periodicals published in this format and display sample OPAC records.

Hands-on Activity

After briefly discussing both the print indexes and/or electronic collections, assign and distribute the resources to the groups. Groups of 3 or 4 students work best. While students are working, walk around the classroom and encourage questions. While you are distributing the resources, have students begin the worksheet by writing down their topic and any keywords they choose.

After the students complete their worksheets allow each group up to five minutes to discuss their findings in class. Each group should choose a reporter to share their answers with the class. The worksheet will take students through developing their keywords and topics, finding a citation, and understanding how to locate a copy of the cited article. Observe students, so if any of them experience problems finding resources for their topic, you can intervene. Often, students do not realize that when looking for primary sources, especially older ones, vocabulary may vary.

If your discussion time is limited, collect the student worksheets, add comments, and return them to their professor. It is important to let each group work long enough with their sources.

Groups were divided and assigned sources as follows:

GROUPS	SOURCES
Group 1	*Poole's Index to Periodical Literature*
Group 2	*Wellesley Index to Victorian Periodicals*
Group 3	*Making of America* (digital collection)
Group 4	*Index to Early American Periodical Literature*

The worksheet (see Supplementary Materials) addresses the following ideas:
* developing a topic and keywords;

- using specific indexes, finding aids, or electronic collections to locate a relevant article or source; and
- learning how to get a copy of the relevant article, whether it is available in print, electronically, or through interlibrary loan.

Evaluation

Both formal and informal evaluation methods are used in this class. The success of the activities and class can be judged through the students' participation, questions, and worksheets. If the class is actively participating, it can be assumed that they are actively learning during the instruction session. Every group should be able to tell their classmates what their source contained, how it should be used, and what their findings included.

Additionally, it is often insightful to collect the students' worksheets and grade them. They are more likely to pay attention to the class and their work if there is a grade attached. Librarians also have the option of having both students and faculty complete a formal survey at the end of a class that gauges how well the topic was covered and whether the information presented was clear.

Supplementary Materials

The materials in this section have been placed on the accompanying disk so they can easily be copied and/or modified to fit the needs of individual libraries and instructors.

- **Handout—18th and 19th Century Newspapers, Periodicals, and Imprints**

- **Worksheet**

Critical Exploration of Periodical Indexes: A Lesson Plan for Active Learning

PATTI RYAN

Political Science Librarian
YORK UNIVERSITY, TORONTO
pryan@yorku.ca

Circumstances for the Instruction

This lesson plan can be used to introduce college or university students to periodical indexes and full-text databases. Using a student-centered, active learning technique, it invites students to discover, through their *own* exploration, the value of using periodical indexes for scholarly research. It is also a useful exercise for illustrating differences and similarities among indexes, and to teach students how to evaluate the appropriateness of a tool for their research topics. It can also be used to introduce keyword and controlled vocabulary searching.

The activity was originally designed for graduate students, but can be easily adapted to meet the needs of undergraduates. It is a particularly effective technique when working with interdisciplinary topics in the social sciences and humanities, but can be modified for science classes. The workshop is designed for classes of 20 to 25 students, and requires at least 90 minutes of class time. It can be incorporated as part of a larger workshop (or series of workshops) on library research, or can be taught as a specialized session on periodical indexes.

The format of the workshop draws heavily from principles of feminist educational theory. Feminist pedagogy, which emerged as a response to traditional educational theory, considers not only *what* is taught, but also, *how* information is presented. Feminist pedagogy posits that authentic learning can only occur when students are actively involved in the construction of their own knowledge. This activity provides an opportunity for this type of learning, and offers an alternative to the traditional lecture format. As such, it will appeal to instructors who are interested in exploring a non-traditional approach to library instruction and wish to experiment with peer-learning techniques.

Objectives of the Instruction

After this instructional session, students will be able to:
- assess the appropriateness of a periodical index for a specific research topic;
- critically evaluate the strengths and weaknesses of several periodical indexes by examining factors such as subject coverage, usability, search functionality, and type of materials indexed;

- construct an effective keyword search using Boolean operators;

- explain and compare the effectiveness of keyword vs. controlled vocabulary searching; and

- understand the importance of using periodical indexes for scholarly research.

Components of the Instruction

Preparation

Prior to the class, select the periodical indexes to be used in the workshop. The number of indexes will depend on class size, but as a rule of thumb, select one index for every four to five students. Using the class assignment or syllabus as a guide, prepare a list of relevant sample searches. Topics should be deliberately broad to allow for the retrieval of at least some relevant hits in each of the selected indexes.

Conduct preliminary searches in all of the selected indexes, paying particular attention to the subject coverage, scope, and search functionality of each database. Note any unique search options (e.g., cited reference searching or important limiters), and/or features that are relevant to the assignment. Ensure that there are an adequate number of institutional licenses for each product, and if necessary, make arrangements to obtain training accounts for the workshop.

If you are working with classes that have not had previous library instruction, it may be useful to distribute a preliminary handout one or two weeks before the class. The handout should provide a *general* introduction to periodical indexes, with instructions on how they can be accessed on the library's web site. The handout could also provide information on accessing databases from remote locations. Do not provide an exhaustive overview of specific tools or the process of searching periodical indexes, as this information will be elicited during the classroom exercise.

Hands-on In-class Activity

Begin the workshop by introducing the concept of a periodical index. In keeping with active learning principles, this section should be kept short – no more than 20 minutes. The librarian may wish to introduce periodical indexes as "gateways" to the literature of a discipline, and explain that they are commonly used to identify relevant research in a variety of formats, including scholarly journals, dissertations, conference proceedings, and association papers. Ensure that students understand the types of materials that may be found in results lists. At this point, it may also be useful to discuss discipline-specific versus multi-disciplinary indexes, and to provide relevant examples of both types.

If it has not yet been introduced, explain the basics of effective keyword searching, using Boolean operators as appropriate. Discuss the benefits of using controlled vocabulary and subject headings and ensure that students are familiar with using the vendor-supplied thesauri. An exhaustive explanation of every aspect of keyword searching is neither required nor recommended—truncation, proximity searching and/or database-specific operators are best left for interested students to discover independently!

After the introduction, divide the class into groups of 3–5 students and assign a specific periodical index to each group. On the chalkboard or flipchart, write down one or all of the pre-selected topics. Interdisciplinary topics work best as they can be searched across a variety of indexes. Instruct the students to "explore" the assigned periodical index as a group by searching one or more of the suggested topics. For upper level or graduate courses, allow students to work with their own research topics.

As they search the assigned databases, ask the groups to consider such things as content, scope, type of material, and search functionality. To guide their efforts, ask each group to complete a "Periodical Index Worksheet" (see Supplementary Materials). The worksheet is designed to elicit information about the index that can then be shared with the larger group. Allow for some flexibility with this task since not every group will be able to complete all the questions. Be sure to tell the groups that they should be prepared to share their findings with the class.

Allow approximately 30 minutes to complete the worksheet. During this time, the librarian may wish to briefly talk with each group and assist with keyword searching and/or database-specific questions as appropriate. At the end of the allotted time, ask one or two people from each group to "present" their index to the rest of the class by discussing the responses on the worksheet, and providing a quick demonstration of the index. Ask the group reporters to summarize what the group believed were the strengths and weaknesses of the index, with particular attention to subject coverage, types of materials indexed, and observable geographic concentration. Allow 10 minutes for each presentation. At the end of each report, the librarian may wish to answer follow-up questions or elaborate on any information provided by the group. After the final presentation, conclude with a summary discussion of the findings of each group and allow for follow-up questions.

Copies of the index worksheets should be made for all participants, offering a unique alternative to the librarian-created handout. Alternatively, the worksheet information could be posted on the class web site or listserv.

Evaluation

Two methods of evaluation could be used for assessment. The librarian may wish to review the index worksheets to see whether the groups identified the key features of the index, as well as its subject and geographic concentration. The worksheet information may also illustrate common problems with keyword or controlled vocabulary searching. A questionnaire could also be distributed to measure student satisfaction with the workshop, and suggested areas for improvement.

Conclusion

This activity offers an opportunity for getting students actively involved in their own learning and takes advantage of peer-to-peer instruction. It also offers a simple way to introduce students to several periodical indexes in a single session. Most importantly, the exercise requires that students think critically about the strengths and weaknesses of periodical indexes rather than simply learning the mechanics of how to search and retrieve results.

The workshop may also yield important benefits for the librarian. The worksheets provide a way of evaluating periodical indexes from the perspective of the researcher, rather than the professionally trained librarian. The activity also allows for observations of how students use periodical indexes for their research. Observations of this kind also provide a backwards glance into the level of success of library instruction in the first and second year of university. By noting performance gaps, information literacy programs can be strengthened for the future.

Supplementary Material

The material in this section has been placed on the accompanying disk so it can easily be copied and/or modified to fit the needs of individual libraries and instructors.

- **Periodical Index Worksheet**

"The Flow of Information:" Understanding How Scholarly Information Is Created and Organized

ANNA MARIE JOHNSON

Reference Librarian/Team Leader, Information Literacy
UNIVERSITY OF LOUISVILLE
annamarie@louisville.edu

Circumstances of the Instruction

This lesson plan was originally created for a library orientation for first-year honors students, but it has also been used with intermediate English classes. Ideally, it would be combined with a companion instruction session in a library's special collections or archives. The central idea is to help undergraduate students understand the difference between primary and secondary sources; that primary sources vary greatly from discipline to discipline; and that scholars use primary sources to create "new meaning" or "new ideas." Another way of stating it would be that scholars work with primary sources to generate questions and the results of their questioning are published in secondary sources.

Understanding the flow of scholarly information lays important groundwork for information literacy by helping students see the big picture. Without this most basic understanding, students may have difficulty grasping how scholarly information is organized and that finding aids (such as catalogs and indexes) are used to retrieve needed information. If students do not understand that the secondary sources they find in research databases are the results of the scholars' interpretation of primary source materials, the students will have difficulty entering into a scholarly conversation.

The unit was designed for a 50–60 minute class but could be shortened or lengthened. The number of students can also vary, but ideally, each group should consist of 4–5 students. The exercise presumes the use of a computer classroom, but it could be adapted to a regular classroom using print indexes.

Objectives of the Instruction

After this instructional session, students will be able to:
- outline the publication timeline of scholarly information;
- understand the difference between primary and secondary sources in a variety of disciplines;
- determine which primary sources can be found in libraries and which cannot; and
- explain how indexes and catalogs organize scholarly information.

Components of the Instruction

Preparation

The librarian will need to create a card set for each discipline s/he would like to have students review (see Supplementary Materials). It is helpful if the examples have local relevance (e.g., articles written by a professor at the university). Otherwise select topics of interest to students. It is important that these examples can be located in indexes that the library has access to in either paper or electronic form for the second portion of the class. Photocopy the *Flow of Scholarly Information* worksheet (either one per group or one per person). The handout in Supplementary Materials is a filled-in example; captions can be removed.

Presentation

Introduce session

This session is designed to be an overview of the scholarly process. It will not teach the students the intricacies of any one specific "tool" such as the catalog. Its intention is to give students the big picture of how the tools organize scholarly information and how they can be used to retrieve the needed information.

Primary versus Secondary sources (20 minutes)

Begin by asking the students if they know the difference between primary and secondary sources since some might know. If not, outline the differences. Keep this discussion very brief.

Divide students into groups of 4–5 and distribute the sets of cards. Each card has a component of the scholarly process starting with the primary source and continuing through a variety of steps to the development of the secondary source. The students' first task is to put the cards in the correct "order." They should also discuss why they chose that order. There may be some room for disagreement depending on the examples chosen. If several groups get done early, have them trade cards with one another.

Distribute the *Flow of Scholarly Information* worksheet and ask the students to take notes on it as the groups report back. They can record the specifics for any discipline which interests them. Remind them that this is a very simplified model and not a precise fit for all disciplines.

Ask several groups to report back (there will probably not be enough time for all groups). After a few groups have reported, guide the students in using that information to define primary and secondary sources based on their discussions. Ask them for differences they saw between the disciplines. Emphasize that what is considered a primary source may vary greatly from discipline to discipline (a painting in art or soil in environmental science or presidential letters in history). Also highlight that some primary sources (like the presidential letters) are preserved in libraries while others (like the painting and soil sample) might not.

Remind the students that some primary sources will be found using finding aids in the library's archives. If time permits, talk about these finding aids and, if available, show an electronic example.

Discuss how some primary sources can be found in a library's general collection. Presidential letters, for example, would be re-printed in book form. Sometimes a person's diary or narratives are reprinted or a library might have an original copy. Some of these things can be found using the library's catalog.

Have the students do some sample searches in the catalog to look for primary source material available in re-printed form in the library. Good keywords are *narratives, manuscripts, diaries, letters,* etc.

Next, instruct students how to use "finding aids" for secondary sources, starting with periodical indexes. Explain the function of periodical indexes. Sometimes it is helpful to start by talking about book indexing because students generally understand that concept.

Encourage the students to remain in their groups and assign each group the index mentioned on the group's set of cards. Try having 1–2 groups use the print indexes while the others use electronic counterparts. The first task is for each group to locate the article cited in their card set. After they have completed this task, have them take notes on what they did and state the source citation. Then, if time allows, have them look up a similar article using keywords of their choice.

Discuss with the students the differences in finding the citations in the print versus the online indexes. What might the advantages/disadvantages be? Ask what other observations the students had about the indexes. It is also helpful to look at subject words and to have a short discussion about brainstorming for a variety of subject words.

Hands-on Activity

The hands-on activities in this exercise included the ordering of the card sets, the filling in of the "flow of information" worksheet, and finding their article in the appropriate online or print periodical index.

Evaluation

Evaluation of this activity was originally done with a separate assignment. The assignment required the students to use material from the library's archives and special collections and combine it with a secondary source on a related topic and draw insights from both of these in a short paper. For example, the students might have found a letter from a WWII soldier and then a scholarly journal article about the psychological scars of soldiers in that war. The student would first discuss the process of finding the material. In the second half of the paper, the student could perhaps comment on the soldier's letter in light of the information in the article. By showing that they could find both a primary source and a secondary source and then begin to create some "new knowledge" from these gave us a sense of whether the exercise had been successful.

Other evaluation options could include a short quiz asking the students to order a set of cards by themselves, define primary and secondary sources, or list the steps one might take in finding either type of source. Pre and post-testing or even quick oral question/answer sessions provide evaluative options.

Supplementary Materials

The materials in this section have been placed on the accompanying disk so they can easily be copied and/or modified to fit the needs of individual libraries and instructors.

- **Flow of Scholarly Information worksheet**

- **Card Sets**

First-Year Web Searching

KIM RANGER
Information Literacy Coordinator
GRAND VALLEY STATE UNIVERSITY, ALLENDALE MI
rangerk@gvsu.edu

MARY K. HILL
Circulation/Inter-Library Loan Librarian
GRAND VALLEY STATE UNIVERSITY, ALLENDALE MI
hillmar@gvsu.edu

Circumstances of the Instruction

This lesson plan was created for CAP 115, a first-year class required for Advertising/Public Relations majors in the School of Communications, but is easily adaptable for any field. The course presents the basic techniques for finding, collecting, evaluating, and using primary data and secondary information relevant to solving communication problems.

Students explore library resources, search engines, government and commercial web sites, corporate documents and databases; use *APA* citation format; and learn presentation methods. It is a semester-long class offered in both fall and winter terms, and each section has about 35 students. The instructors worked with librarians to develop the course initially, and continue to collaborate refining it. A librarian teaches this particular activity in one class session. This instruction session could certainly be altered for other courses.

Objectives of the Instruction

After this instructional session, students will be able to:
- use more than one search engine to find web sites and

- effectively evaluate web sites.

Components of the Instruction

Preparation

The librarian selects three resources for choosing search engines, such as:
> *How to Choose a Search Engine or Directory*—
> http://library.albany.edu/internet/choose.html;
> *Search Engine Resources*—http://searchenginewatch.com/resources/; and
> *Search Engine Showdown*—http://searchengineshowdown.com/.

Two evaluative directories such as the following are also demonstrated:
> *INFOMINE*—http://infomine.ucr.edu/cgi-bin/search and
> *The Scout Report*—http://scout.wisc.edu/Archives/SPT--Advanced.php

A variety of search engines are selected for the students to use as an in-class activity to find good advertising or public relations web sites. Examples are:
> *KartOO*—http://www.kartoo.com,
> *Google* Advanced Search—http://www.google.com,
> *Ask Jeeves*—http://ask.com/,
> *Web Brain*—http://www.webbrain.com/html/default_win.html, and
> *ProFusion*— http://www.profusion.com/.

The librarian directs students to use evaluation criteria such as Virginia Tech's web page "Evaluating Web Information"—http://www.lib.vt.edu/research/evaluate/evaluating.html.

Distribute Handout 1 "Evaluative resources for the Web" (see Supplementary Materials) so students will have this information after this class.

Presentation

The librarian demonstrates the three resources for choosing search engines and the two evaluative directories, pointing out relevant features and constraints of each. For example, *Search Engine Showdown* has a useful comparative "Search Engine Features Chart" and "Search Engine News." *Search Engine Resources* has reviews, but the screen is very "busy." *The Scout Report* is a very small database, bringing back only 1 hit for "public relations." *Infomine* includes many more sites with useful annotations about fees, coverage, and creators, but it is difficult to know what the "score" really means.

Hands-on Activity

Assign students into groups of 2–4 if the instructor has not already done so. Let each group choose a search engine/directory or assign one to each group. Explain that they should use the search engine to find two web sites and use the "evaluating" web site to evaluate them.

Encourage them to take notes on the strong and weak points of their web sites so that they can explain their reasoning to the class (see Supplementary Materials). Give the class 10–20 minutes to accomplish this task. Have each group present the two web sites they chose and explain how and why they designated them "good" and/or "not-so-good."

Out-of-class Activity

Let each student group choose a web site. These sites should be chosen in conjunction with the classroom instructor and the use of the handout *Advertising & Public Relations Sites* (see Supplementary Materials). Each group will investigate, report on, and create an assignment for the rest of the class to use in discovering the "ins and outs" of the site. Explain that they will:
*   examine their chosen web site in more detail outside of class;

- use the "evaluating" web site to evaluate it;
- create an assignment to guide other students through using the site (see Appendix II, ASSIGNMENT CREATED BY STUDENT GROUP FOR CLASSMATES, Student Initiated Activity); and
- present the report and assignment in class at a later date.

Choose the date with the class instructor prior to the library session.

Evaluation

Students answer three questions at the end of the session:
- What was the most important thing you learned in the session?
- What will you do differently in your research process now?
- What questions do you still have about library research?

Librarians review this information for ideas for future classes. The librarians and instructor also discuss the session with each other.

Supplementary Materials

The materials in this section have been placed on the accompanying disk so they can easily be copied and/or modified to fit the needs of individual libraries and instructors.

- **Evaluative resources for the Web**

- **In-class assignment**

- **Advertising and Public Relations Sites**

- **Student-created assignments**

Notes:

Section 2—Case-Based Activities

Information Needs Scenarios

The Scientific Research Process

Evaluating and including Government Publications in Your Research

"Real world: Plagiarism Case Studies

The Politics of Copyright as Learned through Legislative Histories

Ethics of "Real World" Information Seeking & Use

Critically Thinking about the News

"Reading Texts"—Connecting to Research through Art and Artifact: A Course Integrated Information Literacy Lesson Plan

Notes:

Information Needs Scenarios

DAVID ETTINGER, PH.D.
International Affairs and Political Science Librarian
GEORGE WASHINGTON UNIVERSITY
dettingr@gwu.edu

Circumstances of the Instruction

This role-playing exercise, a form of problem-based learning, presents students with realistic research scenarios through real world examples, challenging them to respond to them. As an active learning technique, such concretization of the research process not only enables students to better identify with the material presented, but also involves them intellectually in a manner likely to sustain their interest. At the same time, it allows the instructor to naturally introduce students to information seeking behaviors and resources best suited for particular purposes.

Objectives of the Instruction

After this session students will:

- see the value of research as a problem-solving tool;

- think critically when conducting research for differing problems and situations; and

- be able to use library resources to meet specific information needs.

Components of the Instruction

The exercise is best conducted as an in-class activity. Students are presented with a scenario and, either individually or in small groups, asked to reflect upon how they would go about fulfilling the appointed task. To get things started, the students should be encouraged to think about the kinds of information they are likely to need, and how and where they might go about locating it. The instructor comments on the students' observations and, drawing from them, gradually expands the discussion to cover the various information resources best suited for the case under consideration.

As an example, the professor's research assistant might decide to focus on scholarly sources with a view to compiling a list of major academic literature published during a given time period. Accordingly, students would need to know which databases would be best to search for a particular topic to ensure they found good citations. The instructor can build upon this to engage the class in a discussion of academic sources both generally and within specific disciplines, eventuating in a presentation on how to identify and use subject-specific scholarly databases.

Although the examples provided in this lesson plan were designed for a course in international relations research, they can be easily adapted to other contexts.

Minds-on Activities—Information Need Scenarios

Scenario 1. You are a Foreign Service Officer. The Ambassador is meeting this afternoon with the Indian ambassador for a general discussion of issues of mutual interest and concern between the two countries. He asks you to prepare a background document to prepare him for the session. How would you proceed?

Scenario 2. As research assistant to a professor who has been out of the country on sabbatical, you are requested to compile a comprehensive list of major articles that have appeared in his subject of interest during this absence. Discuss the various ways you might approach this assignment.

Scenario 3. You are a reporter for a major national newspaper. You have been asked to prepare a piece for tomorrow's paper synthesizing previous reporting on a particular issue. How would you go about researching this topic before beginning to write?

Scenario 4. The multinational corporation for which you work is considering investing in a particular country. They have commissioned you to do an analysis of the viability and prospects of this venture. Outline how you would go about doing this.

Scenario 5. As speechwriter at the Council on Foreign Relations, you need to draft a speech on the topic of foreign perceptions of the United States in the aftermath of September 11th. Brainstorm some of the possible sources of information.

Scenario 6. You are the Middle East expert at the Congressional Research Service, the Congressional think tank. A Senate committee is scheduling hearings on the President's Iraq policy. Committee members need you to prepare a briefing book to bring them "up to speed." Walk through the various materials you might include and the steps you might take to compile this information.

Evaluation

If used as the pedagogical foundation for an information literacy course, students should be asked to comment specifically on the instructional technique used as part of the overall course evaluation. In addition, they can be required to do a short final paper reflecting on what they have learned and how it might influence their future research behavior.

The Scientific Research Process

PAMELA ALEXONDRA JACKSON
Reference Librarian
Mathematics and Computer Sciences Liaison
Global Studies and International Student Programs Coordinator
SAN JOSE STATE UNIVERSITY
pjackson@sjsu.edu

Circumstances of the Instruction

Students in this junior/senior-level mathematics and computer science technical writing course often find themselves unprepared for and apprehensive about the research component of the course. Some of the key concepts in the research process for science students are:

- an understanding of and the ability to identify primary or original research;
- navigating the print and online environments to find the full-text of journal articles; and
- developing search strategies to conduct their research.

Technical Writing is taught every semester to approximately 150 students enrolled in seven individual sections at San José State University (SJSU). Working closely with the faculty coordinator for the departments of math and computer science, the librarian teaches a 75-minute instruction session during the third week of classes each semester. Instruction sessions are taught during regular class time. Student attendance and participation is mandatory. Students are required to take the *InfoPower*—http://130.65.109.143/infopower/index.html—and *Plagiarism: The Crime of Intellectual Kidnapping*—http://130.65.109.143/plagiarism/index.htm—online tutorials and submit their scores before the instruction session begins. Class enrollment is limited to 30 in each section and library instruction sessions are taught in the department's computer lab.

Suggestions for other settings: Sections of the hands-on activities included here were refined in collaboration with Charity Hope, Science Librarian at San José State University. She has successfully used the assignment in large, introductory freshman biology seminars.

Objectives of the Instruction

Upon completion of the library instruction session, students will be able to:

- recognize primary research articles in the sciences;
- list differences between primary and secondary research;
- understand various options for obtaining the full-text of journal articles;
- focus their research topic;

- develop a search strategy for their research; and
- navigate at least one database successfully.

Components of the Instruction

Preparation

It is important to work with the class instructor to maximize student learning. This session structure and library assignment work best when students understand their class assignment and have a topic in mind before the library instruction session. It is also helpful to carefully choose sample citations and abstracts that are relevant to the class assignment and that exemplify the key research issues you are teaching. A worksheet is provided to all students and focuses on three important concepts:

- identifying primary resources;
- finding full-text articles; and
- outlining their research process (see Supplementary Materials).

Presentation

Introduction (5 minutes)

Students are first given a brief introduction to library services and how to obtain help. Highlights of the introduction include information about subject specialist librarians assigned to every discipline, the existence of online subject guides to assist students in their research, and the fact that all librarians at SJSU are made aware of this class assignment and can assist them at the Reference Desk. We then move into an almost completely hands-on session that takes them through the research process.

Hands-on Activity (1 hour 10 minutes)

Identifying Primary (Original) Scholarly Research (20 minutes)

Students discuss the Technical Writing course assignment with the instructor. This assignment asks students to pretend they are consultants to a biotech corporation. As consultants, they will evaluate a technology and tell the corporation whether or not this technology will help increase productivity. Research should be based on the primary scientific evidence and not on consumer information.

Students are given a brief introductory lecture on the differences between primary (original) scholarly research articles and secondary research articles. The lecture takes less than 10 minutes; it includes a description of the scientific publishing and peer-review process.

A list of five citations and abstracts are passed out. Working individually or in small groups (they choose as it accommodates more individual learning styles), the students decide if the articles are primary or secondary research and if they would use them for their research assignment in this course. It works well to have a mix of primary and secondary articles, and also an article or two for which a student would have to obtain the full article to make the decision (i.e., it is not evident from the abstract alone).

It is stressed that students must obtain the full-text of the article before making their final decision on whether or not an article constitutes primary research. However, students also learn to read article abstracts for clues that the article is primary scientific research. We discuss clues such as language that describes the experiments being carried out and abstracts that clearly explain original research that is being presented.

The class comes back together as a group and discusses each of the articles, pointing out any tips they learned or questions they had.

Note: A variation on this assignment has been to have students decide whether an article is scholarly or popular.

Finding the Full-Text (10 minutes)

Students are given the scenario that they have been searching in a database and now need to find the full-text of several journal articles. The scenario states that either
    1) the link to the full-text in the database did not work, or
    2) there was no link to the full-text in the database.
Working individually, students are asked to track down the full-text of a number of citations. The librarian chooses citations carefully before the session, giving students the opportunity to find articles in print, online, and via Interlibrary Loan. Students record where they would find the full-text of the journal articles. During this part of the assignment, the librarian walks around the room answering questions and pointing out tips.

Some common mistakes students make when trying to locate the full-text include spelling errors and searching for the title of the article instead of the journal title in the library catalog. The class comes back together as a group and discusses the citations, pointing out any tips they learned or questions they had.

The Research Process (40 minutes)

Students frequently need help focusing their topics and choosing appropriate search terms. As math and computer science majors, Boolean Logic is something they tend to understand. The librarian spends 5–10 minutes discussing topics for the Technical Writing assignment, including topic examples and ways to focus their topics to a manageable level. Also included is a discussion of clarity and the need to use technical language when searching the databases. For example, if one searches for the acronym *GPS*, the database does not know if the student means Global Positioning System or Generalized Processing Sharing.

The librarian gives a brief demonstration of the database that will prove most useful for a majority of the class's technology research topics (in this case, *Compendex* via *Engineering Village 2*). The demonstration includes an overview of the search interface, setting the limits, and a sample search. The sample search provides a great opportunity to pull in Parts 1 and 2 of the exercise. The librarian shows students where to link to the full-text in a database and where to find abstracts to determine if the article is primary research.

For the remainder of the session, students work through the research process for their technology topic. They define their topic, choose keywords on which to search, develop a search strategy, refine their strategies based on their initial search results, evaluate the search results, and begin choosing primary research articles for their class assignment. The librarian answers questions and assists students in narrowing their topic and searching the database.

Evaluation

Check with the students as they complete each part of the assignment to see how it is working for them.

Request feedback from the instructors after the session. Informal feedback from the instructors suggests that students are accurately identifying primary research and submitting quality citations in their papers.

Evaluate reference transactions and questions received by students in the course after the library instruction session. An analysis of librarian reference-by-appointment statistics and documentation suggests a drop in lower-level mechanical questions such as, "How do I get the full-text?" Students are coming to reference appointments more prepared, having employed many of the techniques explored in the instruction section. They have tried searching and experimenting with keywords on their own, something not often seen before launching this assignment. Quite often, the librarian is seeing students who are effectively conducting their research and tend to make appointments for reassurance. This gives the librarian a great opportunity to introduce new ideas and suggest other methods the students can try to enhance their research experience.

Supplementary Material

The material in this section has been placed on the accompanying disk so it can easily be copied and/or modified to fit the needs of individual libraries and instructors.

- **Worksheet**

Evaluating and Including Government Publications in Your Research

SUSAN L. KENDALL

Reference Librarian and Government Publications Coordinator
SAN JOSE STATE UNIVERSITY
susan.kendall@sjsu.edu

PAMELA ALEXONDRA JACKSON

Reference Librarian
Mathematics and Computer Sciences Liaison
Global Studies and International Student Programs Coordinator
SAN JOSE STATE UNIVERSITY
pjackson@sjsu.edu

Circumstances of the Instruction

In the fall of 2002, San José State University (SJSU) launched the Metropolitan University Scholar's Experience (MUSE) freshman seminar program. In this program, students select from a variety of specialized courses designed to help them transition to college life. Library instruction in these seminars introduces students to research at SJSU and starts them on the path to lifelong learning and success. Class enrollment is limited to 20 students.

Students usually take a MUSE course in the fall semester of their freshman year. For many, this is their first experience in a university library. In a MUSE seminar on Hotel Administration, students are asked to research all aspects of travel and tourism for a country of their choice. While the focus of this particular library instruction session is country research, the assignment can easily be adapted to include a variety of government publications.

The instruction session is conducted in a computer lab using the classroom control software Altiris Vision™. This software tool allows the instructor to manage what is displayed on classroom monitors. This device enables the librarian to broadcast specific examples to all terminals, thus having all participants on the same page. When Altiris Vision™ is in its demonstration mode, student terminals are locked, allowing the instructor to share a screen and highlight key concepts. This type of control software diminishes the need for expensive projection equipment, captures the students' attention and affords an up-close, realistic demonstration of the resources needed to teach students research strategies.

Objectives of the Instruction

Upon completion of the library instruction session, students will be able to:
- identify ways to get research help in the library;

- understand the library's web site and where to begin their research;

- search the library's catalog and understand catalog records;

- successfully navigate at least two databases;

- locate information on their topic; and

- understand the availability of government publications and how they can be included in scholarly research.

Components of the Instruction

Preparation

This particular session is team-taught by librarians. These librarians work together before the session to develop the teaching plan, conduct practice searches, and setup the computer lab, ensuring that the Altiris™ software is operating on all terminals.

Students are given a two-part introduction during the library instruction session:
(1) a general overview of the library and library services, and
(2) an introduction to using government publications for their research assignment.
The librarians broadcast their computer screen to the students for the introduction.

The librarians explain that there is a wealth of government information in the online environment. Some of the very best resources can be found at federal government web sites and databases where the information is usually primary sources, current, reliable, in-depth, and free.

Hands-on Activity

The librarians broadcast their screen to show students how to enter and navigate the library catalog. Students are then given control of their computer terminals and are asked to find a book on their assigned country and provide information found in the catalog record, such as the title, call number and whether or not the book is available for check out. This is recorded on the assigned worksheet (see Supplementary Materials).

Next students will learn how to use *CountryWatch* database. The librarians use the Alitris™ software to display the *CountryWatch* database. Students are then given control of their computer terminals and asked to find their country in the database. By correctly navigating the database, students can identify information about their country, such as the largest city and/or examples of cultural etiquette. They again use the worksheet for documenting their findings (see Supplementary Materials).

Once more, the librarians broadcast their screen to show students how to use the *Expanded Academic Index* database. Students are then given control of their computer terminals and are asked to find a journal article about their country, which should be added to the worksheet (see Supplementary Materials). The focus here is not on searching for a specific topic, but to conduct a simple, broad search on their country and learn how to navigate an article database. Students are asked to provide citation information for the article they choose.

Finally, students are instructed to go to the *U.S. Department of State* web site. By navigating the web site to find the "Country Background Notes," students should be able to supply background information and facts about their country in order to complete the worksheet (see Supplementary Materials).

A Step Further

The "step further" section asks students to critically evaluate the information found in *CountryWatch* versus what they found on the *U.S. Department of State* web site and develop their own opinions about the two resources (see Supplementary Materials).

Evaluation

Check with the students as they complete each part of the assignment to see how it is working. All students, the class instructor, and librarian receive library instruction session evaluation forms (see Supplementary Materials). A review of some session evaluations found that students:
- found the hands-on component very helpful;
- learned more about the orientation of the library and resources; and
- found it difficult to distinguish between the article title and journal title in the databases.

The professor of the class thought that the hands-on activity was essential and requested another library instruction session to test the students' comprehension.

Supplementary Materials

The materials in this section have been placed on the accompanying disk so they can easily be copied and/or modified to fit the needs of individual libraries and instructors.

- **Library Worksheet**

- **A Step Further**

- **Library instruction session evaluation – professor**

- **Library instruction session evaluation – students**

- **Library instruction session evaluation – librarian**

Notes:

"Real World" Plagiarism Case Studies

KATE MANUEL

Instruction Coordinator
NEW MEXICO STATE UNIVERSITY, LAS CRUCES NM
kmanuel@lib.nmsu.edu

Circumstances of the Instruction

Ethical use of information, particularly proper attribution of source materials and avoidance of plagiarism, figures prominently in the "Information Literacy Competency Standards for Higher Education:" Standard Five specifies that the "information literate student follows laws, regulations, institutional policies, and etiquette related to the access and use of information resources," as well as "[d]emonstrates an understanding of what constitutes plagiarism and does not represent work attributable to others as his/her own."

Too often, however, plagiarism is presented to students primarily in terms of copying and pasting from the Internet when completing research papers or other written assignments within an academic context (see Hanson 2003; Rimer 2003; Simmonds 2003). This can lead students to the misconception that proper use of sources and avoidance of plagiarism are artificial "academic" constructs, created largely to "torment" students and irrelevant to the "real world."

This activity uses newspaper articles to introduce students to the varied types and consequences of plagiarism within "real world" settings. Newspaper articles are ideal sources because they are generally brief, can be read quickly, and allow students to see society's broader concern with plagiarism—by showing them that newspapers find incidences of plagiarism noteworthy.

Newspaper articles can be selected to highlight the wide variety of types of information plagiarized as well as the occupations of the plagiarist. They discuss plagiarized song lyrics or music, fashion designs, art works, speeches and written texts, as well as musicians, doctors, newspaper reporters, college professors and administrators, and politicians as plagiarists. Throughout the activity, students are asked to consider who plagiarized what, what the consequences of plagiarism were, and whether the consequences were "fair," as well as, ultimately, what "fair" means in relation to intellectual property rights. [Alternately, newspaper articles could be selected to highlight plagiarism within a discipline, such as medicine, for a discipline-specific library instruction session.]

This activity can be adapted for use with students at all academic levels within higher education, from first-year students through graduate students, by the choice of the reading level, length, and discipline-specificity of the newspaper articles selected for reading.

Students are divided into groups which read one or more articles in common, and then answer questions about who plagiarized what and with what consequences. Student groups can consist of two or more individuals, but there should be enough groups that the class can be exposed to at least five different incidences of "real world" plagiarism. This means that class sizes of 10 or more can complete this activity. Twenty to thirty students is often an optimal class size for this activity, although smaller or larger groups can be accommodated.

A basic version of this activity can be completed within 30–40 minutes, although longer variations of it, with further exploration of various issues relating to plagiarism, can easily be constructed.

Objectives of the Instruction

After this instruction, students will be able to:
- identify the types of information (music, art works, fashion designs, oral texts, written texts) that could be plagiarized;

- identify the range of "real world" occupations within which plagiarism can occur;

- recognize common consequences for plagiarism in "real world" settings; and

- articulate some concerns surrounding ownership of intellectual property that make (1) allegations of plagiarism significant and that (2) make particular punishments for plagiarism seem "fair" or "unfair."

Components of the Instruction

Select newspaper articles for the students to read. Articles can be selected with the discipline, academic level, or other features of the class and students to be taught in mind. With first- and second-year students, using articles that highlight the large number of information types that can be plagiarized as well as the variety of fields concerned with plagiarism is often desirable.

The supplementary materials for this lesson plan include a bibliography listing some articles that have worked well in stimulating discussion in prior uses of this activity. Following the citation for the article is a brief annotation indicating the occupational field of the plagiarist as well as the type of information plagiarized. Other articles can easily be found by searching newspaper databases such as *Lexis-Nexis* for stories about plagiarism, or plagiarism and a particular field or type of information (e.g., plagiarism AND medicine, plagiarism AND fashion design).

In terms of getting the students to read the newspaper articles, several options are possible, depending upon situational factors. Students could be provided with photocopies of the articles, directed to a web site where PURLs (persistent URLs) link them directly to their article(s), or instructed how to search for and obtain the article(s) full-text from a database. Similarly, students can be instructed to read the articles prior to the class session, or at the start of the class session. Providing the students with color-coded copies of the newspaper articles (one color of paper for each different article) at the start of the class session and having them read for 10–15 minutes has been highly effective. A kitchen timer or some other timing device can be used to provide a clear signal for when it is time to move from reading to discussing.

In addition to the newspaper articles, students are also provided an activity sheet that lists all the articles being discussed in the class and provides them with a framework for taking notes. The sheet is headed "Plagiarism: Case Studies" and consists of four columns and a variable number of rows (matching the number of articles being read and discussed in the class) printed in landscape. This framework for taking notes is illustrated below; a complete version of the "Plagiarism: Case Studies" notes guide is included in the Supplementary Materials.

What was plagiarized? (Type of resource? Amount of resource? etc.)	Who was involved in the situation? What did s/he do?	What were the consequences of plagiarism in this case?	Reference

Presentation

Depending upon the amount of time involved in the session, a number of presentation options are possible. In shorter sessions, the instructor may simply want to open by engaging the students in a brief discussion of what they already know about plagiarism and introducing them to the objectives and plan for the current session.

In longer sessions, one could open by presenting the "typical" discussion of plagiarism within higher education (as something students do when writing papers by using web resources improperly) and then contrasting this discussion with the reality of concern for plagiarism in various types of information products throughout their professional careers—in fields including news reporting, government work, fashion design, web design, music, and public speaking. In a longer session one might want to open with an archived audio clip, such as the National Public Radio's piece on "The Internet & College Cheating" as an introduction to the "typical" discussion of plagiarism. Also in longer sessions, one could present the traditional discussion of plagiarism via a PowerPoint™ presentation and some activities designed to see if students can recognize plagiarism in written sources or find plagiarism from web sources prior to, or even subsequent to, this activity.

The students should be asked to read the newspaper article(s) in order to detect
    (1) who committed plagiarism (the plagiarist's name and occupation),
    (2) what was plagiarized (the type and amount of source plagiarized), and

(3) what happened to the plagiarist (was s/he punished eventually? by whom? how?).

Once students have individually completed their reading(s), they are asked to work in a group with others who had the same reading(s) to decide what to present to the class about their article(s).

With less focused first- and second-year students, it is often helpful to ask them to mark up their copies of the readings to indicate the "answers" to these questions, as well as take notes on the notes page provided for them.

Finally, while the student groups are presenting, ask students to take notes on each group's presentation on the notes page provided to them—that way each student will have a record of the types of sources that can be plagiarized, by whom, and with what consequences.

Hands-on Activity

The hands-on component of this activity consists of students reading the article(s), presenting their findings about the article(s), and taking notes on their own and others' articles. Collecting the notes pages at the end of the session is an effective way of making sure that students are being attentive to other students' presentations and learning from these.

Evaluation

A one-minute paper serves as a very effective evaluation mechanism for this assignment. Students can be asked to write for 60 seconds, or perhaps a little longer, on the most important thing they learned from this session, as well as the thing that is most unclear to them. Frequency counts of the number of students making particular comments on these one-minute papers can then be used to track how well students learned the materials as well as to cue the instructor to any modifications that should be made to the activity prior to future presentations.

The following multiple-choice question also works well, provided that students are required to explain their answer after making their choice:

You do *not* need to quote words taken directly from someone else's writings provided that

_____

_____.

    a. you use only 5 to 10 words from the source
    b. you include the source in your bibliography/works cited
    c. you do not take a complete sentence from the work
    d. none of the above

Explain your answer:

The materials in this section have been placed on the accompanying disk so they can easily be copied and/or modified to fit the needs of individual libraries and instructors.

- **Newspaper Articles on Plagiarism: A Selective Bibliography**

- **Plagiarism: Case Studies notes sheet.**

- **You Decide ... Is It Plagiarism? worksheet**

- **How Easy Is It to Get Caught? Can you find the source that was plagiarized in each of these student texts ...worksheet**

NOTE: National Public Radio has a number of wonderful audio clips on plagiarism that could also be used in this context, for example, "The Internet & College Cheating" from the May 21, 2002 edition of *All Things Considered* or "Plagiarism in College" from January 20, 2004.

References

ACRL Task Force on Information Literacy Standards. Information Literacy: Competency Standards for Higher Education. *College & Research Libraries News* 61.3 (2000): 207–215.

Hansen, Brian. 2003, Sept. 19. Combating plagiarism: Is the Internet causing more students to copy? *CQ Researcher, 13* (32), 773–796.

Rimer, Sara. 2003, Sept. 3. A campus fad that's being copied: Internet plagiarism. *The New York Times*, pg. B7. Available for sale at http://www.nytimes.com/2003/09/03/education/03CHEA.html.

Simmonds, Patience. 2003, June. Plagiarism and cyber-plagiarism: A guide to selected resources on the web. *College & Research Libraries News, 64* (6), 385–389.

Notes:

The Politics of Copyright as Learned through Legislative Histories

KATE MANUEL
Instruction Coordinator
NEW MEXICO STATE UNIVERSITY, LAS CRUCES NM
kmanuel@lib.nmsu.edu

Circumstances of the Instruction

This case-based, student-initiated, group activity asks students to develop, plan, and implement a search for information on the legislative histories of proposed or enacted legislation relating to copyright. Examples of legislation included are the *Sonny Bono Copyright Term Extension Act* and the *Consumer Broadband and Digital Television Promotion Act*. This activity has been used with students who have experience in basic search strategies and need an introduction either to researching legislative histories or to copyright law. It prompts students to appreciate more fully the relationships between civic responsibilities and information literacy.

Standard Five of the "Information Literacy Competency Standards for Higher Education" specifies that the "information literate student follows laws, regulations, institutional policies, and etiquette related to the access and use of information resources," as well as "[d]emonstrates an understanding of intellectual property, copyright, and fair use of copyrighted material." When copyright law is introduced to students in library and information literacy instruction, students are typically cautioned to abide by the copyright laws when using information. Students are thus introduced to the rights of copyright owners and their own fair use rights (Beck 2001; Bell 2001). Students are not typically introduced to copyright laws as constructed and contested documents, subject to variable interpretations, nor to the roles the politicians elected by voters play in creating copyright laws and confirming judges who interpret copyright laws.

A "legislative history" can be defined as (1) a chronological list of actions that has occurred on a measure or (2) a collection of documents produced as part of the bill's progress to enactment. A federal legislative history should address:

- the original and amended texts of the bill, as well as the timetables for the production of these texts;
- the occurrence and substance of any Congressional floor debates about the proposed legislation;
- the occurrence and content of any Congressional committee hearings, especially the positions taken by interest groups on these issues and their reasons for supporting these positions;
- the sponsors of the proposed legislation;
- the names and party affiliations of those who voted for and against the proposed legislation;

- the existence and content of committee reports and prints produced in relation to the proposed legislation;
- the "intent" of Congress in relation to this legislation; and
- any presidential statement accompanying the signing of the bill into law.

The types of information needed for compiling a legislative history can be found in various places, such as the proprietary database *Lexis-Nexis Congressional Universe,* the proprietary database *Westlaw,* the *Thomas* web site—http://thomas.loc.gov, and the *GPO Access* web site—http://www.gpoaccess.gov/bills/index.html. A number of good guides to finding legislative histories have been developed by various libraries and can be found online. These include:

- Brandeis University's *How to Find Legislative Histories,* http://www.brandeis.edu/departments/legal_studies/research/findleghistories.html,
- The University of Minnesota's *Finding Federal Legislative History,* http://www.law.umn.edu/library/tools/pathfinders/FederalLegislativeHistory.html, and
- Georgetown's *Research Guides: Legislative History,* http://www.ll.georgetown.edu/lib/guides/legislative_history.html.

Legislative histories are especially important to students' understanding of copyright laws as constructed documents by helping to contextualize the creation of these laws: who opposed and favored the laws, and why; contested issues in crafting the language of the law; and, especially, the "intent" of Congress in enacting these laws. Legislative histories help students realize that copyright laws are evolving efforts to deal with the rights and responsibilities of the users and owners of copyrighted materials, not static "givens."

Upper division undergraduates and graduate students are the intended audience for this activity, although it can be used with lower-division undergraduates provided that the instruction is more directive and focused. The number of items of proposed or enacted legislation used in the class can be determined by the number of students in the class. Student groups should consist of 3–5 students, although accommodating more students per group is possible, and at least 4–5 pieces of legislation should be researched per class. This makes the activity most suitable for classes of 12–25 students, or more.

This activity typically takes 75 minutes which can be spread over multiple class sessions. Sixty minutes of this time should be given to student groups for preparing and implementing their plans for retrieving this information. The additional 15 minutes can be spent on either preparing for or debriefing the session, depending upon whether a deductive or an inductive approach is taken to this part of the activity. In any case, the students should be asked to consider their own positions if they were authors of any work—musical, prose, poetry, or any video or audio medium—that was in peril of copyright infringement. The (student) author's position and the possible legal impact might vary considerably.

Objectives of the Instruction

After this instruction, students will be able to:

- identify and address key issues relating to copyright (fair use rights, first sale rights, the need to balance the rights of owners and users of copyrighted content, etc.);

- recognize the legislative history and intent of at least one key piece of recently proposed or enacted copyright legislation;

- appreciate the political and constructed nature of copyright legislation; and

- ideally, to persuade students to become more active participants in civic discussions regarding copyright.

Components of the Instruction

Preparation

This activity rests upon the choice of proposed or enacted legislation given to students as the basis for their explorations. Any proposed or enacted copyright legislation could be used, depending upon the points that the instructor wishes to make with the students. The following examples of proposed or enacted copyright legislation have, however, been used effectively with students on prior occasions.

- The No Electronic Theft Act of 1997, which made those sharing copyrighted files over peer-to-peer (P2P) networks liable for fines of up to $2,500 and prison terms of up to three years if the value of the files exceeds $2,500. Because so many of today's students have engaged in file-sharing, or have acquaintances that do, this piece of legislation generally resonates well with students. It is also provides a good vehicle for discussing the following points about copyright: (1) the balancing between the rights of the creators or owners of copyrighted content and the rights of users of this content, (2) the fact that copyright law has as its root objective "to promote the progress of science and useful arts," not to ensure profits for creators or owners of copyrighted content, (3) consumers' first sale rights, and (4) the role of technology in protecting and violating copyrights.

- Sonny Bono Copyright Term Extension Act of 1998. The CTEA is a good entrée to discussions of the public domain and the "limited times" specified for copyright protections in the Constitution. Originally, copyright protections in the United States lasted for a maximum of 28 years; under CTEA, copyright protections can last for the life of the creator plus 70 years.

Additional examples can be found listed in the Supplementary Materials for this lesson plan.

Once the legislation to be researched has been selected, note the name of each piece of legislation upon a differently colored index card, so that students can be randomly assigned to a group based upon the color of their cards.

Students should also be given an activity sheet asking them to record key pieces of the legislative history relating to their bill. Specifically, each group should be prompted to record (see Supplementary Materials):
- the purpose and effect of the legislation;
- who supported the legislation and why;
- who opposed the legislation and why;
- the language used in the legislation; and
- the margin(s) by which votes on the legislation were decided.

Students will work together to complete the activity sheet. They should be reminded of this—and asked to come up with their own plan for subdividing the work within their group.

Presentation

This activity can be used in presentations introducing students to either
    (1) copyright or
    (2) legislative histories.
When the focus is on copyright, legislative histories are used to introduce students to the real complexities surrounding copyright laws. Conversely, when the focus in on legislative histories, the example of copyright laws is used to introduce students to the processes of researching and compiling legislative histories.

The presentation can be either deductive or inductive in approach. With a deductive approach, students are introduced either to the basics of copyright law or to methods for researching and compiling legislative histories. Students then work in groups to explore the details of copyright law while researching and compiling a legislative history.

With an inductive approach, students are first asked to research and compile a legislative history of proposed or enacted copyright legislation. After they have worked on doing so, the instructor then highlights the key points of copyright law based on the legislative histories students compiled and/or demonstrates how students could complete legislative history research more efficiently and effectively. The latter approach works particularly well with student groups known, or strongly suspected, of being resistant to library instruction on the grounds that they "already know all that."

Hands-on Activity

The hands-on component of this activity consists of students compiling legislative histories for proposed or enacted copyright laws. Students will need to work together to complete the activity sheet. They should be reminded of this—and asked to come up with their own plan for subdividing the work within their group.

Evaluation

A one-minute paper serves as a very effective evaluation mechanism for this assignment. Students can be asked to write for 60 seconds, or perhaps a little longer, on the most important thing they learned from this session, as well as the thing that is most unclear to them. Frequency counts of the number of students making particular comments on these one-minute papers can then be used to track how well students learned the materials as well as to cue the instructor to any modifications that should be made to the activity prior to future presentations.

The following multiple-choice question also works well, provided that students are required to explain their answer after making their choice:

Copyright _____

_____.

    a. protects movies, songs, computer software & architecture, and photographs
    b. protects ideas, facts, systems or methods of operation
    c. requires registration or notice that a work is copyrighted
    d. all of the above

Explain your answer:

Supplementary Materials

The materials in this section have been placed on the accompanying disk so they can easily be copied and/or modified to fit the needs of individual libraries and instructors.

- **Additional Examples for Use with the Copyright Legislative Histories Activity**

- **Legislative histories worksheet**

- **Congressional Universe handout**

References

ACRL Task Force on Information Literacy Standards. "Information Literacy: Competency Standards for Higher Education." *College & Research Libraries News* 61.3 (2000): 207–215.

Beck, Susan E. 2001. Hey, that's no fair! Copyright and fair use case studies. In Trudi E. Jacobson and Timothy H. Gatti, eds., *Teaching information literacy concepts: Activities and frameworks from the field* (pp. 245–247). Pittsburgh, PA: Library Instruction Publications.

Bell, Colleen. 2001. From ethics to copyright law: Protecting intellectual property in the 21st century. In Trudi E. Jacobson and Timothy H. Gatti, eds., *Teaching information literacy concepts: Activities and frameworks from the field* (pp. 249–254). Pittsburgh, PA: Library Instruction Publications.

Ethics of "Real World" Information Seeking & Use

KATE MANUEL

Instruction Coordinator
NEW MEXICO STATE UNIVERSITY, LAS CRUCES NM
kmanuel@lib.nmsu.edu

Circumstances of the Instruction

This lesson focuses upon non-library information seeking strategies that students, particularly business majors, may encounter on the job. It presents them with case studies of actual corporate information seeking strategies (case based activities) and asks them to work in groups (group activities) to explore the ethical implications of these information-seeking strategies. Examples include Avon going through the garbage its competitor, Mary Kay, left in trash bins on public property looking for notes, reports, and memos, and Reuters correctly guessing the URL at which Intentia, a Swedish software company, had posted a financial statement that had not yet been made public. It forces students to engage with multiple types and formats of information, as well as with various ethical and legal issues relating to information.

Standard Five of the "Information Literacy Competency Standards for Higher Education" specifies that the "information literate student follows laws, regulations, institutional policies, and etiquette related to the access and use of information resources," and there are many ethically ambiguous situations in information seeking and use—especially in non-library settings.

This activity can easily be used with any level or number of students and can be completed in as little as 30 minutes.

Objectives of the Instruction

After this instruction, students will be able to:

- describe various ethical and legal standards governing ethical seeking and use of information;

- identify and discuss varied formulations of "ethics" in relation to information seeking and use; and

- recognize potential disjunctions between "ethical" and "legal" considerations in relation to information seeking and use.

Components of the Instruction

Preparation

Students are given individual copies of worksheets describing various "real world" scenarios relating to ethical and legal issues in information seeking and use. Seven scenarios are given on the worksheet included in the Supplementary Materials for this section. Additional scenarios—perhaps based on the discipline-specific needs of students in the instruction session—could be constructed. It is worth noting that all the scenarios used on the worksheet in the Supplementary Materials are taken from "real world" situations. Using "real world" scenarios in this activity is important; being able to point to actual companies in which these situations occurred heightens students' perceptions of the authenticity and relevance of the ethical concerns being introduced to them. Books on competitive intelligence are excellent sources of "real world" situations relating to the ethical use of information.

Presentation

Open the instruction session by asking students what, if anything, they have been told about the ethical use of information. Most students will mention having been told about plagiarism and, perhaps, copyright—but few other concerns in the ethical seeking and use of information.

Give students the worksheet, asking them to discuss their thoughts on whether the information seeking and information use scenarios presented on it are ethical and legal— and justify their answers. Reassure students that they are not expected to know the answers; they are being asked to give their basic reactions to these scenarios and their reasons for these reactions. Students are to work in groups, comparing their reactions and reasons with those of others in their group, eventually coming to a group consensus on the answers.

Once the student groups have completed their discussions, go over the scenarios in class, asking students for their answers and explaining the "correct" answers. It is very important here to discuss with students the "real world" situations from which the scenarios were taken. In many of these scenarios, the information seeking and use described is, technically, legal. Whether the information seeking and use described is ethical is another question, however!

Minds-on Activity

The minds-on component of this activity consists of students debating the legal and ethical propriety of certain scenarios in information seeking and use.

Scenario I: Happens frequently in real-life, as emails are so easily forwarded from their recipients to other people. The copyright to an email belongs to the sender of the email, and any recipient forwarding email has, at the least, infringed the sender's copyrights. Most students have said this is **NOT** ethical.

Scenario II. Happened in real-life. Concerned that Anheuser-Busch was going to make a push into its Rocky Mountain market, Coor's studied Environmental Protection Agency (EPA) filings on wastewater discharge from Anheuser-Busch's Denver-area plants. Perfectly legal: Many government documents, including EPA filings, are available at depository libraries for any who want to examine them. Perfectly ethical, although it may feel like "spying" to some.

Scenario III. Happened in real-life. Avon, a cosmetics company, hired private investigators to go through garbage its competitor, Mary Kay, left in trash bins on public property, looking for notes, reports, and memos. Perfectly legal: Trash left on public property is considered abandoned; it can be picked up and examined by anyone who wants to do so. Feels unethical, as well as illegal, to most students.

Scenario IV. Happened in real-life. Marriott, a hotel company, hired an executive search firm to help it collect information about the economy hotel business. A search firm arranged interviews with managers from companies already in the economy hotel business, holding out the prospect of jobs that *might* be available in the future. The firm thus obtained information about the economy hotel business that it could not have gotten otherwise; no interviewees got jobs. Perfectly legal: Many job interviews find only flawed candidates, none of whom are given the job. Seems unethical to most people confronted with this scenario.

Scenario V. Happened in real-life. From 1987 to 1989, France's equivalent to the U.S. Central Intelligence Agency—the Direction Générale de la Sécuriète Extériere—spied on IBM, Texas Instruments, and other American companies, turning their information directly over to competing French companies. Legal: The French spying, while illegal by U.S. standards, is perfectly legal under French law. Many students have, interestingly, suggested this was ethical because it involved a country looking out for its citizens' economic interests.

Scenario VI. Happens often in real life. In most states, it is perfectly legal for employers to monitor their employees' conduct in the workplace. California is the only state to have systematically given workers rights such that they cannot be subject to employer monitoring without their knowledge. In other states, union contracts may give some workers in some settings protection. Usually sparks heated debate as to whether it is ethical. Some students take the employers' view, while others take the employees' view.

Scenario VII. Happened in real life. A reporter for Reuters was able to obtain Intentia's (a Swedish software company) third quarter 2002 financial results by "guessing" at the URL at which they would be made available before this page was linked to the main Intentia site and the financial results were released to the public. Intentia is alleging criminal wrongdoing and violation of its intellectual property rights/copyrights. No definitive judgment as to the legality of this action has been made. Usually sparks heated debate as to whether it is ethical.

In a longer session, it is worth introducing students to why ethical and legal considerations in information seeking and use matter by giving examples of corporate liability for workers' "failures" to abide by ethical and legal norms for information seeking and use.

Most jobs are now information-intensive: "Today's employees spend an average of 9.5 hours a week obtaining, reviewing, and analyzing information" (Corcoran & Stratigos 2001). Workers are increasingly being held responsible for the accuracy, completeness, objectivity, and relevance of information used by them or supplied to others. Banks, attorneys, doctors, and even city councils have all been held legally liable for their failure to seek relevant information or their supplying of incorrect information to others:

- In the case of Hedley Byrne & Co. Ltd v. Heller & Partners Ltd., an advertising agency successfully sued a bank for giving them a misleading credit reference about a potential client,
- In the case of Smith v. Lewis, an attorney was held responsible for failure to conduct a database search to find additional cases relevant to his client's,
- In Harbeson v. Parke Davis, doctors were punished for their failure to conduct a thorough literature search, resulting in their ignorance of the side effects of a drug prescribed to a pregnant woman, and
- In L. Shaddock & Associates Pty. Ltd. v. Parrametta City Council, the Council was held liable for damages for the financial losses suffered by companies to which it had supplied erroneous information (Pickett & Craig 1993).

Dun & Bradstreet v. Greenmoss Builders is particularly notable among such cases. Greenmoss Builders sued Dun & Bradstreet when Dun & Bradstreet erroneously reported that Greenmoss Builders had filed for bankruptcy. Greenmoss Builders sought – and was awarded – punitive and compensatory damages, successfully claiming that they had been victims of defamation because of Dun & Bradstreet's negligence and recklessness. Interestingly, the person responsible for the error at Dun & Bradstreet was a student worker, who had mistaken a filing for bankruptcy by one of Greenmoss Builders' employees for a filing for bankruptcy by the company itself.

Nor are legal judgments the only consequences of workers' using "bad" information. French police once shot a law-abiding citizen when a database failed to record that a stolen car had, in fact, been recovered and sold (Zwass 1996, 184), while erroneous instructions on an aeronautical chart caused the crash of an airplane into a mountain. The plane's entire crew was killed, the plane was destroyed, and the company that sold the chart ended up paying $12,000,000 in damages (Brocklesby v. Jeppesen) – even though they had not created the erroneous information, merely re-packaged and sold it (Dragich 1989, 270).

Evaluation

A one-minute paper serves as a very effective evaluation mechanism for this assignment. Students can be asked to write for 60 seconds, or perhaps a little longer, on the most important thing they learned from this session, as well as the thing that is most unclear to them. Frequency counts of the number of students making particular comments on these one-minute papers can then be used to track how well students learned the materials as well as to cue the instructor to any modifications that should be made to the activity prior to future presentations.

Supplementary Material

The material in this section has been placed on the accompanying disk so it can easily be copied and/or modified to fit the needs of individual libraries and instructors.

- **Information Ethics: Is It Ethical? Worksheet**

References

ACRL Task Force on Information Literacy Standards. "Information Literacy: Competency Standards for Higher Education." *College & Research Libraries News* 61.3 (2000): 207–215.

Corcoran, Mary and Anthea Stratigos. 2001. *Knowledge management: It's all about behavior.* Information About Information Briefing. Burlingame, CA: Outsell, Inc.

Delio, Michelle. 2002, Oct. 30. Rooting around site with intent? *Wired News.* Available at http://www.wired.com/news/print/0,1294,56079,00.html.

Dragich, Martha J. 1989, Sept. Information malpractice: Some thoughts on the potential liability of information professionals. *Information Technology and Libraries,* pp. 265–272.

Kahaner, Larry. 1996. *Competitive intelligence: From black ops to boardrooms – how businesses gather, analyze, and use information to succeed in the global marketplace.* New York: Simon & Schuster.

Orton, James Douglas. 2002. Manufacturing social responsibility benchmarks in the competitive intelligence age. In Ali Salehnia, ed., *Ethical issues of information systems* (pp. 215–231). Hershey, PA: IRM Press.

Pickett, Marianne and James Pat Craig. 1993. Information malpractice. *Encyclopedia of library and information science* (Vol. 15, pp. 141–166). New York: M. Dekker, 1968–.

Zwass, Vladimir. 1996. Ethical issues in information systems. *Encyclopedia of library and information science* (Vol. 57, pp. 175–195). New York: M. Dekker, 1968–.

Notes:

Critically Thinking about the News

DEBORAH BERNNARD

User Education Librarian and Information Science Bibliographer
UNIVERSITY AT ALBANY, STATE UNIVERSITY OF NEW YORK
dbernnard@uamail.albany.edu

Circumstances of the Instruction

Students are often unaware that the news can be slanted to influence the public's perception of events and/or people. This exercise is designed to encourage students to read and listen to news stories critically, with an eye and ear toward distinguishing between the actual facts that are reported and the ways in which the facts are reported. All information is presented with a bias. If students are able to winnow facts from bias when reading or listening to news stories, they will be better equipped to form their own opinions about newsworthy events and will not be as susceptible to media manipulation.

This activity is suited for any size class. The lesson plan includes a homework assignment that students should work on individually. The activity will work with any level student, but is aimed at high school and lower-level undergraduate students who are beginning to become regular consumers of news.

Objectives of the Instruction

Students will:
- analyze words to determine positive or negative connotations associated with them;
- compare descriptions of an event to determine how names and titles are manipulated in order to influence readers' perceptions of the event;
- evaluate the overall bias of a news publication by carefully examining a selection of stories published by the news organization; and
- critically examine news to differentiate fact from bias.

Components of the Instruction

Preparation

Prior to this class, the instructor should obtain one newspaper story on the same subject from three different newspapers. These newspapers should each have a different bias. Three that work well together are *The New York Times*, The *Wall Street Journal,* and the *Houston Chronicle*. Try to pick a controversial topic that has engendered vocal support as well as opposition. The topic, Same Sex Marriage, works well. Provide a photocopy of all three newspaper stories for each student. Obtain a bias rating scale (see Supplementary Materials).

In-class Activity

Ask the students to read each of the newspaper stories. After each story is read, students should write a brief, one to three sentence summary of the story. Ask the students to then record their opinion on how biased the story is on the bias rating scale.

When they are done rating all three newspaper stories, pair each student with a partner. The partners should read each other's summaries and determine whether or not each student emphasized the same points. Next, have the partners compare their bias ratings. Regardless of whether or not the ratings are similar, students should discuss their reasons for giving the rating.

Choose a few pairs of students to report to the class how they rated their stories and why. At this point, the instructor should point out any evidence of bias that the students may have missed. For example, Are there facts included in one or more of the newspaper stories that are left out of one of the other stories? If a crowd of people is described in a story, does the author describe it as "less than 100 people," "a crowd of 100 people," or "approximately 100 people." Titles that authors assign to people also can denote bias. For example, does the author refer to George W. Bush as Mr. Bush or President Bush? Remind students to pay attention to adjectives because they offer strong clues about the bias of the author.

Homework Assignment

Each student must choose one newspaper to read daily for a week. This can be a hometown newspaper, a regional newspaper, or a national newspaper. Students don't have to read the paper cover to cover, but should pay particular attention to the paper's front page, and its opinion page. Provide each student with the newspaper evaluation worksheet (see Supplementary Materials). This will help each student determine the overall bias of the newspaper.

At the end of the week, students will write a one page essay in which they identify the overall bias of their newspaper and support their findings with specific instances of bias that they found. Alternatively, students can watch the same news program on television every night for a week and write about the bias of the program.

Evaluation

The primary tool for assessment of this lesson is the homework assignment. Students should be able to identify and document at least 7–15 separate instances of bias in their newspapers over the course of a week. These instances should include headlines, story placement, and descriptive adjectives. Ideally students will find other instances of bias that fall outside the parameters of the assignment. This will indicate that they are applying critical thinking skills to their reading.

Supplementary Materials

The materials in this section have been placed on the accompanying disk so they can easily be copied and/or modified to fit the needs of individual libraries and instructors.

- **Bias Awareness Worksheet**

- **Newspaper Bias Scale**

Notes:

"Reading" Texts—Connecting to Research through Art and Artifacts: A Course-Integrated Information Literacy Lesson Plan

DEBORAH M. LAFOND
Social Sciences Bibliographer
UNIVERSITY AT ALBANY, STATE UNIVERSITY OF NEW YORK
dlafonde@albany.edu

Circumstances of the Instruction

Why is content important?

Content conveys meaning across all media and disciplines. The interactive nature of art offers metaphors for learning and can provide possibilities for domain (knowledge) transfer: a conceptual bridge based upon something previously learned or understood can provide a framework to acquire new and different information. In this lesson plan, the use of art imagery is offered as a language to communicate research process.

How can we integrate diversity into curriculum development, particularly within information literacy assignments? How is marginalized experience included or excluded within texts and how can students learn to search for information on under-documented groups? The goal of this lesson plan is to explore methods of creative integration of course content using multiple literacies while offering an environment to explore diverse learning styles.

The subject of African American quilts has only recently been considered worthy of academic interest. Why this is so, and how this development has occurred, relates to the social dimension of information. The development of this scholarship, taken as a subject for information literacy instruction, provides a multi-dimensional case intersecting a variety of personal and cultural knowledge, social movements, and disciplinary traditions. Students who have little or no knowledge of this art or scholarship will have an opportunity to interact with the visual representations of African American quilts, and quilt scholarship, and consider how this development could relate to their own research. This class uses an active learning exercise to encourage interaction with these "visual" texts before the images themselves are discussed.

This lesson plan combines group, case-based, and de-bunking activities. It draws on literacy skills students may already possess and encourages research on under-represented groups, as well as offering an opportunity to integrate new and existing skills. The lesson plan focus is interdisciplinary in nature and could potentially be adapted for instruction in a variety of specializations such as Africana studies, women's studies, art, history, psychology, and many other disciplines.

Although students today are accustomed to highly visual information sources, their understanding of what information is can be enhanced through a broader, more integrated visual focus. Examining text in a variety of formats, whether it be digital or physical, public exhibit space, or printed scholarship on art and culture is relevant to research today—particularly with the emphasis on primary source documents required for research.

Investigating developments in scholarship allows students to see how personal and/or community experience can grow into scholarly dialogue. It also conveys to students how art artifacts can be viewed as primary texts and how the development of this particular area of art and scholarship has occurred. This approach encourages the researcher to consider artifacts of significance from their own experience or community. Students are asked to imagine themselves as potential authors who must consider their experience within the process of scholarship.

By interacting with texts and investigating examples of art scholarship on African American quilts, students are to reflect on the research process—how information literacy principles can assist them in translating their query into a research strategy. The class exercises emphasize how a variety of research tools can assist in the interpretation and analysis of the artistic intention and the artifact itself. Group brainstorming exercises and a review of relevant resources follow the first approach to the material.

The assignment is based on a physical exhibit at the University at Albany Library: "Threads of Scholarship: History and Storytelling in African American Quilts."[1] This permanent exhibit includes a variety of stunning mounted posters on the walls of the Main Library Periodicals Room. The posters are colorful, enlarged photographs representing African American quilts (with docent notes descriptions). Examples of how researchers have used a variety of primary source documents will be discussed.

Sources contained in the exhibit have been cited in the accompanying bibliography (see Supplementary Materials); visual representations of these same quilts are found in books and on the Internet. This lesson plan could expand to include a class project exhibit that includes scholarly resources.

Time for one class: 80 minutes; the ideal is two class periods of 50 minutes each.
Number of students: 5–25 students.
Level: undergraduate or graduate.

---

[1] The theme and exhibit "Threads of Scholarship: History and Storytelling in African American Quilts" and a related 2001 symposium were created and developed by Deborah M. LaFond, Gerald Burke and Brenda Hazard. University Libraries, University at Albany.
<http://www.albany.edu/~dlafonde/women/threadsbibmay.htm>

Objectives of the Instruction

After this instructional session, students should be able to:

- experience less research anxiety by modeling methods of how research questions are formed. Students will generate questions based upon their experience and then formulate research questions using metaphors from their own experience.

- consider relationships between social theories and texts. Students will gain insight into how theoretical frameworks represent past research, conversations, dialogue, and critique. Students will also have an example of how multiple frameworks can be used to develop a research design.

- draw upon and extend their comfort and familiarity with visual texts as a platform to more effectively interrogate, explore, and evaluate multiple texts. Students will be able to consider the broader concept of "text" that includes multiple literacies—art, artifacts, media, print, electronic resources, etc.

- appreciate their insight into the social nature of knowledge creation and will consider how different experiences are valued or discounted.

- understand that diversity enhances research projects; that this focus should not only be addressed only through "diversity courses," but can be integrated to create richer research projects.

- begin to understand components of research cycles (questioning, planning, gathering, sorting and sifting, synthesizing, evaluating, reporting) but will focus specifically on the development of research questions.

- develop problem-solving and decision-making skills. Students will begin to explore key concepts related to an existing body of research and will explore catalogs, databases, and reference sources. Based upon the work of this session, students will identify problems or strategies they foresee for future study and suggest next steps.

- consider their personal connection to their scholarship from the instructor highlighting the importance of personal experience to scholarship and they will be affirmed for recognition.

Components of the Instruction

Instructor Preparation

Organize and prepare instructions for interactive exercise, recitation, discussion, printed handouts, URLs, and guides that include contact information and office hours. Remind the classroom instructor to inform students of the upcoming class scheduled to meet in the library. (Reserve the space for 80 minutes.)

Class Plan

Introduction of the librarian and the class session.
The class introduction includes why the exhibit is here and an explanation of how it was developed. Include an explanation and examples on the discussion and debates of various community or individual agencies within research methodology. Assign numbers to representations of quilts and provide a list of the quilts with numbers. Assign individual students to specific poster images or ask them to count off 1–5 for group interaction.

Instruction to the students.
Based upon your quilt number, please write your assigned number of poster image on your worksheet and begin the "In-Class Assignment" Worksheet (see Supplementary Materials). Allow 15 minutes for this exercise.

After the class assignment is completed, invite participation from students, calling for volunteers. Provide 15 minutes for this discussion. If you need to prompt students, you might ask, "Who will volunteer to share their answers from questions 1 and 2?" Encourage 2–3 students to bring the class to the reviewed poster images in order to share personal reactions. Encourage students to brainstorm on the last question; they don't have to defend their ideas.

Now, have students go back to the sections of the Worksheet they wanted to know more about. From that section, have them make a brief list of 3–4 keywords. Five minutes should be sufficient. Gather search terms and ask for student volunteers to add to the dry-erase board. To bring in the scholarship component, provide two to three examples of theories related to the development of quilt scholarship from a variety of disciplines. Examples:

    Sociology—Patricia Hill Collins, "Everyday Theory"
    English/Folklore—Gladys-Marie Fry
    Art History—Maude S. Wahlman or Faith Ringgold

After students have some keywords and scholarship, provide an overview of the online catalog and databases so students can pursue their topics for the take-home assignment. Distribute the handout on online resources (see Supplementary Materials).

Evaluation

Have students complete the Evaluation handout (see Supplementary Materials). Collect these to review their thoughts on the class. Provide 10 minutes for students to discuss how they evaluate the success of the activities.

Coordinate with the classroom instructor to assign the take-home assignment, "Creating a Class Bibliography." You will need to negotiate grading since these are emailed directly to the librarian who will evaluate what students have learned from the session.

Supplementary Materials

The materials in this section have been placed on the accompanying disk so they can easily be copied and/or modified to fit the needs of individual libraries and instructors.

- **In-class Assignment: Reading Visual Texts: Self-Reflective and Group Exercise**

- **Evaluation**

- **Take-Home Assignment: Creating a Class Bibliography**

- **Bibliography**

Notes:

Section 3—Librarian-Led Activities

"Evaluating Your Search Results: On the Road to the Good Stuff"

International Business Research: Defining Information Needs

Empowering Student Groups with Games

Developing Keywords

Internet Sources versus Subscription Sources

Know Your Library Treasures

The Why, When and How of Citing Sources Using *MLA*

Draw the Internet

Notes:

"Evaluating Your Search Results: On the Road to the Good Stuff"

STEPHANIE STERLING BRASLEY

Information Literacy Coordinator
UCLA, COLLEGE LIBRARY
sbrasley@library.ucla.edu

Circumstances of the Instruction

When searching online resources for books, articles, and other information, undergraduate students are often tempted to select the first few sources, or only those citations that contain the full-text. Librarians endeavor to teach students to evaluate materials in terms of currency, accuracy, point of view, coverage, authorship, and intended audience to assess relevance to fulfill an information need. This exercise enhances students' critical thinking skills as they develop approaches to evaluating items without the need to have the materials in hand. It engages them in the critical, but often overlooked, step of evaluating their initial results in a meaningful way instead of selecting the first few they view. Furthermore, it requires that they articulate why they are selecting particular items.

For this information literacy session, the librarian teaches students how to search for information using either online databases or online public access catalogs (OPACs). Within the exercise, the library instructor focuses on having students evaluate their initial search results using criteria listed on the brief and full records. For example, in the **brief records display**, students would assess potential usefulness of the source by reviewing the author, title, publication information, date, journal name, and other fields.

In the **detailed record display**, information from the notes, abstracts, and subject headings fields should be examined. Using the information provided in the online display, students make the first determination of relevance. Teaching students to evaluate their search results taps into the higher order cognitive skills needed to locate, evaluate, and use information effectively.

This exercise can be used with all levels of undergraduates. The activity may take 10–20 minutes, depending upon the amount of time given for the feedback segment. Several options are offered for eliciting feedback for this activity. All, however, require students to examine their initial search results and to use information from the bibliographic record to assess whether they have enough relevant items to proceed to the next step in the research process or whether they need to revise their search strategy.

The exercise works best in an electronic classroom where students can perform online searches along with the instructor and where students can easily view their results. It may be conducted with large or small groups; however, 20–25 students enable the librarian to receive more feedback from the group.

Objectives of the Instruction

Students will be able to:

- identify the components of a book or article citation that might be used to evaluate its relevance;

- assess the relevance of items from a list, applying some or all of the following criteria—currency, accuracy, authorship, intended audience, point-of-view, language, material or document type, and coverage; and

- analyze the results from a search for books or articles to select the most relevant from the list.

Components of the Instruction

Preparation

The information literacy librarian should identify a sample topic and prepare a search statement for it, based on the IL session content.

- Sample Topic: moral and ethical considerations of human cloning
- Sample Search Statement: human cloning and ethical
  (Note: The actual search statement typed in will depend on the search conventions of the database/OPAC used).

Identify the online database or catalog to be searched and test the search prior to the IL session to ensure that students have an adequate list from which to select the most relevant. This exercise works best after students have been taught: (1) how to narrow or broaden their topics for an effective research question; (2) how to develop an effective search statement using keywords and synonyms from their research question; and (3) how to apply useful search techniques such as Boolean operators and truncation to their searches.

Hands-on Activity

Give students the topic and search statement to enter into an online database or catalog. As a class, perform the search. Students may conduct the searches individually or this may be done as a group exercise. Ask students to carefully review the first screen or first 10–15 results. Let them know that you will ask them which items they would choose for a paper on the given topic and why. Give them 2–4 minutes to peruse the results and instruct them to select at least one citation. The exercise may be completed with or without the accompanying worksheet (see Supplementary Material).

Depending upon the teaching style of the librarian and the information literacy proficiency level of the students, this activity can be implemented in one of two ways discussed here.

If students have had minimal prior exposure to conducting research and have basic or below basic knowledge of searching and interpreting records in electronic resources, the librarian may elect to model the evaluation exercise pointing out some basic features that students might want to consider when evaluating their results.

EXAMPLE:

⌐

1.

Peters, Ted, 1941– Playing God? : genetic determinism and human freedom / Ted Peters. 2003.
(Full Record)

⌐

2.

Clonación humana / Fernando Cano Valle, coordinador. 2003.
(Full Record)

⌐

3.

Biomedical ethics: opposing viewpoints / Roman Espejo, book editor. c2003.
(Full Record)

The librarian may want to begin by asking questions about elements in the record so students learn about relevance. If students are struggling, ask guided questions such as:
- "Does the title give you a sense of whether this might be good for your paper?" or
- "The second source is written in Spanish. Would you choose that book? Why or why not?"

After guiding the students with some basic prompts, allow them to explore other elements of the record that provide more information.

If students have basic or above basic information literacy competency and the librarian feels comfortable using a discovery-based instructional approach, allow the students to conduct the search and complete the worksheet (see Supplementary Material) without first modeling possible evaluative features.

Feedback Segment

The librarian can organize the sharing segment in a variety of ways, depending on the amount of time allotted.

1. Go over each item on the first screen or the first 10–15 results and ask students if they would select those items. Ask for specifics on why they would choose the item—e.g., the title, date, publisher, name of journal, etc.

2. Ask several students at random which item they selected and why. As an alternative approach, select an item from the list and ask students why they did not choose it. By discussing both the positive and negative reasons for selecting or discarding an item, it expands the students' ability to recognize elements of the record that will facilitate their selection of the most relevant items. Also, asking students to verbalize their choices creates a stronger student-centered learning environment conducive to different learning styles.

3. Conduct this idea as a group activity. Break students into groups prior to beginning the search. Have them complete the worksheet with at least two citations and their rationale. Have a spokesperson present the items selected by the group and their justification.

4. As students are conducting their searches and perusing results, the librarian roves and observes the students' actions. S/he selects individuals or teams to demonstrate their evaluation process to the class. This approach allows the librarian to point out noteworthy aspects of the students' search and evaluation process. (Special thanks to Alice Kawakami, UCLA College Library for this approach).

Regardless of the strategy selected, all permit the librarian to provide guided feedback to students about the elements of the online record that can be used to help students evaluate their results. At this point, if students are consistently looking only at the author, title and date of publication, via questioning techniques or direct lecture, the librarian can introduce other record elements that can help the students select relevant sources. These include subject headings/descriptors, a bibliography, the name of the particular magazine/journal/newspaper or edited work for an article or book chapter respectively, article length, availability of an item, etc.

Evaluation

The librarian will know if students understand how to evaluate their results at the initial search result level by looking at the items they select for a paper on that topic and by listening carefully to their process for selecting or deselecting items. As a summary activity, ask students to call out all of the parts of a record or information contained in an online record from which they can evaluate an item. If the worksheet is used, ask them what record elements they used to select their citations. Also ask them to recount additional elements they now think are important to examine when deciding whether an item is relevant to their information need.

Supplementary Material

The material in this section has been placed on the accompanying disk so it can easily be copied and/or modified to fit the needs of individual libraries and instructors.

- **Exercise Worksheet—"Evaluating Your Search Results: On the Road to the Good Stuff"**

Notes:

International Business Research: Defining Information Needs

CHRISTOPHER FRASIER

Reference/Instruction Librarian
WESTFIELD STATE COLLEGE, WESTFIELD MA
cfrasier@wsc.ma.edu

Circumstances of Instruction

Students enrolled in International Business at Westfield State College are required to complete a term project which requires them to choose a U.S. based Fortune 500 company and design a proposal or feasibility study for setting the company up in a foreign country of their choice. Their report is expected to include an analysis of the company, as well as a thorough study of the market they hope to enter. This analysis should ideally touch on issues of demographics, economics, legal environments, cultural gaps, infrastructure, etc.

Early in the semester, students visit the library for a one-shot instruction session specifically related to the term project. The session ranges from 50 to 75 minutes depending on semester scheduling. With so much area to cover in a very limited amount of time, certain assumptions are made of the students' knowledge of the library. Since this is an upper-level college course, there is an expectation that students have been in the library for instruction in one of their earlier business courses and have some experience researching basic company information. This assumption (admittedly not always accurate) provides the ability to focus the session on retrieving information about their intended market.

Before introducing the lesson plan described below, a number of different approaches had been used with these classes over time, each with a focus on introducing students to standard resources in the field of international business research. However, it seemed that students tended to gravitate toward the three or four sources specifically mentioned during the session and spent little time with the others mentioned in their handouts or in searching alternatives on their own. It also appeared as though few had a thorough understanding of the type or amount of research required for such a project. This seemed to be due to the fact that few had taken the time to think about and write down what it was they needed to address and include in their proposal. As such, the objectives for the session were redefined and the lesson plan revamped.

Objectives of the Instruction

Following this instruction session students will be able to:
- determine and define their information need for a given set of circumstances;

- appreciate the variety of resources available and recognize the distinctions between them;

- evaluate these sources as to their usefulness, relevance, currency, scope, etc.; and

- access and retrieve relevant information from business research sources.

Components of the Instruction

Preparation

As always, it is a good idea to speak with the professor in advance of the session to get a feel for where the students are in the course of their project, as well as to get a general idea of the skill level of the group. Much of the preparation involved with this lesson plan deals with creating the resource lists and worksheets the students use throughout the session.

Students are provided with a list of reference sources the library owns on international business, as well as a similar list of web-based resources. The reference resources usually include print reference books, as well as subscription databases, while the web resources focus primarily on freely available web sites providing relevant content. It is helpful to divide each list into sub-categories and annotations should be included which briefly describe the content and scope of each resource. The students will rely heavily on these annotations during the hands-on portion of the session.

The worksheet is fairly simple and straightforward, consisting of brief instructions and two columns of numbered blank lines, one labeled **Information Need** and the other **Source**. In instances where there is extra time, additional exercises can be created to refresh students on their company search skills, or cultivate their "data-mining" abilities (see Supplementary Materials).

Presentation (5–10 minutes)

After greetings and introductions, it is helpful to ask the students to describe the project and its requirements. Having students explain the assignment in their own words provides insight into their view of the assignment. If there are any misunderstandings, this enables the information literacy librarian and/or instructor to clarify the project so all students are on the same page. It also creates a natural segue into the conversation regarding information needs, and can be useful in reinforcing the fact that the session is specifically related to their project and is therefore of immediate value.

Hands-on Activity

As a group, the instructor and students briefly go over the instructions on the worksheet as well as the expectations of the forthcoming discussion. From there, students are asked to brainstorm, as a class, a list of issues/items they should consider in constructing their proposal/report. At this point the instructor takes on the role of moderator, eliciting responses from the students and helping to refine vague or general responses into specific information needs. This may include asking leading questions, providing gentle prodding, questioning students as to why a given issue is important and how it fits into their report, and creating links between related issues. As issues are accepted by the class, they are printed on the board/screen and students enter them in the **Information Need** column on the worksheet (10–15 minutes).

Once the **Information Need** column is filled in, students are asked to consult the resource lists and choose a source that they believe will best provide information for items in the **Information Need** column. Since the term project is group-based, students will often break up into their project groups to complete this portion of the activity. The instructor serves more or less as a proctor at this point, keeping students on track, answering any questions, and where needed, guiding students in the appropriate direction (10–15 minutes).

When the worksheet is completed, students are asked to regroup as a class. The instructor leads a discussion about the previous exercise and takes questions from the class. This allows the student groups to swap notes, and fill in any holes they may have left in their worksheet. It also allows for guidance on the part of the instructor toward more useful sources (5–10 minutes).

For those sessions where time allows, an alternate exercise may follow which can be used to build upon students' skills in company research, or work on their ability to pull relevant information out of useful, but underutilized resources (see Supplementary Materials) (15–20 minutes).

Desired Outcomes

Students leave the session with a tangible product or result — their list of information needs and corresponding sources. This list can be useful as a guide or outline when they begin their actual research for the report. They have also spent a good amount of time critically thinking about the information they need to include in that report and evaluating various sources in which that information might be found. They have defined the scope of their research, and have hopefully created a path or direction for their further research, as well as an awareness of where to look for specific types of information. These are all skills which will serve them well throughout their careers as lifelong learners.

Evaluation

Due to the nature of the activity, and since this is a one-shot session, there is little in the way of formal evaluation or assessment. Assessment in these instances is largely anecdotal and reliant on student and professor feedback, as well as any subsequent reference interactions with students working on the project.

However, the possibility does exist for the professor and instructor to collaborate on a post-instruction quiz to be taken by students in a future class meeting which would help to measure if the objectives for the session had been met. There has been an increase in requests for this type of one-shot assessment in recent semesters and it is an encouraging trend. Such a quiz might necessitate slight changes in the lesson plan however, in order to create tangibly "quizzable" material, since much of the class focuses on critical thinking and evaluation.

Supplementary Materials

The materials in this section have been placed on the accompanying disk so they can easily be copied and/or modified to fit the needs of individual libraries and instructors.

- **Primary Worksheet**

- **Additional Exercises**

Recommended Resources

Print sources available will differ from library to library, but reference lists should include titles that deal with foreign trade statistics, cultural surveys, almanacs, business encyclopedias, industry studies, and international demographics. Particularly useful titles include those of the Library of Congress's *Country Studies* series, the *CIA World Fact Book*, and *Foreign Trade of the United States* published by Bernan Press.

Reference lists should also include any relevant databases to which the library subscribes. EBSCO's *Business Source Premier* and Gale's *General Business File ASAP* both provide in-depth country profiles and economic summaries, as well access to hundreds of trade journals whose articles can often provide that elusive piece of information a student desperately needs.

Web resource lists should include similar content as found in the reference sources. A number of U.S. government agencies provide data and other information related to international trade. The *Country Commercial Guides*, now distributed by the Department of Commerce, provide a great amount of detailed analysis of foreign markets, including economic and political climates, infrastructure, demographics, and how to market American products. There are also a number of useful business etiquette guides on the web. See http://www.lib.wsc.ma.edu/intlbus.htm for an example of the sites provided to students in the session.

Empowering Student Groups with Games

HOLLY HELLER-ROSS

Associate Librarian
PLATTSBURGH STATE UNIVERSITY OF NEW YORK
holly.hellerross@plattsburgh.edu

Circumstances of the Instruction

Playing games is part of human nature. Information literacy instructors can use human playfulness and cooperative and competitive instincts to increase student attention, engagement, and learning. It's just more fun and memorable than a straight lecture and practice session. While librarian invented games could be great, another and frankly easier approach would be to modify current well-known television or computer games. Blatant borrowing…yes. Transparent appeals to pop culture cool…yes, sadly true. Nonetheless…learning games can be just as effective as other teaching strategies. Several enthusiastic accounts of the use of games in information literacy instruction are listed at the end of this lesson plan.

Three modified games were used during the author's winter 2004 section of Plattsburgh State University's LIB101 course, with a class of 20 students. One game was used again in the spring 2004 section, with a class of 28 students. Each game required student collaborative research, demonstrated mastery of one or more information literacy competencies, and was designed to encourage critical thinking. All three were introduced with a verbal statement of objectives, written instructions, and a brief model example for students to follow. All the students knew the original programs and games so they only needed to catch on to the modifications to feel comfortable. The group structure allowed for an empowering sense of cooperative knowledge sharing within the groups along with the spark of competition with the rest of the class.

Objectives of the Instruction

All three of these activity games shared the objective of reinforcing prior learning in a memorable way. Each game reinforced particular information literacy objectives approved by the Feinberg Library Faculty, written into the course syllabus, and derived from standards and objectives published by the Association of College and Research Libraries.

Trading Topics included two specific objectives — (1) to further refine student ability to identify aspects of a topic, and (2) to further explore what makes an interesting and manageable academic research topic in order to effectively complete academic research assignments.

Research Jeopardy reinforced the following four objectives — (1) to practice defining and using the topic/subject/discipline relationship for topic analysis, (2) to reinforce the knowledge that access tools are information resources used to locate other information resources, (3) to further explore access tool variability by subject and coverage, and (4) to select appropriate tools for locating resources in order to fully utilize research resources.

Bibliography Survivor emphasized the following two objectives — (1) to further develop the skill of distinguishing between scholarly, general/popular, and technical/practitioner information resources, and (2) the ability to define and apply the four critical evaluative criteria of timeliness, relevance/specificity, authority, and level of scholarship (type of information).

Components of the Instruction

Trading Topics

The interior design program Trading Spaces was modified into Trading Topics, where student groups traded research topics and re-shaped, re-focused, and spiced up each others topics instead of redecorating each others rooms. Trading Topics focused on the creative aspects of selecting and analyzing a topic, identifying different aspects for research, and identifying possible research questions. Students worked for only five minutes in groups of 3–4 to identify a broad topic, and then traded their topic with another group for analysis and spicing up. The winter section students had 20 minutes to work on the topics before returning them to the original group for judgment.

The game was revised for the spring section based on student suggestions to include a brief check-in with the original group halfway through the game. After 10 minutes of brainstorming and writing down ideas, the groups traded back so that the original group could decide the final research direction for their topic. Once the research direction was set, the topics were traded again for more spicing up. After another 10 minutes, a final trade returned the topic to its original group, where they passed judgment on the revised topic and awarded up to five assignment bonus points. The topics were handed in for grading as an in-class exercise. They were graded on the depth of the topic analysis, creativity and scope of the topic aspects identified, and the quality of the research questions.

Research Jeopardy

The popular game show Jeopardy was modified into Research Jeopardy so that teams of students competed in matching topic questions to research tools instead of to specific knowledge questions. Librarians Tim Hartnett and Debra Kimok had used Jeopardy as an end-of-class review in previous semesters, but this time it was used to provide more engaging practice for the selection of good journal access tools for topics. The focus was on application of the topic/subject/discipline relationship for initial choices on the library web page, which categorizes databases by broad subject, selection of access tools based on subject coverage, and final selection of access tools based on preliminary search results. The class was divided into two groups, each group selected researchers and a spokesperson. One student volunteer kept score of points earned and lost, while the instructor managed the computer display.

As the Research Jeopardy board questions were displayed on-screen, the group members conferred, group researchers searched online, and groups finally selected their best access tool options from the library web pages. A typical question was Science for 600: "Are vitamin supplements beneficial?" Acceptable answers included: "What is the *Health Reference Center,*" or "What is *Medline,*" or "What is *Nutrition Abstracts & Reviews?*"

In another category the choices at our library were more limited. In History for 800: "How critical was the anti-slavery movement as a cause for the U.S. Civil War?" The only acceptable answer was: "What is *America: History and Life.*" There were occasional challenges from the student teams to the instructor's research choices, but that only served to add to the excitement. The winning team earned no money, just the respect of their classmates.

Bibliography Survivor

Finally, the exciting and cut-throat saga of Survivor was modified into Bibliography Survivor, an idea suggested by librarian Carla List-Handley and fleshed out by the author. Teams of students researched evaluative criteria for their assigned bibliography item and argued for its survival and inclusion on the final list instead of trying to keep themselves on the island. The class collectively developed a final class list which was a bibliography.

The focus of this game was on the application of earlier class lessons on information evaluation concepts and practical strategies for locating evaluation clues. For example, after students learned about the importance of evaluating author and publisher authority, they also learned how to follow author links in a database, and how to search the Internet for information about a journal or publisher; information they could use as they made their evaluative judgments.

During the game, student groups had 15 minutes to use the evaluating skills to prepare an argument for the survival of their bibliography item on the final class list. After each group presented its arguments, the voting began. Each round of voting removed one item using the criteria of Level of Scholarship, Authority, Timeliness, and finally Relevance/ Specificity. When the evaluative criteria under consideration was "Authority" for example, each group cast one vote for the least authoritative bibliography item and majority votes ruled.

The game modeled in a group setting the process students would go through as individuals when they created and evaluated bibliography items for inclusion in their final research projects. The game did not work perfectly the first time through. A few teams expressed concern over the quality of their assigned bibliography items and one team clearly drifted off focus after their item had been voted off the bibliography. Several changes were made for future testing with a fall 2004 class, including allowing teams to search for and select their own bibliography item, and allowing team members to join other teams if their item is voted out.

Conclusion and Evaluation of the Instruction

The author/instructor evaluated the three games informally through direct questioning of students as they played. Student comments resulted in the several modifications to Bibliography Survivor noted previously, and an additional check-in with the original team in Trading Topics. The fun and informal tone of the games lent itself to more casual conversational evaluation.

Trading Topics and Research Jeopardy generated the most high-energy group activity, while Bibliography Survivor required more concentrated research and application of information literacy skills. Trading Topics was a graded in-class exercise, while Research Jeopardy and Bibliography Survivor were simply fun learning activities. All three provided an important change of pace in the classroom, moved the emphasis away from the instructor and out to the students, and reinforced critical information literacy objectives. While a steady diet of games would certainly make them less powerful, students responded very positively to these three games dispersed through a one-credit course. So…let the games begin!

Supplementary Materials

The materials in this section have been placed on the accompanying disk so they can easily be copied and/or modified to fit the needs of individual libraries and instructors.

- **Handout LIB101 Trading Topics**

- **WebLink LIB101- Research Jeopardy**

- **Handout- LIB101 Bibliography Survivor**

Suggested Readings

ACRL Task Force on Information Literacy Standards. "Information Literacy: Competency Standards for Higher Education." *College & Research Libraries News* 61.3 (2000): 207–215.

Augustyn, F.J. (2004) Popular culture as a tool in library instruction and analysis. ALA *Cognotes* p. 10.

Behen, L.D. (2003) Who will survive in the library? *Ohio Media Spectrum* 55(2) p. 6–10.

Baker, B. (2000) Use your head. *Book Report* 19(3) p. 36–37.

Miller, P., Johnson, J. (2001) *An SLMC for every learner.* Knowledge Quest 30(1).

Purdy, R. (2003) *Let the Games Begin: Playing on the Web.* Voice Youth Advocates 26(4) p 292–293.

Swan, G., Simpson, C. (2003) Jeopardy in the classroom. *Library Media Connection* Aug/Sept 2003 p. 64.

Developing Keywords

DEBBI RENFROW
Instruction Coordinator
UNIVERSITY OF CALIFORNIA, RIVERSIDE
debbir@ucr.edu

Circumstances of Instruction

When searching for information, students are often very literal in their thinking. They tend to use only those search terms that are in their thesis statement or that an instructor has mentioned in class. They have difficulty expanding their search terms to include synonyms, broader terms, or narrower terms. This prevents them from doing a thorough search of the literature and may cause them to overlook useful information. This activity will prompt students to think of alternative search terms, which will generate a better search of their topic.

This 15–20 minute lesson is intended for lower division undergraduate students. However, it could also be used for higher-level high school students. The lesson can be used in a class with as few as six people or a large class with as many as 40. The length of the activity may vary depending on the number of students in the class. The more students brainstorming the more likely it will take longer.

Objectives of the Instruction

After this lesson students will:

- know how to develop synonyms for their search terms and

- be able to differentiate between broader terms and narrower terms.

Components of the Instruction

Preparation

You will need a can or bottle of Coke, this works best with an actual Coke, as opposed to a Pepsi, 7-Up, etc.; a whiteboard or flip chart with marker and copies of the worksheet for Part II of the hands-on activity (see Supplementary Materials).

Hands-on Activity

Part I (5 minutes)

Ask one student to come up to the whiteboard or flip chart to be the recorder. Hold up the Coke. Ask the students what it is called. Encourage students to shout out responses while the recorder writes them down. You will get a variety of responses, such as coke, soda, pop, beverage, liquid, etc.

Then, lead a discussion about the terms the class came up with. Point out that some terms are broader than others, such as beverage, while others are more specific, such as Coke. In addition, point out to students that there can be several terms to describe one item and that there can be different names for the same thing. Explain to them that the same is true for databases.

Part II (5–8 minutes)

This activity is initiated by the librarian but completed by the students independently. Provide the students with a worksheet. Have them write out their thesis statement, identify the keywords, and then complete the chart on the worksheet (see Supplementary Materials). Have sample thesis statements available for those students that do not have one.

After students have completed their charts, have one or two (depending on time) come to the board to share the terms they came up with.
Note: You could then ask the students which terms are alike and which are different. This could lead to a discussion of Boolean searching.

Part III (Extended Lesson Plan)

Put a thesis statement on the board. As a class, pick out the keywords and write them on the board as a list. Have a student come to the board and lead a second brainstorming exercise to develop synonyms for one or two keywords, depending on time available. This may help evaluate the students understanding of the lesson.

Evaluation

This type of skill is difficult to quantify. The assessment of how well the students understand the concept is evident by observing and interacting with them to see if they are using a variety of search terms. In Part I they should be able to tell the librarian which terms are broader and which are more specific. In the discussion during Part II, the students should be able to identify like terms and unlike terms. If possible, the librarian could collect the students' charts, review them, provide feedback and suggestions and then return them to the instructor. This would have to be done in a timely matter for it to be useful for the students.

Supplementary Material

The material in this section has been placed on the accompanying disk so it can easily be copied and/or modified to fit the needs of individual libraries and instructors.

- **Thesis Statement Worksheet**

Internet Sources versus Subscription Sources

DEBBI RENFROW
Instruction Coordinator
UNIVERSITY OF CALIFORNIA, RIVERSIDE
debbir@ucr.edu

Circumstances of Instruction

Students are often told by professors that they are not allowed to use online sources for their assignments. Therefore, when they come to the reference desk and a librarian directs them to an online database, they are reluctant to use it because it is online. Students do not understand the difference between Internet sources and online subscription research sources. This group activity teaches students the difference between Internet sources and sources accessible online that are subscribed to by a library.

This lesson plan is designed for up to 40 lower-division undergraduate students and should take approximately 20–30 minutes.

Objectives of the Instruction

After this lesson students will:

- understand that an Internet source is a freely accessible source;

- understand that an online database is a subscription source paid for by a library; and

- recognize that there is a difference in quality between Internet sources and subscription sources.

Components of the Instruction

Preparation

The librarian should come prepared with:
- A mock T.V. Guide;

- A "Library T.V. Guide;"

- Make a "Library T.V. Guide" with a couple of subscription databases and two or three free Internet sources (see Supplementary Materials); and

- Whiteboard and marker.

Part I: Using the T.V. Guide (5–10 minutes)

Tell the class to assume they all have satellite television. Give them the T.V. Guide for satellite choices. Tip: When creating the T.V. Guide, make sure there are pay-per-view shows that students would like to see (sporting events, concerts, movies, etc.). Make sure these shows are better than the shows on the regular channels. On a piece of paper, have them rank their top five choices of what they would like to watch, regardless of what channel it is on (see Supplementary Materials).

Once this is complete, have a student come to the board to be the recorder. Through a show of hands, ask students which shows they chose. Tip: It is easier and quicker if you have the names of all the shows on the computer or whiteboard ahead of time. Have the recorder write down the count for each show. Point out any shows they choose that are pay-per-view. Proceed with the following discussion:

Q: Why do they want to watch certain shows?
A: Because they are better.

Q: Why are they better?
A: Because they are more entertaining, more current, have better actors/actress, receive good reviews, etc.

Q: How do you get them?
A: Pay for them.

Explain to the students that sources of information are similar to T.V. shows in that they vary in quality. For example, a movie on a channel such as HBO is considered better, of higher quality, than a show on a network channel such as NBC. The same concept can be applied to library databases. A database such as *PsychArticles* would be considered of HBO quality, whereas a web site would be of NBC quality. The library pays for databases much the same way viewers pay for channels such as HBO.

Part II: Using the "Library T.V. Guide" (10–15 minutes)

Give the students the "Library T.V. Guide." Have them use two web sites and two databases to find information on a specific topic (see supplementary Materials). It is best to have topics that relate to the class or assignment.
- Have them report back on what they found.

Discussion: Ask the students what types of information they found from the databases versus the type of information they found from the web sites. Which sources would they be more likely to use for an assignment? Point out that they only have access to the databases because they are students at that university.

Part III: Using the "Library T.V. Guide" [abridged version] (5–10 minutes)

Rather than having each student use two databases and two web sites, the class could be divided in half. You could pretend that half the class were students of the university, while the other half was not. Have half of the class use two databases to find information. Have the other half of the class use two web sites to find information.

Note: If you use the abridged version, you will need to divide the Supplementary Materials for the Library T.V. Guide activity into two worksheets.

The discussion that follows is the same. You could add a question about which half of the class they thought would do better on their assignment given the sources of information they used.

Evaluation

The qualitative assessment of the students learning from this exercise takes place during the discussion. The assessment can be done using a worksheet to test the students understanding of Internet sources versus online subscription sources (see Supplementary Materials). Were the students able to correctly identify which sources were from the Internet and which were subscription sources? The librarian could collect the Evaluation Worksheet, grade them, and return them to the instructor.

Supplementary Materials

The materials in this section have been placed on the accompanying disk so they can easily be copied and/or modified to fit the needs of individual libraries and instructors.

- **Worksheet for T.V. Guide Activity**

- **Mock T.V. Guide**

- **A "Library T.V. Guide"**

- **Worksheet for Library T.V. Guide Activity**

- **Evaluation Worksheet**

Notes:

Know Your Library Treasures

BARBARA A. SHAFFER

Education Librarian
STATE UNIVERSITY OF NEW YORK AT OSWEGO
bshaffer@oswego.edu

Circumstances of the Instruction

Some academic library collections are very specialized in order to meet the needs of a specific discipline or program. It is important that the target population of students is fully aware of these resources and knows how to identify and access needed materials. This lesson plan was designed to orient the education students at the Oswego campus to collections of materials developed for use in the practice of K–12 instruction — the Teaching Resource Center (TRC) and Juvenile Collection. It could also be adapted to introduce students to collections for law, business, or other specialties.

Ideally, students receive this instruction during the first semester of their teaching methods sequence at the beginning of their junior year. Most students have completed basic information literacy instruction prior to this time, so some familiarity with the online catalog is assumed. Classes include 15–30 students and are 90 minutes long.

To reach the maximum number of students, this orientation is integrated into two required courses, one for elementary and another for secondary education majors in the Department of Curriculum and Instruction. Examples and activities for the library instruction are developed in close collaboration with course instructors and tailored to the specific course assignments for each class. This orientation is also scheduled to coincide with relevant assignments.

Objectives of the Instruction

After this instructional session, students will be able to:

- understand that there is a specialized collection for education students and teachers, and list the types of resources and formats they can expect to find;

- distinguish the differences between textbook and non-textbook materials, and between juvenile and picture book collections;

- locate resources in these collections by call number;

- explain varied ways in which these resources can be incorporated into K–12 classroom practice; and

- demonstrate use of the advanced search function and appropriate document type limits of the online catalog.

Components of the Instruction

Preparation

For the first class activity, prepare a set of 20–25 catalog screen printouts or index cards, each showing the title and call number of a different item in the collection (see Supplementary Materials). The catalog printout is preferable since students will see exactly what they will later need to interpret for themselves.

The choice of these demonstration resources should be based on the points that are discussed here.

- Subject matter and educational level of methods course focus (e.g., elementary social studies).

- Special program concerns of which students should be aware (e.g., interdisciplinary instruction, teaching for social justice).

- Different formats or content the librarian may introduce. Students may not have considered using picture books, posters, videos or sound recordings in addition to books to enhance the lessons or units they are preparing. Other options could be materials on classroom management techniques or instructional strategies.

- Possible inclusion of a few examples from other collections. A book from the main collection or a video from the media collection could illustrate the point that not all relevant materials are in the TRC, especially for secondary level students. Students should be discouraged from thinking of the TRC as the **only** source of good teaching resources.

It saves time to keep several sets of these catalog records on hand (see Supplementary Materials) organized by the general subject matter you are usually demonstrating. I keep one set for elementary social studies, one for elementary literacy (reading), and one for secondary literacy in the content areas (assorted disciplines). You can do a quick catalog search before class to pull out cards for items currently checked-out. Have some extras ready in case something becomes unavailable at the last minute.

Presentation—Part 1

Find the Treasures—Defining the Collection / Orientation to the Collection. Students begin class at the large tables in the Teaching Resource Center where they are given an "armchair tour" of the area including the TRC and juvenile collections. This presentation includes information on the content and purpose of the collections and establishes their relevance to the assignments the students will be completing throughout their academic program.

Various components of the collection and other features of the area (display cases, computer cluster, etc) are described and pointed out. The distinctions between textbook and non-textbook TRC resources and between juvenile and picture book collections are explained in detail. An understanding of these "document types" will be important as students search the catalog and retrieve resources from the shelves. Very basic LC classification information is presented as well. Students are often more successful with browsing of this collection when directed to the appropriate call letters. Finally, circulation and hold policies are defined for these collections.

Hands-on Activity—Part 1

Find the Treasures

Students are each given an index card or catalog printout with the title and call number of a book in the TRC or juvenile collections. (See **Preparation** above for details.) If the class is larger than 20, it works best for them to complete this exercise in pairs.

Students are asked to:
1. Find the listed resource on the Library's shelves.
2. Prepare to report to the group on the question, "How could you incorporate this resource into a lesson you might present in your classroom?" They only need 2–3 minutes to review the materials. This question can also be adapted to fit specific course assignments.

Each student, or pair of students, reports to the class information about the resource they located. They describe where it was shelved and answer the second question listed above. The librarian or course instructor can add to what the students say or make related observations about the collection in order to incorporate all the information that needs to be conveyed.

Presentation—Part 2

Explore the Catalog—Catalog Searching Techniques / Accessing the collection. After an introduction to the physical TRC space and collections, students relocate to the computer-equipped classroom for instruction in the advanced searching techniques necessary for effective identification of subject focused teaching materials. For less complex specialized collections, this instructional component may be unnecessary.

A demonstration of the **advanced search** capabilities of the online catalog is presented using sample topics from the student assignment. This instruction focuses on **document type** limits which allow searchers to easily identify resources in the TRC or juvenile collections. A natural result of this process is a refresher for the students on definitions of the various parts of the collection. During the course of the demonstration, strategies for narrowing or broadening the search are also discussed.

Optionally, other advanced strategies of potential interest to your students may be demonstrated which will vary depending on the functionality of your catalog. Our students especially appreciate learning about special catalog features, such as the

availability filter (which reduces the results list to a list of those items currently checked-in) and the technique of making and printing a **basket** (a printable list of results similar to an online shopping cart).

Hands-on Activity—Part 2
Explore the Catalog
Students have work time on the 15 computers in the classroom, during which they explore the topic of their course assignment. Generally students are beginning bibliographies of teaching resources for use in lesson or unit planning. Depending on the assignment and number of students, they work individually or in groups. Students are asked to conduct searches using **juvenile** and **TRC** document type limits in combination with their keywords, and they are always eager to try filtering for availability and creating a basket.

During this activity, the librarian circulates to help with student searches, most often assisting with identifying appropriate search terms. The class instructor is available to clarify the assignment.

Evaluation

Evaluation for this instruction takes several forms. Informal observation of the classroom activities provides evidence of success, or lack thereof, in meeting most of the objectives. For example, if students can find the resources on the shelves, they are demonstrating an ability to locate materials using call numbers. Any questions or problems arising during the activities provide opportunities for immediate follow-up individual instruction, as well as feedback on student learning.

At the end of the library instruction class, students are asked to complete a brief instruction evaluation form. From this, librarians get information on student perceptions of their learning and skill mastery, as well as their comments on highlights of and possible improvements for the lesson. I am reminded that this lesson is important by recurring comments like "I did not know about the TRC before."

Finally, course instructors with whom we collaborate on this instruction grade the assignments and are very helpful in providing feedback. Based on this feedback, both the library presentation and course assignments have been refined.

Supplementary Materials

The materials in this section have been placed on the accompanying disk so they can easily be copied and/or modified to fit the needs of individual libraries and instructors.

- **Catalog Record Example**

- **TRC Orientation Handout**

- **Alternate Assignments**

- **Supplementary Activity**

Notes:

The Why, When and How of Citing Sources using *MLA*

KARI NYREN MOFFORD

Instruction Coordinator/Information Technology Librarian
WENTWORTH INSTITUTE OF TECHNOLOGY, BOSTON MA
moffordk@wit.edu

Circumstances of the Instruction

This session was created for computer science majors in a Database Management course but could be altered for use in other disciplines. The professor requested an information literacy session after receiving research papers that contained very poor citations, if any. This class covers the entire process of how to properly cite sources using *MLA* citation style through a combination of lecture, group discussion, and an activity. It works for any level of undergraduate class, but the size should be 20 or fewer, if possible. It works best in an 80-minute session, but can be adapted for 50 minutes.

Objectives of the Instruction

After the instruction the student will be able to:

- correctly cite sources using parenthetical documentation and
- create accurate *MLA* citations.

Components of the Instruction

Preparation

The room should have an LCD projector, projection screen, PC (or Mac) with MS Office™, and an Internet connection. Also, during set-up, make sure the font size is large enough for the students to see the examples. This activity works best if large tables can be arranged in two sections, but individual desks could be gathered together to make two groups. There are four handouts (see Supplementary Materials):
- an *MLA* style guide;
- two plagiarism decision tree handouts; and
- a list of web sites about citing and plagiarism.
 In addition, students receive a copy of a bibliographic record of a book retrieved from the online catalog.

Presentation

Discuss why it is important to cite sources in academic assignments. This is a good time to bring up plagiarism issues. Reinforce that whether it's accidental (not realizing you have to cite a paraphrase) or blatant (pulling the paper right off the web), both instances are considered plagiarism and can carry the same consequences. Also, talk about the importance for readers to get good citations since the citation acts as an 'address' to the original material.

Give the students an example of real world use such as having them imagine themselves in a few years reading a professional journal and needing to get the material cited in one of the articles. What if the one they wanted was poorly cited and they couldn't track down the original work? How much valuable time would be wasted?

Talk about using direct quotes briefly, but focus on paraphrasing. Explain why a paraphrase needs to be cited in the same manner as a direct quote. Show students how to properly paraphrase, which entails synthesizing source information with their own ideas within the paper, rather than changing a word or two and not citing. Emphasize that someone else's 'idea' is as important as their 'words.' Give the students the decision tree handouts (see Supplementary Materials) and go over the process with them. The "Decision Tree" handouts are included in this text at the end of the lesson plan.

Next, help them learn how to paraphrase correctly by displaying examples of direct quotes with examples of good and bad paraphrasing of that quote. Have the students report on which paraphrase is better. You can take it a step further and provide a quote, which they can paraphrase and supply a hypothetical topic to put it in context. Also emphasize that they need to give documentation after each sentence rather than just once at the end of a paragraph. Otherwise, how would the reader know which ideas were the author's and which were paraphrased? End this section by presenting some good web sites that provide more detail on paraphrasing, good writing habits, and citation practices (see Supplementary Materials).

Pass out the *MLA* style guide and point out basic information of how a citation is structured (author, title, publication information, punctuation, spacing, etc.). Explain that citing a print journal article uses different information than the same article retrieved from an online database and why citing the medium enables the reader to locate the correct version.

Also, go over how to cite web pages. Point out the structure of the citation style, "Do you notice how strict *MLA* is with punctuation, spacing, and the type of information each citation needs (author, title, pages, volume, etc.)?" Ask the students why *MLA* is so much more lenient about what kind of information is needed for web pages. Ask them if they think they will find all the elements listed. Explain that if a URL is changed, you need to have more information to get your reader to the page. Then move on to the activity.

Hands-on- Activity

An *MLA* citation competition.
Split the class into two groups, Team A and Team B. Give everyone a copy of the bibliographic record. Both teams have to figure out how to cite the book using the *MLA* style guide. Team A will choose a representative to come up to the PC and type the citation into MS Word™ so it will be projected onto the screen at the front of the class. Once Team A is satisfied with their citation, Team B then gets a chance to challenge Team A's results and point to any mistakes. If there is more time, do another round with a different source, such as a journal article, but let Team B lead and Team A challenge.

Evaluation

The short-term evaluation of this class is to see how well the students do in the *MLA* competition. Often the students are so into the competition that they are able to spot most if not all errors (usually Team A will omit something). But the real evaluation comes from the actual papers the students hand in to the professor. Follow-up with the professor and see how well they did. Request permission to see the actual papers, or at least the works cited page(s).

Supplementary Materials

The materials in this section have been placed on the accompanying disk so they can easily be copied and/or modified to fit the needs of individual libraries and instructors.

Note: The Decision Tree handouts are only printed in this book by permission of the publishers, Pyrczak Publishing, an imprint of Fred Pyrczak, Publisher, A California Corporation. The full citation is listed below in Endnotes and Resources.

- *MLA* Handout—http://www.wit.edu/library/ref_sources/MLA6ed.htm

- Web site handout—"Web Pages on Plagiarism and Source Citation"

- "Decision Tree" handouts (From *The Plagiarism Handbook, Appendix C,* p. 155, 158) included at end of this lesson plan.

Endnotes and Resources

Harris, Robert A. *Plagiarism Handbook: Strategies for Preventing, Detecting, and Dealing with Plagiarism.* Los Angeles, CA: Pyrczak Publishing, 2001.

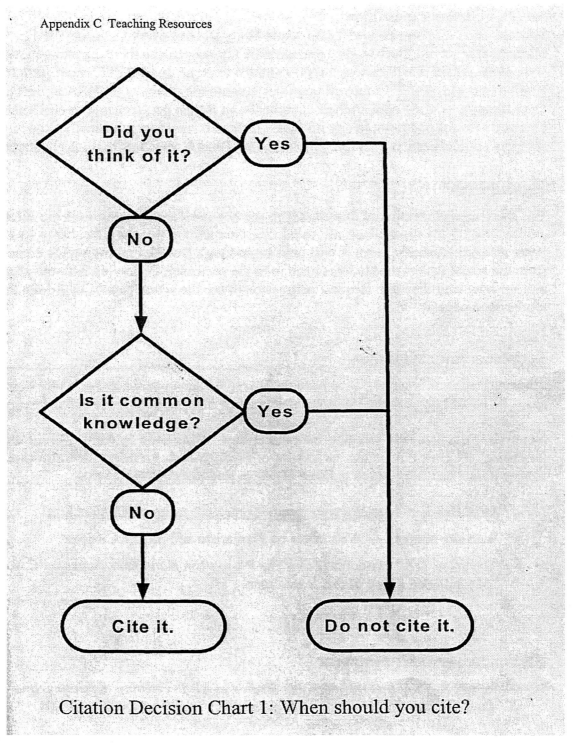

Citation Decision Chart 1: When should you cite?

• "Decision Tree" handouts (From *The Plagiarism Handbook, Appendix C*, p. 155

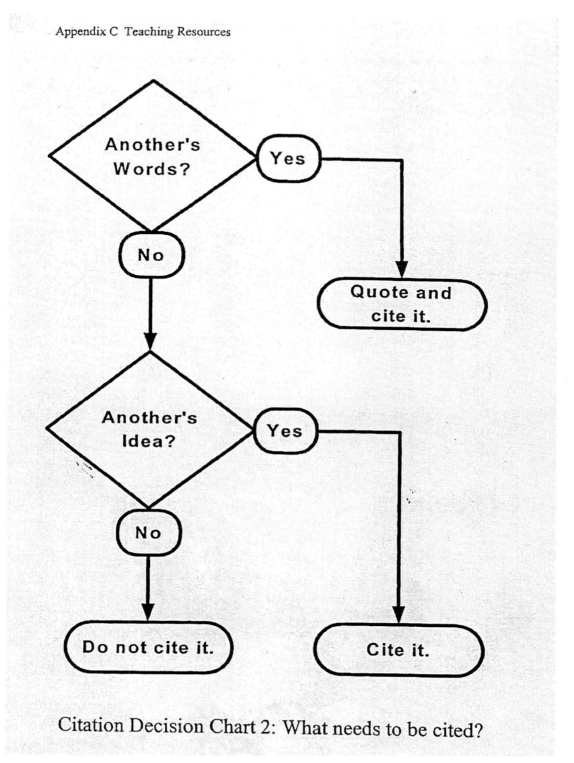

Citation Decision Chart 2: What needs to be cited?

"Decision Tree" handouts (From *The Plagiarism Handbook, Appendix C,* p. 158

Notes:

Visualizing the Internet

CAROL ANNE GERMAIN
Networked Resources Education Librarian
UNIVERSITY AT ALBANY, STATE UNIVERSITY OF NEW YORK
cg219@albany.edu

Circumstances of the Instruction

The fact that students regularly use the Internet is an understatement! Even though many of them started using this electronic resource at an early age, they may not know the answers to questions like:

- What is the Internet?
- How does it function?
- What distinguishes free and research-based subscription resources, both easily available via the information superhighway?

For this latter question, knowing the differences between using research databases and conducting a global Internet search are often unknown. This is extremely important since the research databases will benefit students when writing papers, creating speeches, and developing other academic projects. As librarians, we need to teach students about these resources and how helpful they are for completing assignments. This lesson plan focuses on providing students with an understanding about how the Internet works and the differences in materials accessed via the Internet so students can make better choices when navigating the web.

One of the critical components of this instructional session is having students visualize or draw their impression of the Internet prior to lecturing on the subject. This enables students to compose their thoughts and then later reflect back on their initial interpretations. The second part of the exercise provides an opportunity for students to conduct an identical search on the Internet and then use a research database to compare results. Again, this gives students the opportunity to use different electronic tools and then evaluate the quality of those resources.

This session is conducted in a computer classroom, since students will be navigating web search engines and other electronic resources. The room also needs a document projector for displaying student work. The ideal size of this class is 25 students. The first part of the session (visualizing the Internet) can be used with any student level, from kindergarten to graduate school. However, with the second part (comparing Internet/subscription sources) should be taught to students above the middle-school level. Since the class is made up of two distinct activities, they could be taught in separate classes. Class time for both parts averages around 90 minutes.

Objectives of the Instruction

After this instruction, students will be able to:

- understand the infrastructure of the Internet;

- comprehend the distinctions between free web resources and subscription research tools available through the Internet; and

- recognize key elements within a database record (e.g., descriptors) when conducting searches.

Components of the Instruction

Preparation

Make sure to photocopy enough of the handouts for the class, including "Draw the Internet," "Comparing Internet and Electronic Database Sources" and "Search Choices" (see Supplementary Materials). For the "Search Choices" handout, either highlight or circle assigned searches for individuals or groups. You will also need to bundle crayons in packs of three or four to be distributed to all students.

Prepare a lecture/discussion that includes a brief history and the infrastructure of the Internet. The content of this material can be found in *The Internet encyclopedia* and the on the web page, *How Internet infrastructure works*, hosted by howstuffworks.com (see References). In addition, the instruction needs to include a comparison of Internet resources and fee-based research databases. As with any Internet-related instruction, you should have print backups of examples in case you lose network access.

Presentation

At the start of the class session, each student is given the "Draw the Internet" worksheet and three crayons. They are instructed to draw their impression of the Internet and given five minutes to complete this task (this exercise will produce giggles). Once they are finished, the sheets are collected and displayed using a document projector unit. Students are asked to discuss the representations. Interestingly, the drawings often contain a variety of patterns. These include the expected pictures with shapes (nodes) and connecting lines. However, many students draw other images. Some write the names of their friends with linked lines. Others will draw a desktop image. Some make lists of information available via the web (e.g., news, sports). These mirror four main concepts:

    networking computers (the node examples);

    communication (emailing friends);

    personal computer (desktop); and

    information retrieval (news, etc.).

Prompt students for these patterns and in the follow-up discussion add the historical and infrastructure elements of the Internet.

Next, have students work individually or group them in pairs. Distribute the "Comparing Internet and Electronic Database Sources" handout as well as a designated search on the "Search Choices" handout. Before students begin working on this exercise, briefly describe how to access the Internet search engines and research databases from your library web page. Allow 20–30 minutes for students to complete the handout. Most importantly, they need to evaluate the difference between the two tools. Regroup and have students report their findings. Ask specific questions about the searches to bring up differences (i.e., Why does the Disney/Snow White search retrieve commercial resources on the Internet as compared to research articles in *MLA*?). At this point, review the fee/free aspects of the Internet. You may want to let students guess the costs of the database subscription and then tell them the actual costs.

Evaluation

Since this is a two-activity session, you should be able to ask some questions about the first activity discussion/lecture during the second half of class to determine if students have grasped the instruction. There are several additional options for evaluating this instructional session. By using the "In This Class…" worksheet (see Supplementary Materials), you can have students quickly write down what they feel they have learned in the class and what they'd like to know more about. By asking for more detail on each of these statements, you will be able to better assess what they have learned.

Work with the class instructor to have students complete the "Research Reporter" handout (see Supplementary Materials), which should be done after a student completes a research assignment. While some of the information reported in this form could be determined through students' bibliographies, it provides students with the opportunity to identify the finding aids they used. Answers will let you know if they think *PsycINFO* is a search engine or *Google* a database.

Supplementary Materials

The materials in this section have been placed on the accompanying disk so they can easily be copied and/or modified to fit the needs of individual libraries and instructors.

- **"Drawing the Internet" Worksheet**

- **Comparing Internet and Electronic Database Sources**

- **Search Choices**

- **In This Class…**

- **Research Reporter**

References

Bidgoli, H. (2004). *The Internet encyclopedia.* Hoboken, N.J.: John Wiley & Sons.

Tyson, J. (n.d.) *How Internet infrastructure works.* Retrieved May 10, 2004, from http://computer.howstuffworks.com/internet-infrastructure.htm

Section 4—Debunking Activities

Web Evaluation Class

Plagiarism Detectives

Scientific Discovery as Portrayed in Popular Media

Notes:

Web Evaluation Class

ELOISE BELLARD

Reference Librarian/Coordinator of Instructional Services
ADELPHI UNIVERSITY, GARDEN CITY NY
bellard@adelphi.edu

Circumstances of the Instruction

With the increased accessibility of personal computers and Internet connections on campuses and at home, many students today rely on commercial search engines for academic research. Students using free vs. fee-based information do not understand the need to evaluate the resources they find. Moreover, students do not always know how to make distinctions between the variety of sources they find, or between the quality of resources published on the web and materials found in the library. Consequently the sources students use may fall short of faculty expectations and requirements. In addition the teaching faculty are often unfamiliar with the reliability and validity of web sites students use to complete their assignments.

Learning the skills to analyze the content of web sites has become critically important in the information seeking process. This lesson was created to instruct students on how to properly evaluate web sites and was incorporated into one of our Freshman Orientation Library sessions. The class has become so popular on its own that it has been requested by faculty in History, Political Science, Honors English, Journalism and Social Work. It has also been used as a demonstration for a class on Information Literacy Instruction and several instructors from that class have asked for the site information and lesson.

The class employs both "hands-on activities" and "minds-on" elements so a classroom equipped with individual computers is best suited for this lesson, but a classroom with computer and projector could be used for the librarian-led activity. Throughout the class, it is important to solicit and pose questions like: Do you trust the information you retrieve from a search engine or database? Do you think it is important to confirm or validate the information you find there? What are some of the things you currently do to check the reliability of information on a web site?) The answers and discussions that ensue require students to be actively engaged in the learning process.

Many other sites, similar in nature but better related to an assignment or discipline, can be used in order to teach this class with great success.

Objective of the Instructions

The goals of this lesson are to enhance the students' ability to locate reliable web sites and to teach them how to examine web sites for accuracy, relevancy, and appropriateness in order to utilize the information found in an effective and ethical manner.

At the conclusion of this instructional session, students will be able to:
- understand the importance of critically evaluating information including Internet-based resources;

- deconstruct the elements of a URL (Uniform Resource Locator) and describe how it can determine credibility;

- determine the objectivity or bias of a web site;

- validate a web site based on its affiliation, author, content, and currency; and

- apply the criteria to specific web sites to determine whether they are sources acceptable for academic research.

Components of the Instruction

Presentation

After an introduction, lead a brief question and answer period asking students if they use the Internet for research and why? What are some of the advantages/disadvantages? How much information on the Internet is credible: all of it, some of it, or none? Included in this lesson is a short PowerPoint™ Presentation (see Supplementary Materials). The presentation provides an overview of the different types of resources available on the Internet, what they provide, and where the information originates. This mini-lecture gets them thinking about the tools they use when seeking information and its relation to academic research.

At this point, students are asked to list a variety of different resources and why they might use them in order to complete a research assignment. This discussion may be centered on a specific assignment that students must complete. We talk about what undergraduate or graduate research means, and how it might differ from other information needs. It is important to try to get students to think about their information needs before actually starting their searches. Have students answer the following information seeking questions:
- Who am I writing this for? Identify the audience that the paper is being written for. Is it for the general public or subject specialists?

- What resources do I need to complete the project? Identify the sources necessary to complete the assignment. Are scholarly journals, historic documents, primary sources, books, newspapers, or internet sources necessary?

- When is the assignment due? Identify and plan adequate time to complete the project.

- Where are my resources likely to be available? For example, will I find my information in online databases, special collections, the internet, or library stacks?

After this initial assessment of their informational needs, students are more likely to critically evaluate the sources they locate. Provide them with copies of the "Five Criteria for Web Evaluation" (see Supplementary Materials) then review them together. Ask students for examples or supply them wherever possible as you discuss the criteria in class. Spend about 20 minutes in this discussion.

Hands- on-Activity

Librarian led Activity and Debunking Activity (10–15 minutes)

Direct students to individually open their browsers and go to the web site for *Encyclopedia Mythica*—http://www.pantheon.org and together you can apply the evaluation techniques learned in class. The librarian should guide them through the evaluation process asking questions about the site, incorporating items from 'criteria handout' to highlight a variety of things to look for on a web site.

Encyclopedia Mythica is a site that most students initially think is a print encyclopedia available online. It is copyrighted and looks quite academic. Under closer scrutiny, it becomes evident that many of the entries are done by middle school children. Even the entry for "Zeus" which is well written and has a good bibliography comes from a questionable source. It was written by Ron Leadbetter. Mr. Leadbetter is an attorney and author of *Journey to Noah's Ark* a book which documents his trip to Turkey, where he believes he found the Ark buried on Mount Ararat. This site is listed as a source by many reputable organizations such as NYPL. Which brings up the issue of what criteria libraries and other organizations use to list web site links. Often there are no standards for these listings other than individual preference; students are often surprised by this. This site offers a wealth of ways to challenge and provoke some pre-conceived notions about web sites.

Group Led Activity (10 minutes)

Students are given a list of sites (see below) related to mythology, or asked to find a site on their own that would be used to find information on a variety of myths and mythological figures. They are asked to evaluate it using the criteria and methodology employed with "*Encyclopedia Mythica*." They could also be divided into groups and given one of the specifically listed sites.

  http://pubpages.unh.edu/~cbsiren/myth.html
  http://www.pitt.edu/~dash/mythlinks.html
  http://www.timelessmyths.com/index.html

Additional Activities

If time allows, demonstrate ways to locate more reliable web sites by teaching students to use the "advanced search" screen on search engines to limit their searching or introduce them to:

>*Infomine*—http://infomine.ucr.edu/ and the
>*Scout Project*— http://scout.cs.wisc.edu/.

These are just two wonderful sites for academic resources on line.

Evaluation

Observing students reactions to the *Encyclopedia Mythica* is a real eye opener. Students are often surprised when some of their preconceived ideas about web sites are put to the test and scrutinized. Sources they may originally think acceptable can often turn out to be sources that are not really reliable or academically sound. This class often accompanies a web assignment. Students are asked to supply a valid site on their topic and validate the site for their next class. Feedback from faculty has indicated that students used the evaluation and criteria handout for their assignments with excellent results.

If a follow up assignment is not scheduled, the group-led exercise is a perfect way to evaluate what the students have learned. Observing the process students employ in evaluating the web sites and having groups report their findings will demonstrate how students have incorporated the learning objectives. Lastly, an assessment of student learning can be achieved with the "one minute paper" evaluation handout. Ask students to jot down things they learned in the session and what still needs clarification.

Supplementary Materials

The materials in this section have been placed on the accompanying disk so they can easily be copied and/or modified to fit the needs of individual libraries and instructors.

- **Five Criteria for Web Evaluation**

- **Web Evaluation Power Point™**

References

1. Alexander, J, Tate, M.A. *Evaluating Web Resources.*
   http://www2.widener.edu/Wolfgram-Memorial-Library/webevaluation/webeval.htm
2. Barker, J. *Finding Information on the Internet: A Tutorial Evaluating Web Pages: Experience Why It's Important.*
   http://www.lib.berkeley.edu/TeachingLib/Guides/Internet/EvaluateWhy.html
3. Yildiz, M.N. *Searching the Web: An askERIC Lesson Plan.*
   http://www.eduref.org/cgibin/printlessons.cgi/Virtual/Lessons/Information_Literacy/IFO0202.html

Plagiarism Detectives

CAROL ANNE GERMAIN
Networked Resources Education Librarian
UNIVERSITY AT ALBANY, STATE UNIVERSITY OF NEW YORK
cg219@albany.edu

Circumstances of the Instruction

If you tap into any teaching listserv, attend a conference session on instruction, or browse through any recent library or educational journal, the likelihood of coming across the topic of plagiarism is quite high. Over the last decade, electronic access to information has grown exponentially. Students regularly use these resources to meet their information needs, especially in course work. It is very tempting for students to cut-and-paste digitized materials for use in academic assignments. Unfortunately, students often overlook citing sources correctly, neglect to use quotations, and incorporate large chunks of other authors' works to create their "own" work.

Teaching students that plagiarism is an inappropriate practice is an essential component of information literacy. The Association of College and Research Libraries (ACRL) addressed this issue by including it in the ACRL Information Literacy Competency Standards for Higher Education. Standard five of this document notes that, "the information literate student understands many of the economic, legal, and social issues surrounding the use of information and accesses and uses information ethically and legally."

The second performance indicator of this standard states that it is necessary for students to "follow laws, regulations, institutional policies, and etiquette related to the access and use of information resources." One of the outcomes of this performance indicator clearly states that an information literate individual "demonstrates an understanding of what constitutes plagiarism and does not represent work attributable to others as his/her own."

Librarians play a key role by providing instruction that helps students think critically about what sources they use and how to properly cite them. This lesson plan focuses on the issue of plagiarism and strives to deter students from engaging in this practice. It can be used with any student level and works best in a class of 15–25 students. Students can work independently or in groups. It is ideal in a 90-minute instructional session but it can be conducted in 50 minutes. This session should be taught after students have attended a class on using digital library resources, such as the catalog and research databases, since they will need to use these to track down the plagiarized materials in the mock paper.

Objectives of the Instruction

After this instruction, students will be able to:
- understand the ethical issues surrounding plagiarism;

- use techniques to help avoid plagiarizing; and

- distinguish the correct way to paraphrase and cite sources.

Components of the Instruction

Preparation

Prepare enough handouts for students and the course instructor. These include the "Would You...?" questionnaire, the "Avoiding Plagiarism" handout and the mock "N.A. Hurri " paper (see Supplementary Materials). "N.A. Hurri" is a paper that was created by cutting and pasting text from Internet sites, database abstracts, and full-text resources. No print resources were used in this document. Librarians can create their own mock paper, using resources and topics of their choice.

This session needs to be scheduled in a computer classroom since students will be using electronic resources to locate elements of the mock paper.

Presentation

One of the main objectives of this session is to teach students the issues surrounding plagiarism. At the beginning of the class, each student completes the "Would You...?" handout. This usually prompts a lively discussion about ethical behavior in the real world as well as in scholarship. The elements of plagiarism are reviewed so students become aware of what is correct or incorrect in proper citing practices as well as acceptable paraphrasing. Provide examples so students can determine what is right and wrong. This discussion should include campus policies and rules surrounding cheating behavior.

Next, students are divided into groups and each takes on the role of **plagiarism detective**. All students receive a copy of the "N.A. Hurri" paper and are instructed to use electronic resources to find the plagiarized components of the text. Students are required to document where they located the plagiarized material and reasons for this decision (e.g., incorrectly paraphrased; no quotations, etc.). In a credit course, extra points can be offered to the team that finds and verifies the most plagiarized sources. This is an excellent motivator and needs to be negotiated with the course instructor prior to the session.

Once students have located enough of the plagiarized mock paper components ("N.A. Hurri" has eight different plagiarized sources), the class regroups to discuss their findings. You may want to ask them to rate how difficult it was to locate these sources. This will make them aware of how easy it is to locate plagiarized materials. Finally, distribute the "Tips for Avoiding Plagiarism" handout and review these useful techniques.

Evaluation

The latter group discussion of this instructional session will determine how much students learned about plagiarism during the "Would You…?" lecture section presented at the start of the class. To determine how much students retained from this session, ask the course instructor to include this material in a follow-up quiz. Questions for the quiz can be generated from the "Avoiding Plagiarism" handout and/or class examples.

This class provides an additional assessment component for the session students previously attended. By observing students during the searching component of this session, the librarian can determine the extent of resources and strategies learned in the first class which covered digital library resources.

Supplementary Materials

The materials in this section have been placed on the accompanying disk so they can easily be copied and/or modified to fit the needs of individual libraries and instructors.

- **Would You…? Handout**

- **Plagiarism Essay — N.A. Hurri paper**

- **Tips for Avoiding Plagiarism**

References

ACRL Task Force on Information Literacy Standards. "Information Literacy: Competency Standards for Higher Education." *College & Research Libraries News* 61.3 (2000): 207–215.

Notes:

Scientific Discovery as Portrayed in Popular Media

JILL GREMMELS
College Librarian
WARTBURG COLLEGE, WAVERLY IA
jill.gremmels@wartburg.edu

Circumstances of the Instruction

Everyone is a consumer of science information. Each day, it seems, we hear about some new study that tells us what foods to eat or refuse, what habits to adopt or avoid. It's possible to become jaded about all the contradictory information and conclude that scientists aren't sure about much of anything. This lesson, which dovetails nicely with units about the scientific method, requires students to compare a scientific journal article about a new discovery with a newspaper article announcing the same discovery. Students have the opportunity to reflect on how dependent we are on the mass media to digest scientific advances and how unreliable the media can be at this task.

The assignment also requires students to consider the role that mass appeal plays in the media deciding what is worth covering. The lesson works well for general education scientific reasoning courses. It has been used with students at all levels of undergraduate education in groups of 25–55. It can be introduced in a one-hour session or adapted for slightly shorter sessions, and it is quite flexible in terms of outcomes and implementation.

Objectives of the Instruction

As a result of this assignment, the student will be able to:

- describe the process of scientific discovery;

- compare a popular article announcing a scientific discovery with the scholarly paper written by the scientists themselves;

- understand and paraphrase the gist of an article in a science journal, requiring some research time, and use of secondary sources; and

- think critically about the similarities and differences in how scientific information is communicated to specialists and laypeople.

Components of the Instruction

Preparation

Create a handout of library sources that provides overviews of science topics and definitions of scientific terms. Include plenty of sources about medicine, as many of the articles students work with will be health-related. Develop a display (overhead, projected Word™ document, or PowerPoint™) of the main components of a research article (see

Supplementary Materials for a sample). Decide how you want students to get their articles. Librarians at Wartburg College maintain a collection of newspaper articles, clipping them from newspapers we read. An alternative is to have students browse newspapers to find their own articles; Thursday and Friday editions work particularly well.

News magazines can also be sources. Sigma Xi, as part of its Public Understanding of Science project, offers a service called *Science in the News*, which digests newspaper articles about science—http://www.mediaresource.org/news.shtml. Not all, or even most, of the *Science in the News* links to online newspapers yield articles describing scientific discoveries, so librarians using this source need to select carefully. Transcripts from news programs will work, too, but National Public Radio transcripts should be avoided because they are too good; there will be few points of contrast. Wherever the articles come from, they should report on a new scientific discovery and reference a journal the library carries ("as reported in today's issue of *Science*," for example).

Next, decide if students will find the corresponding scientific article themselves or if you will locate the articles. Your choice may depend on the classroom faculty member's assignment (see below). Having the students look for the articles themselves will save you a lot of time and give them practice finding journals in your library, although they will probably need some help selecting the right articles. Often, the article title in the science journal is long and technical and not easy to match with the terms used in the popular article. If the popular article quoted one of the authors of the study, it is helpful to look for that person's name.

Presentation and Hands-on Activities

Ask students to share what they learn about science from the popular media. You may need to prime the pump with the latest announcement, whatever it may be. Reflect on the subject areas that the media cover (health issues are heavily reported; astronomy, environmental issues, and computing issues sometimes; other fields rarely, if ever). Ask why they think this occurs—"Are there never any advances in theoretical physics?" The goal is to elicit, interactively, an understanding of the limited view of science provided by the media in response to the media's perception of the public's interests.

Partner with the classroom faculty member to teach students the process of scientific discovery and the typical format of research articles. It is important that students understand the requirement that other scientists be able to replicate the study. It is also important that students understand the relatively modest claims scientists make from their findings. If the students have not already had the opportunity in your information literacy curriculum to compare popular magazines and scholarly journals, this is a good place to include it.

Give students copies of newspaper articles announcing scientific discoveries (or however you have planned to do this). Students can work in pairs or triads. Give them the handout of secondary sources for reference use. This is a good place to reinforce search strategy and to remind students that educated people have strategies and resources to which they can turn when confronted with material they find difficult to understand.

Provide students with copies of the scientific articles or help them find the articles (however you have planned to do this). Distribute copies of the classroom faculty member's assignment. Let students work and ask questions.

Assignments (see Supplementary Materials)

One faculty partner requires students to write a four- to five-page critique including the following steps:

- explain the issue so a layperson would understand it;
- analyze the scientific study;
- critique the newspaper article;
- compare and contrast the newspaper and journal articles in specific ways;
- summarize the analysis and critique; and
- create an original newspaper article.

Another faculty partner gives students the scientific journal article, has them write their own newspaper article, and then gives them the published article for a three-way compare and contrast exercise.

Evaluation

The entire assignment will take students longer than the typical class period, and the most challenging work will likely not have been encountered at the end of the session with the librarian. The evaluation that is most helpful to the librarian, therefore, can occur only after the students have completed the assignment and the classroom faculty member has had an opportunity to examine the students' work. Evaluation forms (see Supplementary Materials) facilitate this kind of feedback. Distribute the forms at the end of the session and direct students to fill them out **after** they have finished the project and to turn them in with their completed papers. A reminder or two from the professor along the way is also helpful.

If students write a critique, they can turn in two copies, one for the professor and one for the librarian. When the particulars of the assignment are known, librarians can develop a rubric or Primary Trait Analysis, in partnership with the professor or on their own, to assess the information-seeking and critical thinking skills the students demonstrate.

One-minute papers or "murkiest point" papers could be used at the end of the session for additional assessment. Assign a one-minute paper in which students recap the scientific method and apply it to the newspaper and journal articles they have selected. This indicates whether the students understood the first part of the assignment.

Supplementary Materials

The materials in this section have been placed on the accompanying disk so they can easily be copied and/or modified to fit the needs of individual libraries and instructors.

- **Typical format of research articles.**

- **Two sample assignments.**

- **Sample student and professor evaluation forms.**

Section 5—Empowering through Assessment

"Thumbs Up, Thumbs in the Middle"

Understanding Controlled Languages

Information Literacy Self Assessment

Research Log

Notes:

"Thumbs Up, Thumbs in the Middle"

STEPHANIE STERLING BRASLEY
Information Literacy Coordinator
UCLA, COLLEGE LIBRARY
sbrasley@library.ucla.edu

Circumstances of the Instruction

This active learning technique can be used in a variety of information literacy (IL) activities to engage students and to elicit their evaluative feedback. The value of this technique is that students are engaged in a group activity that encourages peer interaction and coaching. More importantly, students must critically evaluate the information they are given and provide beneficial feedback to fellow classmates about it. Also, it provides a mechanism for all students to participate, especially those who would not normally be vocal. This feedback technique will be demonstrated using a Topic Narrowing group activity.

This technique works well with undergraduate students, both lower- and upper-division. It can be used with any number of students, as students are using a visual cue to voice their opinion. However, the number of students may become a factor, depending on how much time the librarian instructor wants to devote to eliciting comments from students. Based on a class size of 20–25 students, using this technique with a topic narrowing exercise, the activity may take approximately 20–25 minutes.

Objectives of the Instruction

Students will be able to:

- construct a research question utilizing topic narrowing strategies such as concept map/clustering, questioning and brainstorming, or criteria-based topic selection and

- articulate their feedback about an information literacy concept to classmates.

Components of the Instruction

Preparation

Select 1–3 broad topics pertaining to the course content that can be distributed to students. Select a topic narrowing strategy (see below). Prepare an example of a broad question and resultant research question to model to students.

Presentation

The class is given an IL assignment/exercise to complete (e.g., topic narrowing, distinguishing between magazines and journals, primary versus secondary sources, identifying different types of citations, etc.) that utilizes active learning approaches including collaborative groups and think-pair-share.

Divide students into pairs or groups. Explain that after completing the exercise, they are going to be giving and receiving feedback from their fellow students on the assignments. Tell them that they need to have a recorder and a spokesperson. One student can assume both roles; the group may decide. Have students complete the assignment to the point where they need to give group feedback.

Feedback Segment

Tell students that they are to listen attentively and to evaluate how well their classmates completed the exercise. After listening, they will vote in one of two ways: Thumbs Up (Thumb pointing upwards) or Thumbs in the Middle (thumb pointing sideways, not down). Thumbs Up signifies that the student agrees with the group's work product. Thumbs in the Middle signifies that there is some revision needed. If a student votes Thumbs in the Middle, then he/she must be prepared to articulate what he/she thinks is wrong or what would improve the group's work product.

The basic purpose of this activity is to have students refine a broad topic. Lead students through a topic narrowing activity. During an IL session, you may assign different topics to each group. However, assigning the same topic for each group can be extremely illuminating as students recognize the variety of research questions that can be developed from one single broad topic.

Hands-on Activity

Topic narrowing exercises include:

- Concept Map/Clustering/Brainstorming. Model this approach and then provide students with a broad topic to narrow into a research question. Divide students into small groups to complete the exercise.

- Criteria-Based Topic Selection. Select by time period, geographical location, perspective or discipline, person or group, event. Model this approach and then provide students with a broad topic to narrow into a research question. Divide students into small groups to complete the exercise.
    Note: For more information on using this topic narrowing exercise, see: Grassian, E. (1998). Modeling Topic Selection In Gradowski, G, Snavely, L. and Dempsey, P., (Eds.), *Designs for Active Learning* (pp. 149–150). Chicago, IL: ACRL, A Division of the American Library Association; or UCLA College Library help guides, Topic Narrowing:—
    http://www.library.ucla.edu/libraries/college/help/topic/index.htm

- Questioning. Students generate questions pertaining to what they do and don't know about the topic. Encourage them to think like a journalist and ask questions using Who, What, Where, When, How, and Why. Model this approach and then provide students with a broad topic to narrow into a research question. Divide students into small groups to complete the exercise.

Once the small groups have developed their research question, explain to students that they will need to give feedback using Thumbs Up or Thumbs in the Middle. Have each group report their research question. Have students vote. Those voting in the middle must provide feedback on whether the research question is still too broad or too narrow and how they might fix it. The librarian instructor also uses this time to give feedback as well.

Evaluation

The primary evaluation (i.e., how the librarian instructor will know that students have grasped the concept) will focus on the quality of the students' work output. For example, in the case of the topic narrowing exercise, a well-developed research question will demonstrate that they understood this concept. Also, in terms of evaluating the Thumbs Up/Thumbs in the Middle technique, the lucidity of their feedback will enable you to assess whether students understand the concept well enough to provide feedback on it to their classmates.

Notes:

Understanding Controlled Languages

DEBBI RENFROW

Instruction Coordinator
UNIVERSITY OF CALIFORNIA, RIVERSIDE
debbir@ucr.edu

Circumstances of Instruction

This lesson plan will teach students about controlled languages and their advantages by using chat room acronyms. Students traditionally come to the reference desk because they need help finding information for a class assignment. One of the things students struggle with when researching is using appropriate search terms to find information. When conducting research, students often find too much, too little, or the wrong kind of information. Many times this is because they are not using appropriate search terms; they are not "speaking" the language of the catalog or database.

Additionally, students will focus on a specific word or phrase and do not think about using alternate search terms for their topic. Generally students do not realize that in a library catalog, books are described using a controlled language. The same is true of discipline-related databases (*ERIC* for example). This lesson plan aims to enlighten students to the concept of controlled languages and to the use of subject headings and descriptors.

This 15–20 minute exercise is intended for lower division undergraduate students. However, it could also be used for upper-division undergraduates as well as graduate students.

Objectives of the Instruction

After this lesson students will:
- understand the concept of controlled languages;
- know how to identify and use controlled languages; and
- be able to develop alternate search terms.

Components of the Instruction

Preparation

For this information literacy lesson, you will need:
- a list of chat room acronyms (a good selection is found at *AcronymsOnline*— http://acronymsonline.com/lists/chat_acronyms.asp);
- a list of keywords;

- the *LCSH* volumes; and

- copies of the handouts (see Supplementary Materials).

The classroom you use will need a computer with projector and a whiteboard with marker or a flip chart with marker.

Hands-on Activity

Part I

Give students a list of chat room acronyms only. Try to give them a few acronyms they are likely to know as well as a few with which they are not likely to be familiar. Ask them what some of them mean. Either fill this information in on the computer or write down their responses on the whiteboard or flip chart.
Tip: It saves times to have the acronyms already on the computer or written on the board/flip chart.

Ask students what they do when they encounter an unknown acronym that someone has used in a chat room. Ask them how it affects their conversation. Explain that chat room acronyms are a type of controlled language, where you have to know what the combination of letters means to continue the conversation (i.e., LOL, BTW, etc.). In order to effectively have a 'conversation' with a library's catalog, it helps to know its language.

Part II (approximately 5 minutes)

Explain that the controlled language used in an academic library's catalog comes from the *Library of Congress Subject Headings*. Give students a list of topics or search terms.
Tip: If you know student topics, give them a list of terms that relate. If not, give them a list of terms that have LC subject headings they might not have known. For example, give them Native Americans, where the subject heading is actually Indians of North America.

Have the students search the library's catalog using the terms you gave them. Have them write down the number of results they retrieved. Also have them briefly look at a few of the titles to determine if they appear relevant or useful to what they were looking (see Supplementary Materials).

Part III (5 minutes)

Next, have the students use either the library's catalog or the 'Big Red Books' to find the *LCSH* equivalent for their terms. Ask students to do another search using the subject headings they found, writing down the number of results retrieved and quickly review the relevancy and usefulness of a few of the titles (see Supplementary Materials).

Evaluation

Evaluation of the Students Learning

The evaluation portion of this lesson plan is built into the hands-on activity where students have to find subject headings and evaluate the relevancy and usefulness of the titles. Were students able to find the appropriate subject heading(s) for their search terms? If the students found the most appropriate subject heading for their search terms, then they were successful.

If time permits, the librarian could collect the worksheet for Part II & III, evaluate the subject headings the students felt best matched their assigned search terms, and return the worksheet to the instructor with comments. If the students did not find the best subject heading, the lesson should be reinforced and practiced. Evaluation can also take place through discussion on the relevancy of the titles returned. If the students recognize that the titles were more relevant when subject headings were used, then they were successful.

Evaluation of the Lesson Plan

The success of the lesson plan may be dependent on the search terms given to the students as well as the willingness of the particular class to participate and become engaged.

Supplemental Lesson Plan

This lesson plan can be adapted to teach database symbols, such as truncation, wildcards, etc. However, rather than using chat room acronyms, use emoticons as examples of symbols that are used to represent certain sentiments. An excellent source for these can be found at *the canonical smiley (and 1-line symbol) list*—http://www.astro.umd.edu/~marshall/smileys.html

Supplementary Materials

The materials in this section have been placed on the accompanying disk so they can easily be copied and/or modified to fit the needs of individual libraries and instructors.

- **Student's Thesis Statement (Keywords)**

- **Worksheet for Part II & III—Keyword versus Subject Heading Search**

Notes:

Information Literacy Self Assessment

DAVID ETTINGER, PH.D.

International Affairs and Political Science Librarian
GELMAN LIBRARY, GEORGE WASHINGTON UNIVERSITY
dettingr@gwu.edu

Circumstances of the Instruction

From the librarian's perspective, one of the most frustrating aspects of providing information literacy instruction is the differential knowledge base of students. Some are very adept at particular aspects of research, while others are notably lacking. For their part, students are often ignorant of, or oblivious to, the various steps in the research process. Inspired by and adapted from ACRL Information Literacy Competency Standards for Higher Education— http://www.ala.org/ala/acrl/acrlstandards/informationliteracycompetency.htm, this self-reflective exercise (see Supplementary Materials) allows students to evaluate themselves on various research competencies.

Objectives of the Instruction

As a result of this exercise, students will be able to:
- review and reflect on their research behavior and abilities;
- recognize some of the major competencies underlying the research process; and
- better understand what it means to be information literate.

The instructor will be able to:
- identify common gaps in students' library skills;
- compare students' self-perceived research abilities; and
- incorporate student input in planning for library instruction.

Components of the Instruction

The self-assessment exercise should be administered during the first of a series of instructional sessions. Either the simplified or advanced version can be used depending on the audience, the latter being more focused and detailed and thus better suited for upper-level undergraduates and/or graduate students.

Students should be encouraged to fill out the form as honestly as possible. If class time and physical space allows, a Human Likert Scale can be conducted to dramatize the results—students position themselves in rows according to their responses, providing a visual indication of how they rate themselves in comparison to others.

Evaluation

Bearing in mind that students tend to overestimate their abilities, the instructor collects the self-assessment forms and reviews them following the session, tabulating the results to identify those areas where a majority of students believe their skills are most wanting. These can be taken into account when preparing for future classes by suggesting particular areas for instructional emphasis.

Supplementary Materials

The materials in this section have been placed on the accompanying disk so they can easily be copied and/or modified to fit the needs of individual libraries and instructors.

- **Self-Assessment Exercise—How Information Literate Are You? (Simplified Version)**

- **Self-Assessment Exercise—How Information Literate Are You? (Advanced Version)**

Resources

ACRL Task Force on Information Literacy Standards. Information Literacy: Competency Standards for Higher Education. *College & Research Libraries News* 61.3 (2000): 207–215.

Research Log

DAVID ETTINGER, PH.D.
International Affairs and Political Science Librarian
GELMAN LIBRARY, GEORGE WASHINGTON UNIVERSITY
dettingr@gwu.edu

Circumstances for the Instruction

This lesson is intended as the culminating exercise of a semester-long information literacy course or final assignment following a series of library instruction sessions. The research log assignment provides students with an opportunity to demonstrate mastery of the various skills and concepts they have learned. A chronological bibliographic trail qua personal narrative or diary recording individual progress, problems, and frustrations as they research a specific topic, it provides an excellent holistic introduction to the research process. Guided by the instructions set forth in the Supplementary Materials, students proceed incrementally to produce a detailed, ongoing account of their research experiences, reflecting on their work both as they go along and retrospectively.

Objectives of the Instruction

At the conclusion of this exercise students will:
- recognize research as an iterative, integral, self-reflective process;
- know how to develop a research methodology and adapt it as they go along; and
- demonstrate specific research competencies and critical thinking skills.

Components of the Instruction

The instructor distributes the assignment during the first class session and goes over it carefully. Make sure to point out that although there is no prescribed format, the questions should be used as guidelines to help structure the content. It is important to emphasize that the main focus is the methodology and thought process underlying the research being chronicled; therefore, students should be as candid as possible in recounting their experiences, both positive and negative. Encourage students to work incrementally rather than rush to complete the assignment at one sitting. Monitor progress at subsequent classes by inquiring how things are coming along, reminding students to contact you at any point for assistance or clarification.

Evaluation

Expectations are explicitly set forth in the assignment so students should be clear about what they need to do. As already stated, the major assessment criterion is the instructor's estimation of how well students have demonstrated critical thinking skills as they work through the research process. Although this is, admittedly, a somewhat subjective determination, there are certain identifiable benchmarks.

A good paper would, for example, provide evidence that the student proceeded in a systematic, methodical fashion, having thoughtfully considered the steps involved, refined or adapted his or her approach, identified appropriate databases to search, constructed search statements using advanced techniques such as Boolean logic, and reflected on his or her progress as documented by specific examples.

Supplementary Material

The material in this section has been placed on the accompanying disk so it can easily be copied and/or modified to fit the needs of individual libraries and instructors.

- **Research Log Exercise**

The Research Process: Getting Into the "Flow"

GERALD T. BURKE

Bibliographer of Humanities
UNIVERSITY AT ALBANY, STATE UNIVERSITY OF NEW YORK
gburke@uamail.albany.edu

Circumstances of the Instruction

As the number of information resources available to students increases, the need of students to understand the research process becomes more vital. Anyone teaching Information Literacy will attest to students' misconceptions of the fundamental process at the heart of research.

It is one thing to describe the research process, but it is something different for students to internalize it into their own research methodology. Whether or not they have been taught to do research correctly, students often develop their own method, frequently starting (and sometimes ending) with the Internet.

In this lesson plan, they will have the opportunity to examine how their current methods of doing research compare with their peers. They will also have the opportunity to compare and discuss their methods with a standard fundamental model of research represented by a flow map.

Objectives of the Instruction

After this instructional session, students will be able to:
- understand the research process;
- recognize that research is not a linear or static process; and
- compare their current research process to the basic fundamental process of doing research.

Components of the Instruction

Preparation

1. Prepare a handout for the exercise. The handout should leave most of one side of an 8 1/2 by 11 sheet of paper blank. Simple instructions and a definition of a "flow map" should be written at the top, something like: Draw a "flow map" of **your** research process. A flow map is a visual representation of a process. I want to know what **your** current research process is.

2. Prepare a handout of a flow map that shows the essential elements of the research process (see Supplementary Materials).

Presentation

Because this lesson is designed to allow students to discover the fundamental process of research, there is no need for a preliminary discussion or lecture.

First, hand out a copy of the flow map exercise to each student. To help get students started, draw a simplified flow map on the board. Make it simple to avoid giving away too much of how the process works; for example, draw three circles and connect them with arrows, then label them beginning, middle, and end. Secondly, after the students have finished with their flow maps, ask for three volunteers to draw their process flow maps on the board (you can have more depending on the classroom space). At this point you can begin a discussion with students about the maps on the board and about their own. Discuss similarities and differences or any consistent patterns in the students' diagrams.

During the discussion, be supportive of students and remind them repeatedly that this exercise is not so much about correctness, but learning about their own current process. You can repeat this with three new students. Next, give each student a handout with a standard flow map of the research process (see Supplementary Materials). Review the handout so they can compare point by point how his or her process is similar or different from the standard one. Then have all the students write a short paragraph comparing and contrasting the two.

Evaluation

The exercise works in a number of ways. First, it allows students to see explicitly what they have internalized as their current research process that, while seeming logical to them, is probably radically different from the standard process. Secondly, it allows students to spend time working with a correct model of the reference process. Finally, if the instructor collects the flow maps and paragraphs, he/she could evaluate the level of follow-up work needed to reinforce and supports students' understanding of this significant aspect of information literacy, and, for that matter, general literacy as a whole.

Supplementary Material

The material in this section has been placed on the accompanying disk so it can easily be copied and/or modified to fit the needs of individual libraries and instructors.

- **Basic Research Process Flow Map**